W9-CAR-164

DISCARDED

Persistent Inflation

Historical and Policy Essays

Persistent Inflation

Historical and Policy Essays

Phillip Cagan

1979

Columbia University Press • • New York

Library of Congress Cataloging in Publication Data

Cagan, Phillip.
Persistent inflation.

Bibliography: p.
Includes index.
1. Inflation (Finance)—United States.
2. Wage-price policy—United States. 3. United States—Economic policy. I. Title.
HG538.C175 332.4'1'0973 79-1017
ISBN 0-231-04728-2
ISBN 0-231-04729-0 pbk.

Columbia University Press
New York Guildford, Surrey

Contents

Preface

THESE ESSAYS were written at roughly one year intervals since 1968. Other than Part I, which gives an overview of the nature and cause of inflation, the historical surveys in Part II and the policy analyses in Part III are presented in the sequence in which they were written. Although they represent my views on the role of monetary influences, I shared the general concern over continuing inflation and the prevailing interpretations of events. More than would be possible if they were written today, these essays reflect the perception of the problem of inflation, and the prognoses and disappointments, that were widely held at the time, while the final two chapters represent my present views on policy. Minor revisions were made to avoid repetition and unneeded detail. Yet, to preserve the chronological assessment of developments seen as they unfolded, I have made no other changes in the original texts, not even in the few places I would now change to take advantage of more recent research. Lacking the perspective and concerns of an earlier period, we too easily impose the perceptions of a later time and misunderstand the reasons for earlier policies.

In the early stages of the Vietnam inflation it seemed important to stress the monetary cause of rising prices and to correct the misapprehensions and policy mistakes that obstructed a proper management of aggregate demand. For a while it appeared that the burgeoning inflation could have been easily arrested. Even though such an emphasis on the strategy of monetary control is still important, it nevertheless overlooks how intransigent inflation had become. A change in the behavior of prices had occurred since World War II which made inflation more resistant to monetary restraint and slack demand. Now that this change in behavior is evident, policymakers are aware that curbing inflation takes time. Decreases in monetary growth first reduce output and employment, and only begin to affect most prices after a considerable time. Long accustomed to dealing with current disturbances in the economy, however, policy has not yet adjusted to the necessity of preventing an overexpansion of aggregate demand and of maintaining some downward pressure on rising prices over a long period. Only a firm commitment to subdue inflation, no matter how long it takes, is likely to change the inflationary expectations which have made the initial effects of restraint on inflation so weak. Various alternatives to an extended period of economic slack for combating inflation continue to be discussed, and in 1978 tried again, but they hold no promise of being successful. Even though the economic capability of subduing inflation exists, it is not encouraging that, after more than a decade of escalating inflation, a political consensus in favor of an effective anti-inflationary policy has still not formed.

Predictably, a chronicle of repeated failures to eradicate inflation ends pessimistically. Continuing failure can only result in extremely high rates of inflation—a prospect so alarming, one hopes, that further discussion and understanding promoted by these and other essays will finally bring the needed consensus.

Persistent Inflation

Historical and Policy Essays

Part I

The Nature and Cause of Inflation

1

Emergence of the "Problem" of Inflation

At the close of World War II many people, including professional economists, thought that the U.S. economy, no longer stimulated to overfull employment by armament expenditures, would return to its prewar condition of depression. Ironically, this widely accepted and gloomy projection of the future was dead wrong—as is often true of projections at historical turning points. The postwar period brought prosperity and rising prices, not depression and stagnation. The overhang of war-related scarcities and the lifting of price controls in 1946, followed by scare buying at the outbreak of the Korean War in 1950, set off bursts of inflation, and high aggregate demand kept the economy at or above the threshold of inflationary pressures for most of the 1950s. For the general public the specter of depression faded and persistent inflation became the major concern.

During the 1950s fears of recurrent inflation could still be viewed as exaggerated, because timely changes in future policy seemed capable of avoiding the overexpansions in aggregate demand that started inflationary movements. Indeed, the inflationary pressures of the 1950s withered in the next half-decade, and concern with inflation abated. During the first half of the 1960s price increases were quite moderate. The wholesale price index fluctuated around a flat trend, and the consumer price index rose only 1.25 percent per year.

Yet it was also apparent that fewer sizable declines had been appearing in the aggregate indexes for some time. After the 1930s

Adapted from a pamphlet originally published as *The Hydra-Headed Monster: The Problem of Inflation in the United States*. American Enterprise Institute, Domestic Affairs Study 26, October 1974.

such declines occurred only during the 1949 recession and in wholesale prices following the scare buying induced by the Korean War. Without periodic declines, the trend of prices in the 1950s and 1960s was unmistakably upward.

Then in 1965 the Vietnam War set the stage for another round of inflation. Although monetary restraint finally engineered a business recession in 1970 and price controls were imposed in 1971, these policy actions made little enduring headway against the inflation. The failure was alarming. "The rules of economics are not working in quite the way they used to," complained the chairman of the Federal Reserve Board.[1] No one could doubt that inflation had become worse. After the continuing rise of prices during 1970–72 despite a slack economy, the public was shocked when prices then skyrocketed in 1973, thrusting the wholesale price index up 18 percent that year. The prospect that the United States might not be able to avoid the perpetual high rates of inflation that had engulfed many other countries after World War II was now seriously contemplated by middle-of-the-road professionals and widely feared for the first time by the public.

How and why had inflation become worse since World War II? Had it become uncontrollable?

Post–World War II views of the inflation problem evolved through several stages before they reached the present belief that the nation is prey to unending and perhaps escalating inflation. This chapter surveys these developments and assesses what we know about inflation and what, lacking sufficient evidence, we can only conjecture. Although the postwar inflation has been a worldwide phenomenon, the United States was until recent years largely insulated from foreign monetary influences. The discussion is confined to domestic developments, without any intention of denying international similarities and interrelationships. The emphasis is on changes in the behavior of prices and the associated problems of effectively controlling inflation in the United States.

Historical Changes in the Behavior of Prices

An overview of postwar U.S. price movements is provided by figure 1.1. It shows rates of change in wholesale prices for three stages of production and in consumer prices. The series have been smoothed by a two-quarter moving average of the quarter-to-quarter rates of change. The shaded areas represent periods of business recession, including the minor downturn from the fourth quarter of 1966 to the second quarter of 1967 which did not qualify as a full-fledged recession but produced a significant effect on prices. The figure shows that inflation has surged and subsided over periods of several years' duration. The surges generally came first in wholesale materials prices and gradually worked through the price system to consumer prices. Consumer prices have had a higher average rate of increase mainly because the long-run increases for services and housing have been greater than those for basic commodities and manufactured goods. These differences in price trends among components of the indexes reflect long-run supply conditions largely unrelated to general inflation.

Four major inflationary movements have punctuated the postwar period. They originated in (1) the strong expansion of aggregate demand associated with World War II but partially delayed until the removal of price controls in 1946, (2) the outbreak of the Korean War in 1950, (3) an investment boom in 1955, and (4) the escalation of the Vietnam War in 1965. When the demand pressure eased, the price increases moderated but continued to ripple through the economy for some time.

Table 1.1 compares these developments in all wholesale prices for business cycles going back to 1890. Even in times other than the two world wars and the major depressions of 1920–21 and 1929–33, the amplitude of cyclical fluctuations in the rate of price change has varied appreciably. No trend either way appears until the 1950s, but then the amplitude diminishes for both expansions and recessions. As the averages reported at the bottom of the table demonstrate, the six cycles from 1921 to 1949 had much larger amplitudes on the average than the four from 1949 to 1970. (The 1973–75 recession, not covered in table 1.1, is discussed in chapter 6.) The problem of persistent inflation is reflected in the fact that the attenuation of rates of price decline during recessions was greater than the moderation in the rates of rise during expansions. As a result, the change in rates of change from each expansion to the ensuing recession became less negative and, in the last two cycles, the change became positive—that is, the rate of price increase in the recession exceeded that in the expansion, perverse cyclical behavior not exhibited

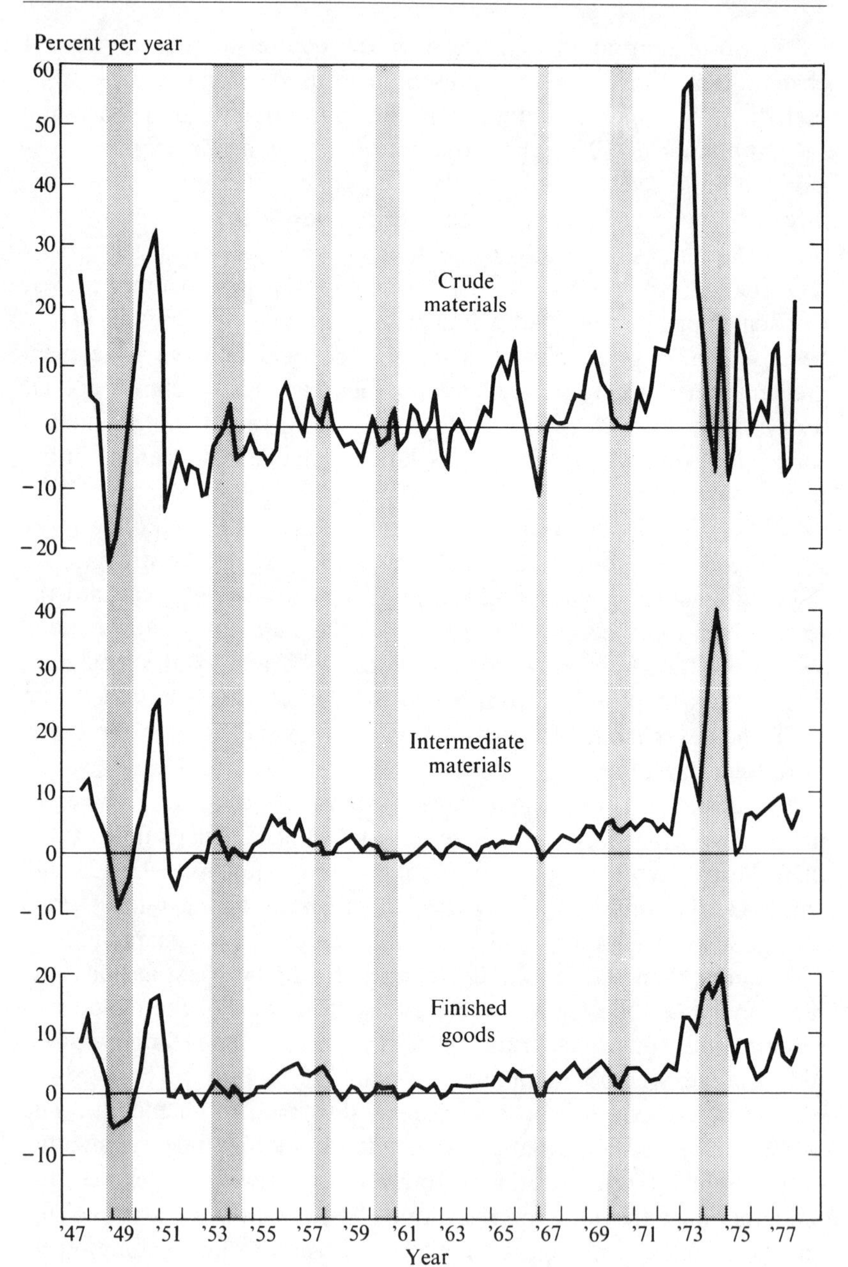

Figure 1.1 Quarterly Rate of Change of Wholesale Prices, 1947–1977 (centered two-quarter change at annual rate)

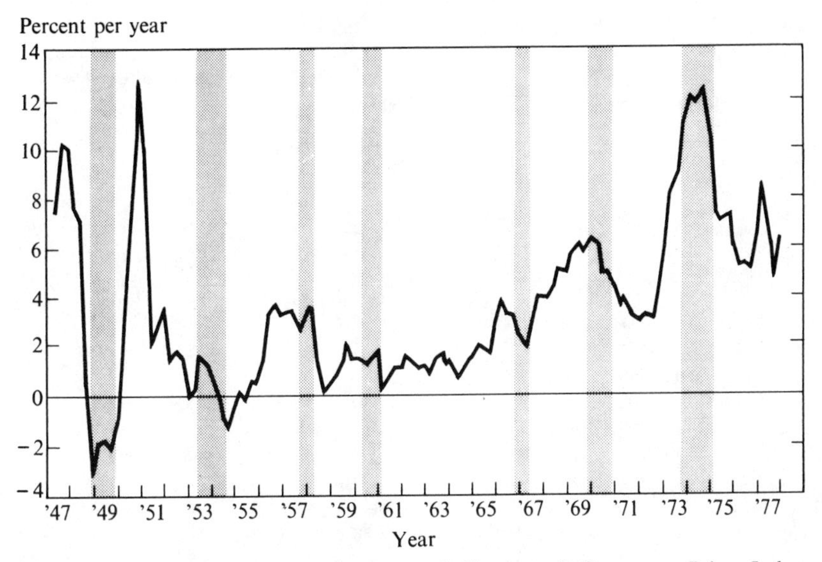

Figure 1.1 ***(Concluded)*** Quarterly Rate of Change of Consumer Price Index, 1947–1977 (centered two-quarter change at annual rate)
NOTE: Shaded areas denote business contractions.

before. The distinctive feature of the postwar inflations has not been that prices rose faster in periods of cyclical expansion—many previous expansions had much higher rates—but that they declined hardly at all, or even rose, in recessions.

Recessions in business activity have been milder on the average since World War II than formerly, according to various measures of aggregate activity.[2] The moderation accounts in part for the attenuation of price fluctuations—but not fully. The mild cycles in the 1920s were about as severe as those in the 1950s in terms of activity, yet price changes in the latter had a much smaller amplitude, as is shown in the last two rows of table 1.1.

The consequences of this altered cyclical behavior for the total change in prices over business expansions and recessions are shown in columns 4, 5, and 6 of the table. The total price change in postwar business expansions was small compared with previous expansions, while the total change for postwar recessions was (except for 1948–49) typically positive though small. The total increase in prices over full cycles was not great in most of the postwar cycles, but recessionary declines did not offset the expansionary increases, and

Table 1.1 Wholesale Prices over Business Cycles, 1891–1970

Business Cycles [a]			*Rates of Change* [b] *(percent per year)*			*Total Change (percent)*		
Trough	*Peak*	*Trough*	*Expansions* (*1*)	*Recessions* (*2*)	*Recessions minus Expansions* (*3*)	*Expansions* (*4*)	*Recessions* (*5*)	*Full cycle* [c] (*6*)
May 1891	Jan. 1893	June 1894	−0.9	−12.4	−11.5	−1.5	−19.2	−21.0
June 1894	Dec. 1895	June 1897	1.7	−4.5	−6.2	2.5	−7.0	−4.3
June 1897	June 1899	Dec. 1900	6.3	5.0	−1.3	13.3	7.7	22.0
Dec. 1900	Sep. 1902	Aug. 1904	4.6	−0.7	−5.3	8.4	−1.3	7.0
Aug. 1904	May 1907	June 1908	3.7	−4.0	−7.7	10.6	−4.5	5.9
June 1908	Jan. 1910	Jan. 1912	8.3	−4.0	−12.3	14.1	−8.3	5.3
Jan. 1912	Jan. 1913	Dec. 1914	6.1	−1.8	−7.9	6.3	−3.6	2.6
Dec. 1914	Aug. 1918	Mar. 1919	18.8	−4.1	−22.9	98.9	−2.4	94.0
Mar. 1919	Jan. 1920	July 1921	19.9	−33.8	−53.7	18.1	−66.0	−40.6
July 1921	May 1923	July 1924	4.8	−5.3	−10.1	9.1	−6.4	2.5
July 1924	Oct. 1926	Nov. 1927	1.6	−2.6	−4.2	3.6	−2.9	0.6
Nov. 1927	Aug. 1929	Mar. 1933	−0.1	−13.2	−13.1	−0.1	−60.3	−60.3
Mar. 1933	May 1937	June 1938	9.0	−10.1	−19.1	45.8	−11.5	30.6
June 1938	Feb. 1945	Oct. 1945	4.4	1.2	−3.2	33.9	0.8	35.0
Oct. 1945	Nov. 1948	Oct. 1949	13.6	−7.1	−20.6	51.9	−6.7	42.3
Oct. 1949	July 1953	Aug. 1954	3.2	0.0	−3.2	12.5	0.0	12.5
Aug. 1954	July 1957	Apr. 1958	2.3	1.7	−0.6	7.0	1.3	8.3
Apr. 1958	May 1960	Feb. 1961	0.1	0.3	0.2	0.2	0.2	0.4
Feb. 1961	Nov. 1969	Nov. 1970	1.4	2.6	1.2	13.5	2.7	16.5
			Averages					
By period								
6 cycles 1921–49			5.6	−6.2	−11.7	24.0	−14.5	8.4
4 cycles 1949–70			1.8	1.2	−0.6	8.3	1.0	9.4
By period and similar severity [d]								
2 cycles 1921–27			3.2	−4.0	−7.2	6.4	−4.6	1.6
2 cycles 1954–61			1.2	1.0	−0.2	3.6	0.8	4.4

[a] National Bureau of Economic Research dates.

[b] Changes are calculated between average levels for three months surrounding peaks and troughs. The series is the Bureau of Labor Statistics index of all wholesale prices, seasonally adjusted.

[c] The percentage for the full period approximates but does not exactly equal the sum of the percentages for the two subperiods in the preceding two columns.

[d] Severity of business recessions is based on Moore (1961), p. 104, and (1973), p. 18.

hence the price level consistently rose over each cycle. The cumulative increase in wholesale prices over the two decades 1949–70 was 40 percent, which was on a par with the gold-expansion inflation from 1897 to 1914. Price increases since 1970, however, far exceed previous U.S. experience in peacetime.

Consequences for Policy

The diminishing response of prices to recessions, and by inference to periods of slack demand in general, compounds the problem of curbing inflation. Although stabilization policies since World War II have moderated cyclical expansions and the associated price increases, sporadic inflationary movements have not disappeared and by all indications are going to last longer in the future, while offsetting declines in prices no longer occur. The long-run trend of prices has tilted upwards. At the same time a given amount of restraint applied to the economy takes longer to curb inflation than it used to. Not only has inflation worsened since World War II—particularly since mid-1960—but the means to combat it have become less effective. In 1973 the Council of Economic Advisers labeled inflation a hydra-headed monster because it accelerated in successive sectors of the economy and defied price controls. To be sure, the 1973 surge reflected several unusual circumstances and, by itself, neither initiated new trends nor signaled a new era. But 1973 marked a further step in the evolving persistence of inflation. Faith in the capability and determination of policymakers to subdue inflationary movements weakened. From a long-run view, inflation had become a monster, not because of the outburst in 1973, but because it was developing greater resistance to the traditional remedies.

Evolution of Explanations of the Inflation Problem

Why has inflation become more persistent and more difficult to subdue since World War II? The answer is to be found in the way inflation is transmitted through the economy rather than in its sources, which remain the same as always. Let us first look briefly at the sources of inflation.

The Monetary Conditions Necessary for Inflation

The persistence of inflation for many years at a time is not new. Indeed, prices have risen through most decades of recorded history, whereas extended periods of deflation such as that from the 1870s to the 1890s are the exception. The underlying conditions for a rising trend of prices are not in dispute. They can be summarized in three widely accepted propositions: First, when aggregate expenditures expand faster than the flow of goods and services, the expansion pulls up prices and supports a rising price level. Second, excess aggregate demand may originate from a variety of developments, such as an increasing government budget or a vigorous cyclical expansion in private expenditures. And, third, a rise in the money supply in excess of the growth in demand for money balances is necessary to support, and given time will produce, excess aggregate demand. Some inflationary movements that originate from scare buying, as in 1950 with the outbreak of the Korean War, or from a business boom, as in 1955, may continue for a while without a commensurate increase in the money supply, but higher and rising price levels cannot be maintained for long without monetary expansion.

An emphasis on monetary expansion as necessary and sufficient for inflation makes money a proximate cause but not in any simple sense *the* fundamental cause of inflation. There remains the question why in each instance the money supply expanded so rapidly. A few historical examples will clarify the difference between proximate and fundamental cause. Following major gold discoveries in 1849, the money supplies of the gold-standard countries expanded rapidly, pulling prices up in the 1850s and 1860s. This sequence was repeated from the last decades of the nineteenth century into the second decade of the twentieth. Had a country abandoned convertibility into gold and allowed its currency to appreciate in relation to inflating currencies, it could have prevented most of its own inflation. The appreciation of the foreign exchange rate would have prevented most or all of the surplus in the balance of payments that led to the importation of gold specie. Here the gold discoveries in combination with the decision not to demonetize gold led to inflation.

Another example, characteristic of business cycles mainly before World War II, arises from the fact that expansions in economic activity generate rising demands for bank loans that can be accommodated to the extent that banks possess excess reserves and, to that extent, the money supply can be increased and inflation fueled. If excess reserves were to be absorbed by the regulatory authorities, the inflationary expansion could be stifled. Here cyclical expansions combine with banking practice and regulatory policies to produce inflation. A more recent example of money expansion as a proximate cause relates to the Federal Reserve policy during World War II, and some years after, of supporting the prices of Treasury securities. In achieving its purpose of keeping Treasury borrowing rates low, this policy let the market determine the money supply. As market demands for credit expanded, the Federal Reserve was powerless to exercise monetary restraint through the usual practice of selling Treasury securities, lowering their price, and raising interest rates; instead, the policy of support required the Federal Reserve to purchase Treasury securities in whatever amounts the market offered them. Monetary institutions and policies can thus work to accommodate the money supply to expanding economic activity, a process that creates new money to support rising expenditures.

The lessening importance of gold in the monetary systems of most countries since the 1930s is a precondition of the more rapid expansions of money supplies since then, but it is not the immediate reason for the expansions. In most countries today central banks have ultimate control over the money supply. In the United States the Federal Reserve controls the issue of currency and the quantity of bank reserves directly. It thus exercises effective control over the total money supply, though unanticipated changes in currency use and bank operations will in the short run put the supply above or below the targeted level. The problems of short-run control of the money supply have been extensively discussed in recent years.[3] Over longer periods of, say, four to six months, control of the money supply is virtually complete and, if monetary expansion supports inflation, it is because the Federal Reserve has allowed it to happen.

Why, then, does the Federal Reserve allow inflation to continue? No one wants inflation, least of all the federal caretakers of the nation's money. Nevertheless, they may acquiesce in a depreciation of money through inflation because forecasting ability and stabilization techniques are not sufficiently advanced to guide the economy to full employment and at the same time prevent sporadic inflation that, once under way, cannot be subdued except by subjecting the economy to a protracted period of idle capacity and unemployment. Forced idleness is political dynamite. A compromise is necessarily struck between a slow and moderate cooling of inflation on the one hand and a temporary restraint of economic activity on the other. If inflation cools more slowly now than formerly, as the evidence presented above indicates, policymakers are pressed to cut short the agony of restraint before price stability is achieved.

The Perverse Behavior of Prices when Demand Is Slack

Paradoxical as it seems, inflation has become a serious problem, not because prices rise faster than they used to in periods of business expansion, but because they are so slow to decelerate when demand is slack. The weak response to demand restraints is an exasperating puzzle to the public, a nightmare to the monetary authorities anxious to obtain quick results, and a challenge to economic theory. It is clear why prices rise when the quantity demanded comes to exceed the quantity supplied at the preexisting price. Here the excess demand raises prices. The relationship between demand and supply goes a long way toward explaining virtually all large price changes, the level of prices relative to each other in the long run, and day-to-day prices of commodities traded on exchanges by open bidding. But prices for many products often do not fall, and some even continue to rise, when capacity lies idle and the quantity that both idle and employed resources are capable of producing exceeds the quantity demanded at the current price. To be sure, costs may continue to rise in an industry after it encounters slack demand because previous inflation is still working through the economy or because strong demand elsewhere in the economy raises resource costs. In general, however, persistent excess capacity in an industry has traditionally been thought to force first a deceleration of price increases and then a fall in the level of prices.

The steel industry offers a famous example of rising prices in the face of slack demand. From 1955 to 1960 the wholesale price index of iron and steel rose 21 percent while the index of all wholesale prices rose 8 percent. Over the same period, steel output fell 22 percent, and capacity utilization was estimated to range around 80 percent after 1955 and even lower during strikes and recessions. The price increases kept up the profit margin on sales despite the decline in output, but the rate of profit on equity fell, though not nearly as much as that for most other manufacturing industries.[4] Apparently the reported price increases were genuine and were not subject to the discounting prevalent in most industries when demand is slack.[5] Steel companies were accused of being a major contributor to "creeping" inflation, as steel prices accounted for 52 percent of the rise in the total wholesale price index from 1953 to 1958.[6] The industry became exhibit number one of the consequences attributed to cost-push inflation and of the evils of corporate profit grubbing. This reputation no doubt exacerbated President Kennedy's outrage when the industry raised prices again in 1962 following the administration's success in orchestrating a moderate wage settlement. (Direct pressures on the companies produced a rollback of these increases, whereupon the stock market plummeted as investors feared that other corporations might be subjected to similar treatment.)

The steel companies claimed that the price increases reflected earlier increases in costs and a need to restore profit margins that would attract capital to the industry. But that did not explain why prices had not adjusted much earlier, at the time that costs rose, nor why the price increases were so much larger in this industry than elsewhere in the economy. No single explanation for the unusual behavior of steel prices in that period is widely accepted, and the issue continues to be debated.

Steel prices have not "misbehaved" since then on so grand a scale, and it is tempting to dismiss the episode as an aberration, inexplicable but of no continuing significance. Yet the phenomenon of rising prices in slack markets is quite common. Furthermore, sometimes prices even rise faster in slack markets than in preceding periods of high demand. Wholesale prices rose faster in the 1970 recession than in the preceding cyclical upswing, even though the recession slackened demand in most of the economy (table 1.1). If prices respond less to recessions, a given decline in aggregate expenditures means a greater accumulation of inventories and cutbacks in production schedules accompanied by layoffs. Thanks in part to improved stabilization policies, recessions have been milder in real terms since World War II, but the reduced response of prices to postwar recessions implies that milder fluctuations in aggregate expenditures have had a proportionately greater effect on output than on prices.

If demand has not expanded, the public typically views a price increase as a plot by sellers to bilk buyers. But economic theory does not support such an interpretation of price increases. In general, maximum profit is achieved by lowering the price when the demand curve shifts down. This is especially so in the short run, when the size of plant is fixed and marginal cost falls with a decline in output, provided that the shift does not also appreciably decrease the price elasticity of demand for the firm's product (which usually is not to be expected). In large-scale manufacturing, marginal costs may remain fairly constant with sizable changes in output, and input prices may be fixed in the short run, so that a decline in demand would not reduce the profit-maximizing selling price very much. But the price would ordinarily fall a little and would not, on these considerations, remain constant or rise. Of course, collusion among sellers to maintain a higher price can, if successful, allow them to share monopoly profits, but, far from being automatically easier, collusion generally becomes more difficult when demand weakens. It therefore hardly seems sufficient by itself to explain the broad strength of prices in slack markets.

Large changes in output in most industries at the same time suggest that prices are not fully clearing markets in the short run, in the sense of equating the amount producers would like to supply with the amount demanded. Other clearing mechanisms then come into play. With excess demand, inventories are depleted, unfilled orders rise, and queues form. With excess supply, inventories accumulate, soon inducing curtailment of output and employment, with snowballing effects on aggregate income and expenditures. The Keynesian theory of the multiplier depicts this process, and recent research on the theory of economic adjustments shows how it works its way from industry to industry across the economy.[7]

In the literature on output adjustments, the failure of prices to change enough to clear markets on a short-run basis is largely taken as given. But that assumption is in fact the key to the problem of ending inflation. Why do prices not clear markets in the short run? Or, specifically, why do many prices respond sluggishly to shifts in demand? For prices fixed by contract, rates charged by regulated utilities, and most wages, the answer lies in institutional practices; but what is the explanation for the rest? While manufacturing prices have at times fallen precipitously, as in the business contractions of 1920–21 and 1929–33, usually they do not. To be sure, the available data do not record the secret discounting and shading of prices in slack markets, and actual transaction prices undoubtedly undergo larger fluctuations than the reported quotations suggest. The difference between reported and actual market prices is discussed further below. It does not appear to be important enough, however, to invalidate the observed insensitivity of most prices to shifts in demand.

The perverse behavior of prices raises three separate issues: First, why do most prices respond sluggishly to short-run shifts in demand? Second, why do many prices actually rise in the face of slack demand? And, third, why have prices reacted less and less sensitively to a slackening of demand since the early 1950s? The next section outlines an answer to these questions, and subsequent sections develop it further.

The "Costs" of Changing Prices

If, despite standard considerations of profit maximization, firms disregard short-run fluctuations in demand in setting prices, it must be that there are some "costs" to changing prices which they wish to avoid. But this merely pushes the question of sluggish response back one step: What are these costs? Price changes obviously entail administrative costs, particularly for firms that offer a long list of items. The price for each item must be decided and transmitted to salesmen and customers; and prices charged by competitors must be monitored so that undesired differences can be eliminated. Minimizing price changes thus undoubtedly makes life easier for sellers (and perhaps too for regular buyers), assuming that prices never stray too far from their long-run optimal paths. But under most circumstances these administrative costs cannot pose a major deterrent to price changes.

For an industry with only a few firms, some writers argue that price reductions are avoided in an effort to prevent price wars that reduce profits for all in the industry. But sluggish prices appear broadly throughout the economy and they are sticky on the up side as well as the down side. Any special behavior of oligopolistic industries does not suffice as an explanation for the broadly observed failure of price changes to occur as often or as much as demand conditions appear to warrant.

The phenomenon needs a more general explanation, a theory of industry price adjustments in which the uncertainty over where the market "equilibrium" price is, and the disruption to the market if every firm were to search for the equilibrium on its own, promote methods of coordinating price changes among firms in the industry. Although some industries can tolerate price differences, coordination generally appeals to sellers, because few can afford a reputation for charging more than their competitors for the same product and service. If all sellers simply charged the same, on the other hand, prices that are not determined on an open exchange would have no mechanism for changing. A method of coordinating price changes that takes all firms in an industry to a new price in unison is a benefit from the sellers' point of view.

Such a mechanism involves the dynamics of price adjustments, a subject on which economic analysis has not advanced very far. Some practical methods of facilitating coordination are well known, however. Certain events may trigger changes—a new industry wage contract, for example, which focuses the attention of all sellers on setting a mutually acceptable price, or a rise in the costs of other commonly used resources. Certain firms may become price leaders that the rest of the industry is willing to watch and follow. As a last—and illegal—resort, a discussion among suppliers may produce advance agreement on price changes. Other, more sophisticated, methods may be employed. The more nearly perfect the coordination, the easier it is to keep prices continually in line with market conditions. Of course, such coordination is not likely ever to be perfect or easy. When it is imperfect but not absent, it works to reduce the magnitude as well as the frequency of responses to short-run shifts in demand that are regarded as reversible, and thus can help explain the observed weak response of many prices to slack demand.

Which industries are likely to exhibit this behavior the most? The coordination of price changes is a problem for markets in which the pricing decisions of one firm affect those of the others. In the terminology of economic theory, these firms are usually price setters as distinct from price takers. Price setters are generally associated with a monopoly or oligopoly situation, in which the market gives firms leeway in setting the price, and price takers are associated with a situation closer to perfect competition, in which the impersonal forces of demand and supply set prices. But the association is only suggestive. Most industries lie in between these two extremes and are hard to classify. Furthermore, monopoly bestows the power to extract quasi-rents above resource costs—a very different process from a slow or nonexistent response to demand shifts, which reflects the dynamics of market price adjustments. Analysis of the effect of industry characteristics on the short-run behavior of prices also is not yet very advanced. Although prices react almost immediately in a highly competitive market and slow response may be possible only where the number of firms is limited, it is not clear a priori whether effective coordination of price changes among a few firms should mean larger or smaller changes in the short run.

It turns out that concentrated industries (defined as industries in which the largest few firms account for a high percentage of sales) do display less amplitude of cyclical price changes (see chapter 3). This fact suggests that the greater coordination made possible by a smaller number of firms reduces the flexibility of prices. But the common conclusion that price inflexibility reflects increasing industrial concentration does not appear justified. Price inflexibility is not new,[8] although it has received greater attention since the 1930s. Perhaps it appears to be more important because products characterized by less flexible prices have become a larger fraction of the total over the years, but even this is not clear. The diminished responsiveness of prices since World War II pertains to nearly all products, the main exception being raw materials traded on commodity exchanges. Increased inflexibility cannot, therefore, be explained by a supposed growth of concentration or big firms in the economy, but must, rather, be laid to a change in the operation of the price system.

With inflation now more persistent, will it foster more effective methods of changing prices frequently and of speeding adjustments to fluctuations in demand? Under inflation, firms no doubt tend to change prices more often to follow upward trends in costs. Such changes are anticipated and can be easily coordinated. But adjustments to unanticipated deviations from the trend may remain difficult to coordinate and continue to be ignored. Therefore, although prices are continually rising in an inflation, they may decelerate slowly as an inflationary upswing subsides, because they still respond sluggishly to short-run changes in the rate of growth of demand. Indeed, since uncertainty about market prices is likely to make coordination more difficult, and since inflation—unless it is unusually steady—heightens uncertainty, prices may tend to deviate from anticipated trends less frequently during inflation than at other times, prolonging the transition to price stability. Thus, the very inflation that necessitates frequent changes in prices may at the same time foster an uncertainty that accounts for the dampened response of prices to fluctuations in demand since World War II.

The Dependence of Prices on Cost

Insofar as the coordination of price changes reduces the response to short-run shifts in demand, it makes prices relatively more dependent on influences from the cost side. The preceding interpretation of price adjustments is therefore consistent with, and provides a rationale for, the apparent prevalence of unit-cost pricing in manufacturing industries.[9] Empirical studies have long found that short-run shifts in demand have small and often insignificant effects, and that, instead, costs play a dominant role. The most common form of this evidence is a statistical regression of price changes on changes in unit wage and materials costs and on a proxy for demand shifts (usually changes in the quantity sold or unfilled orders).[10] The latter variable usually has a small, and often statistically insignificant, regression coefficient, while the cost variables are highly significant and account for most of the total correlation. The implication of these studies is that prices largely reflect costs and are generally unresponsive to short-run shifts in demand.

Of course, by standard accounting practice, price per unit is distributed among the unit cost of labor, materials, and capital, and a profit margin, and must equal their sum. In terms of this accounting identity, a change in quantity sold due to a shift in demand affects the price and at the same time is reflected in costs and profits. Consequently, in the long run, changes in demand cannot be identified by the preceding regression unless they happen to be in the same direction and amount as the omitted capital and profit variables, which is not likely.

In the short run of a quarter or even a year, however, wage rates and materials prices do not react fully to changes in output. The profit margin rises and falls in the short run with changes in output, and the quantity variable represents the effect of changes in demand on the profit margin. Therefore, the fact that the coefficient of the quantity variable is unimportant in these regressions strongly suggests that industry prices respond very little to changes in demand and are set largely to reflect unit costs.

Costs per unit of output also change as production is raised to higher and less efficient levels to meet increases in demand. These studies do not make clear whether such demand-induced changes in unit costs affect prices. One view is that they do not, which would mean that demand plays no indirect role either. This view implies that prices are determined by unit costs at a "standard" level of capacity utilization, with a markup over variable cost to cover fixed capital costs and to provide a target return on equity.[11] Since plants are designed to be most efficient at standard levels of output, prices in this view will equal minimum average cost in the short as well as the long run.

The empirical results thus do not imply a departure from traditional theories of *long-run* price determination, according to which prices gravitate toward long-run average cost. But the finding that demand also plays little or no role in the *short run* does depart from traditional theories. While these results suffer from deficiencies of the data, they support the proposition that manufacturing prices are not very responsive to short-run shifts in demand.

The empirical results that prices are closely correlated with unit costs but not with proxies for demand tie together with the notion that the coordination of price changes among firms is responsible for the unresponsiveness of prices to short-run shifts in demand, because one way to coordinate price changes is to base them on changes in the wage rates and materials costs that are similar for all firms in an industry. This dependence of prices on costs clearly exists in regulated industries and under "pass-through" price controls, where cost increases, but usually not an expansion of demand, can be used to justify higher prices. Most manufacturing industries also appear to relate prices to costs, though in varying degree according to their incentive and ability to coordinate price changes, and thus to disregard short-run shifts in demand.

This view of industry pricing in the short run is not derived from the standard theory of demand and supply but is inferred from empirical observations. It is incomplete in not providing a theoretical explanation of where and when it applies. But it is appealing because it describes behavior that is consistent with important characteristics of the inflationary process—namely, a slow response of prices to shifts in demand and continuing increases to catch up even after demand slackens.

The Transmission of Inflationary Pressures through Costs

The dependence of prices on costs can account for the fact that, once under way, inflation travels from earlier to later stages of production, rather than the reverse, even though most inflationary movements originate in excess aggregate demand for finished goods and services. An increase in aggregate demand first elicits an expansion of output and transmits increases in demand back to resource inputs. This process can take place even at full capacity, because under stimulus the economic machine can always turn out a little more by drawing on spare plants and equipment, overtime, and marginal workers. There is no sharp barrier of "full employment" at which prices begin to rise. Some prices begin to respond, though slowly, to the first signs of recovery from a recession. At first, as an expansion of demand spreads to lower stages of production, prices begin to rise in markets that respond quickly, most prominently those for raw materials. Later, wage rates begin to increase faster as selected labor markets tighten, but the response is delayed by union contracts and the traditional reluctance of firms to raise the pay of some and not all workers. Most firms raise prices only as their input costs are increased. Then, after the prices of final goods and services rise, workers bargain for cost-of-living increases in the next contract, which in turn are passed through the pipeline of costs to prolong the upward spiral.

A slowing of inflation due to restraints on aggregate demand is transmitted in the same way and entails the same delays. Output is reduced, factor demands decline, and unemployment rises. Prices nevertheless continue upward, because cost increases are still working forward through the price system. The first prices to weaken are generally those of raw materials and of other goods sold in highly competitive markets. The upward pressure on costs in subsequent stages of production thus eases, weakening prices first for intermediate goods and finally for finished goods at the retail level. Wages resist still longer, and service prices that are tied closely to wages are usually the last to reflect a change in aggregate demand. While there are always many exceptions to this pattern, it is broadly confirmed in the price indexes by subsectors.[12]

Since wage rates are slow to reflect changes in the growth of aggregate demand and are a major component of manufacturing costs, it might seem that manufacturing prices cannot decelerate much before wages do. In fact, these prices do decelerate ahead of wage rates, because demand restraints retard the rise in unit labor costs. A slackening of business activity leads firms to trim costs, chiefly by using workers more efficiently. This process is at first concealed by the retention of skilled workers who are not fully employed but who are held in the work force against the day when output again expands. In the ensuing recovery, unit labor costs decelerate rapidly, relieving a significant pressure on prices. As the rise in prices eases, the slower increases in the cost of living feed back on wage rates, allowing the process of deceleration to continue after the benefits of cost cutting have run out.[13]

The 1970 recession generally followed this sequence. Output per hour of labor (an overall indicator of efficiency) had actually declined during the peak of the cyclical expansion in 1969, and unit labor costs (private nonfarm sector) rose 8.2 percent in that year while compensation per hour rose 6.9 percent. Output per hour began to increase in the second and third quarters of the 1970 recession, but the drop in output resulting from the General Motors strike in the fourth quarter, as well as the continuing recession, held the increase to 1.7 percent for the year. Thereafter output per hour of labor began to advance sharply, so that from the first quarter of 1970 to the second quarter of 1971 it rose at an annual rate of 3.8 percent, and it accelerated to 5 percent per year in the first half of 1972. Although compensation per hour rose about the same in 1971 and 1972 as in 1970, the advance in unit labor costs dropped from 8.2 percent in 1969 to 5.0 percent in 1970 and to 2.2 percent per year overall in 1971 and 1972. Because profit margins began rising in 1971 from their depressed levels, the deceleration in unit labor costs had little immediate effect on most prices. But the rate of increase in the private nonfarm deflator peaked in the fourth quarter of 1970, and inflation began to subside slowly; the deceleration continued well into 1972, though the imposition of price controls in August 1971 obscured the normal pattern of events. As we now also know, what might have been a happy ending to the restraint imposed on the inflation by the 1970 recession was shattered by the explosion of prices in 1973.

Costs as Initiators of Inflation

According to the preceding view of the inflationary process, many prices rise in slack markets because they undergo a step-by-step adjustment to a new equilibrium over a period of time and continue catching up well after the initiating period of excess demand has ended. Yet, because inflationary movements subside so slowly, it is often concluded that costs have a tendency to rise on their own. This cost-push theory of inflation merits attention because it is time honored, still very influential, and the source of important observations on the behavior of prices.

A large part of the literature on inflation is devoted to cost-push forces. They were cited often in the late 1950s, when demand pressures seemed insufficient to account for rising prices in slack markets. The prime sources of cost push are supposed to be labor unions with bargaining power to achieve rising incomes for their members and large corporations with at least some monopoly power to raise prices in pursuit of higher profits.

It is important to distinguish between costs as a possible independent source of inflation and as a channel for transmitting inflation. As noted earlier, many firms base prices on costs, which is sufficient to give the appearance that costs initiate inflation even when the culprit is excess demand. Whether some costs are, in addition, a major independent initiator of inflation is open to doubt. The doubt arises first from the implausible consequences for relative prices and wages of such a phenomenon. (Other reasons for doubt are discussed later.) Although unions and firms with monopoly power undoubtedly gain income relative to those without it, any such group is likely to seek the maximum amount in a once-and-for-all jump, whereas inflation is a continuing process. In particular industries monopoly power could cause inflation during the period when it is first exercised, but how could such an inflation continue and recur?

Inflation is sometimes thought to stem from the intricate battle among incompatible claims of various monopoly elements for larger shares of total output. Such a battle might be described as starting with contracts for higher wages won by strong unions. Firms pass the increased costs through to prices, which reduces the purchasing power of the higher money wages. At the existing level of aggregate demand, the higher prices threaten to reduce output and employment, events that the monetary authorities attempt to forestall by expanding aggregate demand. Unions then bargain to recapture their initial real gains in the next contract, and wages and prices thus follow one another up a spiral of inflation.[14]

Conceivably this scenario applies to some European countries where strong union power blankets most of the economy and the nation's politics forces an aggregate demand policy of full employment at all times. But even in some countries where the power to set wages and prices is centralized in union and industrial associations, international trade often exposes the domestic economy to outside competition and inhibits a full-blown cost-push inflation. Such a scenario hardly applies to the United States where only a fifth of the labor force belongs to unions (and not all of them have strong bargaining power), where periods of rising unemployment occur and are tolerated even though deplored, where few firms can lay claim to monopoly power or anything close to it, and where power to set wages and prices is not centralized in nationwide associations. All these factors discourage the development of cost-push inflation in the United States, even though until recently the small importance of international trade provided the insulation behind which it could have occurred. To be sure, many unions and firms have long had the power to influence wages and prices within limits in their industry. And some nonunion firms that are subject to potential unionization may keep pay scales in line with union wage rates. Nevertheless, the maintenance of cost-push inflation in most of the economy when aggregate demand is not excessive requires a prevalence of monopoly that has never existed in the United States.

The sequence of U.S. inflations, furthermore, does not point to costs as the source. Periods of slack demand in which prices are rising have invariably followed strong inflationary surges that can be attributed only to excess demand, and the price increases have eventually begun to decelerate after demand slackens. Wage increases have adjusted slowly to inflation and, after catching up, have moderated. These are not the patterns of cost-push inflation.

Much of the cost-push literature has focused on the pressure on prices exerted by corporate giants seeking higher and higher profits. The steel industry in the late 1950s has been the prime example; but, in fact, there are few other examples and none of equal importance. A study of machinery prices in the same period attributed their extraordinary rise to strong excess demand.[15] Moreover, the average profit margin for all manufacturing firms peaked in 1955 at the height of that inflation and was lower for the remainder of the 1950s and the early 1960s, contrary to the view that it was responsible for the continuing rise in prices.

This evidence does not mean that unions and large corporations play no role in the inflationary process. But their role is not that of initiators of inflation.

Unions and wages. Unions lengthen the time it takes an inflationary impulse to work fully through the price system, and in later stages they appear also to strengthen each impulse. When inflation is rampant, union leaders agitate for large wage increases. Labor militancy hardens, bitterness deepens, and strikes become crusades. Rather than fight a long battle, employers often surrender. Construction wages in the late 1960s provide a dramatic example. The construction industry contains many separate unions, each in control of a critical skill. As the Vietnam inflation progressed and wage contracts escalated, the relative wages of different skill groups came to diverge from traditional patterns. As each group sought to reestablish its relative position, there began a leap-frogging sequence that, with each new contract, catapulted the bargaining union ahead of others. Negotiated first-year increases reached 21 percent in the second half of 1970 and averaged 14.8 percent during 1969 to 1971, compared with 8.8 percent for negotiated first-year wage changes in manufacturing. Municipal unions exerted a new power over their wages during this period. Here in particular it was hard to distinguish among the effects of a strengthened bargaining position due to a favorable turn in demand and supply conditions, a new militancy reflecting the acquisition of political power, and ordinary wage push.

When slackened market conditions remove the justification for the maintenance of previous rates of wage increase, union members do not suddenly become receptive to a slowing of wage increases and their leaders do not moderate contract demands at once. In the construction trades, for example, union leaders took no public steps to dampen the exorbitant increases noted above, although privately they welcomed the Construction Industry Stabilization Committee, set up in March 1971 by the government as a means of bringing reality to the industry and of untangling a wage spiral that was pricing union workers out of jobs. Construction wage settlements then came down dramatically after the first quarter of 1972 to a range of 4.5 to 6.5 percent per year.

Although wage increases decelerate slowly after markets slacken and in that respect continue to push the inflation along, they do not generally accelerate on their own and so do not intensify the inflation. Historically, the number of strikes has declined when the economy has weakened. If inflation then speeds up, wages are slow to respond on the up side as well. The inflationary surge of 1973 illustrates this tendency. During that year, despite the strong advances of wages in 1971 and 1972 to regain the ground lost in the first stages of the Vietnam inflation, average hourly earnings in the private non-farm sector (adjusted for interindustry shifts and overtime in manufacturing) continued rising at the 1972 rate of 6 to 7 percent per year. In the first half of 1974 the rise in hourly earnings accelerated only to 7.25 percent per year. In real terms this was equivalent to a 3 percent rise for long-run productivity growth and 3 to 4 percent for cost-of-living increases, which as it turned out was too little. Insofar as controls helped to hold wages down during 1973, they reinforced the usual lags and required a subsequent catch-up, which prolonged subsequent efforts to curb the inflation.

The lagging and catch-up behavior of wages reflects their delayed adjustment to the effect of inflation on workers' cost of living. Broadened experience with the reality of inflation since World War II has gradually intensified anticipations of persistent inflation, which retards the deceleration of wages after each new round of inflation, thus prolonging inflationary movements and impeding the return to price stability. Even if some overshooting of wages occurs, however, it is not the same as initiating the movements. To blame unions for inflation is to blame them for catching up with past price increases and for seeking protection against future increases. Commodity prices that keep astride of inflation and thus do not have to catch up later illogically escape blame. Unions are not praised, as well they might be, for letting wages fall behind in the first place.

The fear has frequently been voiced that, if wages were all tied to automatic cost-of-living escalators, they would transmit inflationary pressures more rapidly and thereby intensify inflation. However, for a given inflationary pressure from excess demand, quick adjustments, while they speed up the price increases, do not necessarily push the ultimate level any higher. On the other hand, negotiated wage gains to cover anticipated increases in the cost of living over the life of the contract, which become more common in a long-lasting inflation, pose a problem for subsequent policy efforts to reduce the rate of inflation. Lagged adjustments of wages to inflation may therefore be worse than immediate ones, because they may lead to overshooting and also, in prolonging the process, make a tough policy of restraint harder to carry through to completion.

Unions contribute to the problem of inflation, therefore, by reducing the flexibility of the rate of wage increase. This is not the same as the downward rigidity of wages or the upward push of which unions are often accused. In the first place, downward rigidity is of no importance, because price reduction is no longer considered a desirable policy objective. The problem, rather, is to halt further rises in prices, a goal that is not inconsistent with wage gains that hold to the 2 percent long-run rate of growth of productivity. In the second place, wages show few signs of exerting upward push, except in the special sense of maintaining rates of increase in the later stages of inflation whose justification has been removed by slackened market conditions.

In short, labor unions do not initiate inflation, and the problem would not disappear even if their power were severely curtailed; but they exacerbate the problem by perpetuating inflation once it gets started.

Administered prices. Misconceptions similar to those about unions surround the public's view of large corporations. It is natural to attribute power to organizations that are big, whether or not they have any power; and wage and price increases are often seen as arising not from the pressure of general excess demand, as they usually do, but from the exercise of individual market power. The mystique of the powerful corporation is reflected in the concept of "administered prices," which supposedly generate cost-push inflation. Despite its questionable applications, I believe this concept is still important to an understanding of the inflationary process, though not as it is commonly presented.

The concept of administered prices was first introduced by Gardiner Means in the 1930s to describe the tendency of prices of manufactured goods to decline less during the Great Depression than did prices of raw materials.[16] Means advanced the proposition that some industries can administer prices—that is, set them where they please—in contrast to competitive industries, whose prices are determined by the impersonal market forces of demand and supply. Administered prices are less sensitive than market-determined prices to declines in demand and to excess capacity. But the accusations against administered prices go beyond their failure to decline in slack markets, and make them responsible for spearheading cost-push inflation.

The market structure that fosters administered prices has never been pinned down. It has variously been identified as (1) an industry with monopoly; (2) less strictly, an oligopolistic industry (that is, one with a small number of major sellers as indicated by a "high" concentration of industry sales in the top few firms—a definition that embraces the industries with large manufacturing corporations); and (3) somewhat circularly, an industry that for one reason or another does not change prices very often. I find the second view the most suggestive as well as the most useful, since data on industrial concentration make it possible to classify prices for empirical analysis.

As noted earlier, prices in concentrated industries respond less to shifts in demand. Such price inflexibility is not unique to concentration. It occurs also in connection with durable products (presumably because of the existence of inventories); and also in connection with long-term contracts for labor and, in certain industries, for raw materials and energy supplies. Prices associated with all of these conditions tend to fluctuate less over business cycles than do other prices. This phenomenon is neither new nor rare. In historical data back to the 1890s prices of manufactured goods have generally displayed a smaller amplitude of fluctuation than have those of raw materials;[17] and the smaller amplitudes are very likely characteristic of the more highly concentrated industries as well.

But the fact that they exhibit less price fluctuation does not mean that concentrated industries or large corporations spearhead inflation. Quite the opposite: in general they tend to slow it down. Because of their slower responses to changes in market conditions, prices in such industries lag behind in the initial stages of inflation and catch up only as the inflation subsides. It was this catching up in the waning phase of the 1955–59 inflation that fostered the view that such industries were an independent source of inflationary pressure. This popular diagnosis went astray, because it misread evidence accumulated over too short a period. With the benefit of longer observation, later studies showed that the catching up was completed by the early 1960s, after which, allowing for differences in labor and materials costs, concentrated industries no longer manifested price increases greater than those in other sectors.[18] (Why would these price increases, *if* due to cost push, ever end, as they did in the early 1960s? One explanation attributed the ending to the price guideposts of that period; but in fact the guideposts had no more than a marginal effect.[19]) To the extent that prices are set to reflect costs, the timing of price increases gives the appearance that inflation is due to rising costs when excess demand is the main source of the pressure.

A repetition of the pattern of first a lag and then a catch-up in these prices appeared during the Vietnam inflation. From 1967 to 1969 price increases for the more concentrated industries, after allowing for differences in labor and materials costs, were smaller, but in 1971 they became larger in a characteristic catching up as the inflation subsided.[20] Prices in concentrated industries fell behind in 1972, presumably because the price controls instituted in August 1971 had a greater effect on them than on other industries; and they fell behind again in 1973 as the inflation speeded up.

Administered prices have long been recognized as having such a lag and catch-up pattern. Yet the catch-up phase continues to be blamed as an independent source of cost push that can and should be restrained by price controls.[21] Such a policy makes no sense. In general, over the long run, administered prices gravitate toward a level consistent with profit maximization just as all other prices do. Some firms with monopoly power may administer their prices to obtain monopoly profits, but that has nothing to do with the rising prices experienced in inflation. Prices that lag should be allowed to catch up and reestablish the relation to other prices that demand and supply conditions generate in equilibrium. The new equilibrium will be attained eventually, and the sooner the better. Restraining the catch-up of administered prices will only delay it to no purpose.

The concept of administered prices is useful in the analysis of short-run dynamics, to refer to prices that tend for certain reasons to be unresponsive to short-run shifts in demand. But the concern long focused on administered prices as the source of a cost-push inflation has diverted attention from important developments in the inflationary process and the associated policy problems.

Integration of the Evidence on Costs and Concentration

What are the implications of these various pieces of evidence on price behavior for the process of inflation? They can be interpreted as indicating that concentrated industries are more likely to be characterized by some discretionary price setting by firms, as distinct from the highly competitive markets for many agricultural products and raw materials, which are characterized by market-determined prices. The existence of inventories, as well as other characteristics of industries, may also be relevant to this dimension of the behavior of prices. The importance of price setting is that firms in industries where it is the rule appear to coordinate price changes with each other so far as possible. The various methods of coordination require these firms to disregard short-run shifts in demand and to depend instead on changes in costs. As a consequence, their prices exhibit smaller fluctuations over the business cycle and less sensitivity to increases and retardations of general inflation. They appear to be less flexible, and they impede the propagation of inflationary pressures through the economy. Their lags of adjustment are evident in an inflationary upswing by the fact that basic commodity prices move earlier and faster. As inflationary pressures wane, they make catch-up increases that present the paradox of rising prices at a time when demand is slackening and when many prices in "competitive" markets are stable or declining.

On this interpretation inflexible prices do not initiate inflation; but they play a crucial role in transmitting it and in delaying the success of policies to curb it. The transmission of excess demand initially through increases in output and then in costs influences the dynamics of inflation by stretching it out. As wage rates catch up to past inflation and are passed through as further price increases, the cost of living goes up and feeds back on wages in a subsequent round of labor contracts. Thus the sequence of adjustments to inflation can appear to be unending and impervious to policies of restraint to unwind it. The persistence of inflation in the face of the 1970 recession and subsequent price and wage controls showed the extended and exasperating road that policy can follow in pursuit of price stability, in this instance only to end in failure.

Downward Rigidity and Asymmetry of Price Changes

The greater public sensitivity to unemployment since the Great Depression, as attested by the passage of the Employment Act of 1946, has made the pursuit of policies of high employment politically attractive. These policies, together with a dependence of prices on costs and the accompanying slow response to shifts in demand, generate a potential for persistent inflation. The slow deceleration of an ongoing inflation when demand slackens means that output and employment are initially cut back to absorb most of the impact; and if signs of these cuts induce policymakers to take steps to expand aggregate demand, monetary support is provided for the existing level of prices, whatever it may be. The potential for inflation in high employment policies was widely associated in the 1950s with the "downward rigidity" of prices.

Downward rigidity is a corollary to the dependence of prices on costs: if costs never move downward, neither do prices. Allegedly, price changes can decline from a positive to a zero rate but not to a negative rate. When in the recessions of 1954 and 1958 the aggregate index of wholesale prices failed to decline in the historical fashion that had held true as recently as 1949 (see table 1.1), the failure was attributed to downward rigidity. The new behavior had alarming implications. If during recessions prices and wages remained rigid at the levels attained in the preceding cyclical expansions, the economy could not return to full employment in the ensuing recovery without a commensurate expansion of aggregate demand. Yet if monetary policy provided the necessary stimulus to aggregate demand to achieve full employment, prices would begin each new expansion on the level attained at the end of the last one. Even should cycles in aggregate demand be miraculously ended, the composition of demand would be bound to fluctuate among industries. As demand in certain industries expanded, their prices would rise, while the prices of industries experiencing a complementary slack would not fall. The consequences of this scenario are clear: inflationary episodes are bound to occur sporadically; if prices do not decline between such episodes, they must trend inexorably upward.[22]

While the observed dependence of prices on costs implies that the short-run influence of demand is slight, if not necessarily nonexistent, the notion of downward rigidity even more pessimistically implies that most prices never fall in response to a decline in demand. The obvious examples are wages[23] and utility prices determined by contract or set by regulatory commissions, none of which change at all until renegotiated. Industries vulnerable to public opinion or subject to government regulation may eschew price reductions for fear of inability to raise prices later, or as a safeguard against the imposition of price controls. If firms believe all declines in demand to be brief and increases to be permanent, the asymmetry in price changes is explained. But a belief in a rising trend of demand would mean that any deviations from the trend would be perceived as brief, and the rigidity would take the form of small and infrequent deviations from the upward trend in the rate of price change, not the specific form of an asymmetrical barrier to *negative* rates of price change. As a general rule for most industries, a pricing strategy that precludes a decline in prices seems difficult to rationalize.

Downward rigidity of prices is often attributed to oligopolistic industries. A common argument is that oligopolies could expand production and reduce their average costs, because they face downward sloping demand curves and production settles at the point where the demand curve is tangent to the downward sloping portion of the average cost curve. Attempts of any one firm to sell more, cutting into the shares of competitors, could bring on a price war that would reduce profits for all. Price stability thus requires general acceptance in the industry of the market shares resulting from nonprice forms of competition.[24] Since reductions in price threaten that cooperation, they are avoided, while increases occur more freely.

Although the danger of price wars may be greater under oligopoly, it does not follow that price changes are more difficult to coordinate and more assiduously avoided. Industries with only a few major competitors may even find it easier to coordinate price changes. In any event, as already noted, the prices of more concentrated industries identified with oligopoly do appear to lag during inflationary movements; but they appear to respond more slowly to changes in demand in *both* directions, and not asymmetrically less to decreases than to increases.

Nevertheless, the prevalence of downward rigidity is widely assumed. It is thought to be confirmed by the large number of reported prices that change very little during recessions. There is no doubt that prices of manufactured goods change infrequently compared with the day-to-day or even hourly changes of commodities traded on organized exchanges. Yet the very large number of prices that remain unchanged during recessions raises questions about the validity of these data. One argument is that the data do not reflect the secret discounting and shading that are presumed to occur in actual transactions for industrial products when demand is slack.

In a major study of this question, Stigler and Kindahl collected from buyers actual prices paid for industrial products and, from these, constructed price indexes for the period 1958–63.[25] Their indexes move differently from the corresponding series compiled by the Bureau of Labor Statistics using reports of sellers. It is clear that widespread market discounting occurs from list prices, and that downward rigidity of prices largely disappears in the data collected from buyers: in a comparison between sixty-two price indexes for manufacturing industries constructed by Stigler and Kindahl and corresponding BLS indexes, 31 percent of the BLS indexes did not change at all in the 1958 recession while only 3 percent of the Stigler-Kindahl indexes showed no movement; in the 1961 recession the percentages were 39 and 5, respectively (see chapter 3). The individual price series of the Stigler-Kindahl data show numerous small declines in periods of slack that do not appear in the BLS reported quotations, and the Stigler-Kindahl data do not show a major asymmetry in the dispersion of price changes.

These observations in no way refute the fact that many prices have been less volatile and less sensitive in recent recessions than they once were. But a less sensitive response of rates of price change to short-run shifts in demand is not the same as a downward rigidity of price levels. While most manufacturing prices show small *changes* in average rates of price change over a period, they do not display a barrier to negative rates or an asymmetry in the direction of response. As is shown in chapter 3, changes in the rates of change of individual prices from expansions to ensuing recessions are not predominately zero, and exhibit a similar dispersion in most post–World War II cycles.

While the tendency of rates of price change to resist going below zero was thought to be the main problem in the mild inflation of the 1950s, in recent experience a similar resistance appears at higher rates of inflation: now prices take almost as long to decelerate from, say, 6 to 3 percent per year as they once did from 2 to −1. This suggests that the problem is not so much a downward rigidity in price *levels* as a resistance to changes in either direction away from the going *rates of increase*.

The Tradeoff between Inflation and Output

As it became clear during the second half of the 1960s that inflation had become something more than a simple reflection of downward rigidity in prices, the problem came to be seen as the tendency of prices to continue rising in the face of slack demand. Output took the brunt of declining aggregate demand. The choices thus presented to policy were represented by a tradeoff between output and inflation:

restraint undertaken to reduce the rate of inflation would also substantially curtail output. Similarly, stimulation applied to expand output would increase the rate of inflation.[26] As an example, the low rate of price change in 1962 and 1963 was associated with an unemployment rate of 5.5 percent, and the subsequent reduction of unemployment to 3.5 or 4 percent in the 1965–69 period by expansive policy actions led to a rise in the average rate of change in the consumer price index from 2 percent per year to 6 percent. The tradeoff relationship was a simple quantitative expression of these associated changes in output and the inflation rate.

The tradeoff between output and inflation depends upon the stage of the business cycle. At the bottom of a business recession when many resources are idle, output recovers with less upward pressure on costs and prices than is true in the advanced stages of expansion that depend mainly on overtime work. At high levels of capacity utilization, bottlenecks develop, unfilled orders rise, delivery times lengthen, and prices are pushed and pulled up at a quickening pace. The stage of the business cycle can be partly taken into account by weighting the quantitative relationship to show a greater effect on output when the economy is depressed and a greater effect on prices when the economy is booming. This is usually done by expressing the tradeoff as a relation between the rate of inflation and the gap between the actual and the potential level of output. Potential output is a reference point intended to approximate normal productive capacity ready for use at the moment. Even at so-called "normal" levels of capacity utilization, output can expand through a temporary "overuse" of productive facilities, though usually with substantial price advances. Hence potential output is not a barrier, and a negative gap can exist in which actual output exceeds the potential level. The gap is intended to measure the presure of idle or scarce resources on prices. When the gap is large, the rate of inflation is low; as it narrows, inflation increases.

To be sure, this gap does not account for all price movements. At the bottom of cyclical contractions and despite a large overall gap, the first signs of recovery usually bring sizable price increases in markets for sensitive raw materials, partly as a recovery from previous deep declines due to distress selling and partly in expectation of higher sales to come. After these initial increases, prices in these markets may then stabilize until supplies become tight in the later stages of the cyclical expansion. Intermediate and finished products do not uniformly pass on these early increases in the cost of materials. While competitive industries respond directly to demand influences, others may not increase prices until tightening factor markets raise costs substantially above prerecession levels. Despite the variety of response patterns, price increases spread and speed up as more and more idled resources are put back to work. Thus a cyclical upswing elicits an expanding wave of price increases along the way.

The division of aggregate demand between output and prices depends in large part, therefore, upon the amount of idle capacity. Capacity involves both capital equipment and labor, though usually the measurement takes only unemployed labor into account. In assessing past experience on the tradeoff, one difficulty has been the changing level at which the labor force can be considered to be fully employed. Trends in the composition and mobility of the labor force have increased the incidence of unemployment. During the Korean War inflation, unemployment ranged from 2.5 to 3.5 percent, while under the higher inflation rates of the Vietnam War it ranged from 3.5 to 4 percent. In the 1972 recovery, prices began to accelerate before unemployment fell to 4.5 percent. Labor force developments have shifted the measured tradeoff between inflation and the gap between actual and potential employment, where potential is calibrated according to earlier experience. (These developments are discussed in chapter 8.) Insofar as the shift reflects the changing character of the labor force, however, it does not imply a change in the behavior of prices.

"Full employment" is a vague concept and difficult to measure precisely; policy discussions undoubtedly would be less confusing without it. But, even allowing for changes in the full employment point, the adjusted tradeoff appears to have shifted over the postwar period toward higher inflation rates for a given gap between actual and potential employment. Allowing for the difference in levels of full employment, the United States has experienced high rates of inflation in recent years compared with much lower rates in the past at the full employment levels then prevailing.

The inescapable implication of the recent escalation of inflation at higher levels of unemployment, as well as at conceptually comparable levels of full employment, is that wage rates are rising faster, presumably in response to the greater general inflation of prices. One reason is that wages respond with lags but gradually make up for past inflation as it is reflected in the cost of living. In addition, wages (and other prices, too, for that matter) also incorporate anticipations of future inflation, which can fundamentally affect the whole process.

Effect of the Anticipated Rate of Inflation on Prices and Wages

The phenomenon of anticipatory wage and price increases has received considerable attention in recent discussions of inflation. Anticipations of inflation are obviously relevant to any economic transaction fixed in dollar terms for a period of time, and therefore particularly relevant to wages. Due to both custom and union contracts, wages are changed infrequently, which makes the degree of inflation over the period until the next negotiation crucial to the current one if the purchasing power of workers' incomes is to be sustained. Anticipations of inflation prompt workers to bargain for wage increases sufficient to allow at the outset for anticipated increases in the cost of living over the life of the contract; or they seek escalator clauses, which automatically keep wages in line with the cost of living.

Although an effect of anticipations on wages used to be denied, there can be no doubt today that some anticipated rate of inflation has been built into wages, and that this accounts for continuing high rates of increase after the initial catch-up. Unemployment averaged 5.5 percent from 1962 to 1964 while compensation per hour in the private economy was rising 4.5 to 5 percent per year. From 1964 to 1969 the unemployment rate fell to 3.5 percent and compensation escalated to 7.5 percent per year; conceivably the tradeoff was at work. Then from 1970 to 1972 the unemployment rate again rose to 5 percent and above, but compensation accelerated almost to 7 percent per year, and in 1973 to 8 percent with unemployment still at 5 percent. These high wage increases can be reconciled with historical experience only by recognizing that the inflation rate had risen and was expected to continue to be as high.

It is difficult to distinguish catch-up from anticipatory increases, to be sure, because each adjustment in wages tends to compensate for unanticipated increases in the cost of living since the last adjustment. Catch-up increases bring wages up to previous levels in real terms and do not add to existing inflationary pressures. Anticipatory increases take real wages above previous levels on the supposition that prices will soon catch up. Some evidence on anticipations is afforded by multi-year union contracts, since they are usually front loaded with especially large increases in the first year to compensate fully for past inflation. In 1970 and 1971 the first-year increases were running above 10 percent, but by 1973 they were not much above the second- and third-year increases provided in multi-year contracts (though the duration of contracts understandably shortened). The later-year increases in contracts negotiated in 1973 averaged from 5.5 to 6.5 percent per year, which indicated anticipations of continuing inflation, though by hindsight these increases were too low and subsequent contracts again had to include catch-up adjustments.

Anticipatory increases in wages can be confused with an ordinary wage push that is thought to initiate inflationary pressure. They have the same effect; the main difference is that they are an attempt merely to offset an expected inflation-bred reduction in purchasing power rather than to raise *real* wages. They also differ in timing and origin from ordinary wage push: they usually come in the later stages of inflationary movements, after wages have begun to adjust, and they are not generally confined to the strongest unions but appear to germinate widely throughout the wage and salary structure.

Anticipatory increases in prices as well as wages avoid the money illusion of treating a dollar as a dollar when its purchasing power is falling. They can work to reinforce the dependence of prices on costs and to reduce the influence of short-run shifts in demand. The argument earlier was that the costs and difficulties of coordinating price changes in less than fully competitive markets foster a reliance on changes in unit resource costs as the best guide to the equilibrium price path. Although prices will be changed more often in inflationary periods, each new quotation will have to anticipate the future so that it stays reasonably close to the average equilibrium price until the next likely change. Since cost inflation in particular industries reflects the overall rate of inflation, anticipations of changes in particular costs will rely heavily on anticipations of general inflation.

To the extent that they are raised to allow for cost increases to come, prices follow an upward trend irrespective of market transactions. In this way the price system adjusts on a current basis to the anticipated rate of inflation and need not wait for the emergence of excess demand in each market to pull prices up. Anticipatory increases are the mechanism by which the price system adapts more efficiently to inflation. If the price adjustments are accurate, they clear markets on the average over time, and discrepancies due to short-run variations in demand from anticipated trends are absorbed by the usual fluctuations in inventories and unfilled orders. Obviously, real-world inflations are not so smooth as to make it easy for firms to track the market-clearing price levels, but, unless prices are changed very often, a prolonged inflation tends to induce anticipatory adjustments.

Anticipatory price and wage increases help to explain the persistence of inflation and the recent shift in the tradeoff between output and inflation. A short-run tradeoff exists because faster growth of aggregate expenditures raises the rate of inflation and expands the demand for labor at the existing money-wage structure while real wages decline. Hence employment and output initially rise. As wage contracts come to reflect the higher demand for labor and rate of inflation, real wages recover and cut back the expansion of employment and output. The initial reduction in unemployment is gradually lost even though the rate of inflation remains higher. In this way increases in the anticipated rate of inflation over the postwar period have shifted the tradeoff toward higher inflation rates at any given gap between actual and potential employment.

Anticipations are by their nature based on perceived trends and so do not change quickly. The price increases they induce are transmitted through the economy as higher costs to other products, just like any other increases, and thereby add to inflationary pressures. Anticipations thus build a momentum into inflationary movements that takes time to abate and that further shifts the initial impact of monetary restraint from prices to output. The restraint to subdue inflation works more slowly, because it must first retard the more responsive prices and then gradually penetrate the anticipations that are pulling up the others. Inevitably, the distortions and dislocations due to the differential impacts of restraint are serious and protracted.

The Tradeoff in the Long Run

Anticipations of the rate of inflation are bound to change as events unfold. What happens over time? The short-run effect of a policy restraint on aggregate demand reduces output and only gradually slows inflation, in large part because of anticipations; with time the price deceleration accumulates, and the longer-run effect on prices is bound to be stronger. Hence the *longer-run* tradeoff is more favorable to a policy of reducing inflation and achieving high employment. In the opposite direction, when policy stimulates aggregate demand, the effect on inflation will also be stronger in the long than in the short run; hence attempts to raise employment beyond a certain point will be inflationary in the long run even though the short-run effect on employment is favorable.

The final long-run consequences of the tradeoff have been sharply debated. In one view policy could institute some stable growth of aggregate demand to produce any selected long-run average rate of inflation, even zero, while output and employment would approach the same growth path of reasonably full utilization of resources whatever the rate of inflation. The argument is based on the proposition that the public eventually "catches on" to continuing inflation. All prices and wages in time come to anticipate the trend rate of inflation completely, which removes any influence on long-run output and employment of the level of prices or their trend rate of change; hence, ultimately, *no permanent tradeoff exists*. In another view this full adjustment to inflation is never reached, particularly for wages. Consequently, price stability requires a permanent gap between actual and potential output that is larger than the minimum attainable; smaller gaps can be maintained, but they entail a permanently higher rate of inflation.

There are two issues here. The first is whether the level of unemployment that is consistent with price stability should be viewed as "full employment" and accepted as satisfactory even though lower levels are attainable. One answer is no, and the reason offered is that prices start to rise well before cyclical unemployment becomes zero and when the number of job seekers exactly matches job vacancies. The reason for this incipient inflationary pressure, aside from certain instances of union power, would have to be that variations in tightness among labor markets affect wages asymmetrically: "unemployment retards money wages less than vacancies accelerate them."[27] This would mean that at full employment—defined in this case as equality between the number of unemployed workers and job vacancies—the average wage rate rises faster than productivity growth.

The second issue is the question of whether there is some "natural" level of unemployment to which the economy gravitates irrespective of the level or rate of change of nominal wages,[28] so that a faster growth of aggregate demand and the accompanying higher rate of inflation would not permanently lower the level of unemployment. The short-run effect of an expansion in aggregate demand on unemployment is so evident over the business cycle that a permanent effect may also seem obvious to the man in the street; yet a permanent effect contradicts the economic principle that all prices and wages eventually anticipate the trend rate of inflation completely because workers and consumers are free of money illusion and adjust fully to demand and supply conditions.

Could the adjustment be incomplete? One argument is that the economy always harbors marginal workers who are ready to accept employment and who will be employed if the real wage for all workers falls. A step-up of inflation reduces real wages if money wages do not rise proportionately. But would employed workers accept this reduction? Failure of the supply of labor to respond to such a reduction in real wages implies an irrational money illusion on the part of the workers, at least up to some threshold level, and is usually assumed away in economic theory. Some economists, however, do not think that such an insensitivity in labor supply is entirely implausible. Except for renegotiated union contracts, employers are the originators of changes in nominal wages, and for various reasons they may allow reductions in real wages due to inflation to persist. Most workers will not quit when their real wages fall due to inflation, because they are mainly concerned with relative wage levels vis-à-vis each other and do not pay close attention to real purchasing power of their wages so long as it does not change substantially or continually.[29]

The evidence on these issues is difficult to interpret. When inflation intensified in 1973, for example, wages did not immediately rise commensurately. What appeared to be an incomplete response, however, may have been only a slow response. A change in the inflation rate is not viewed as lasting until it has persisted for a time and, insofar as expectations are based on past and current experience, they are adjusted to that experience with a lag. Whether wages eventually adjust *completely* to the trend rate of inflation cannot be concluded from short-run behavior. Attempts to estimate the long-run outcome econometrically[30] have not been successful because of problems in measuring the anticipated rate of inflation.[31] Therefore, whether the adjustment is complete in the long run or not is uncertain, and the existence of a long-run tradeoff between inflation and unemployment remains an open question.

Recent discussions sometimes seem to imply that inflation is preferable to monetary restraint no matter how the long-run tradeoff turns out. It is argued that, so long as anticipatory adjustments to inflation are incomplete, inflation provides benefits in the form of reduced unemployment. That is what the tradeoff means. Then, if and when anticipatory adjustments are completed, inflation has no permanent effect on unemployment, but neither does such fully anticipated inflation affect the allocation of resources or the distribution of incomes. Inflation is virtually painless![32]

That is a rose-colored view. The reality of inflation is far from appealing. The dispute over the long-run tradeoff has unfortunately detracted from the serious problems of dealing with inflation in the short run. At any given time, adjustments are far from complete and, judging by the public outcry, inflation is extremely painful; at the same time bouts of higher unemployment are not highly effective against inflation. (The temporary reduction in unemployment induced by inflation is all a net benefit only if it is not necessary or desirable later to subdue the inflation.) Whatever the outcome of the long-run tradeoff, anticipations of inflation clearly prolong it in the short run and aggravate the problem of curbing it. Even if anticipations have so far been slow to incorporate the full intensity of actual inflation, they have nevertheless kept prices rising faster in periods of restraint on aggregate demand, and thus have compromised the immediate effectiveness of policies to curb inflation and compounded the difficulty of carrying them through to success.

Anticipations of Inflation and Uncertainty

Anticipations of inflation are a problem for policy, therefore, because they are slow to adjust and can keep wages and prices rising faster for a time than the rate justified over the longer run by policy restraints on demand growth. Yet this problem could lessen with various developments. Except for prices fixed by contract, the only direct constraints on the frequency of price changes are minor administrative costs, and presumably changes could be coordinated more frequently to prevent prices from straying far out of line in a rapidly changing inflation. The duration of contracts could be shortened. The pay provisions of union contracts could be negotiated more often. (Indeed, the duration of wage contracts has declined in recent years.) In addition, escalator clauses could help to keep wage and price contracts in line with a general index of prices, although selection of a single, universally applicable, index is difficult.[33]

Escalator clauses—so far more talked about than used—are said to reduce public resistance to inflation, because the benefited groups would be protected against inflation and the nation's determination to undergo the hardships of subduing inflation would fade. In this view, inflation would increase. While escalators reduce lags in the transmission of inflation and would speed up the adjustment of the price and wage structure to inflationary pressures, they also speed up the response to an *easing* of inflation. Whether escalator clauses would make the rate of inflation any different over the long run is not clear. In any event, there is no justification for opposing them for groups that fall behind in inflation, even if the result is to speed up inflation for others who manage to maintain their relative position without them.

Neither a rise in the anticipated rate of inflation over the postwar period nor the spread of escalator clauses can account for the diminished response of prices to recessions since the 1950s. A higher anticipated rate of inflation makes the actual rates of price and wage change higher but would not affect their tendency to decline when markets slackened. Escalators might, if anything, hasten this decline. The dampened response appears to reflect instead a strengthened, general belief that inflationary movements will not be subdued quickly, as distinct from anticipations of a particular rate of inflation. Such a belief pertains to the likelihood of rising prices, but may well be accompanied by greater uncertainty over the particular rate of rise. Its acceptance has undoubtedly spread since World War II because of the demise of the traditional gold standard, which over the long run kept the growth of money stocks and therefore of prices more or less in line with the expansion in the gold stock. In recent decades, with money and prices no longer tied to gold, governments have been free to pursue full employment policies largely unconstrained by gold reserve requirements. The consequences of such policies are probably the most important reason for the prevalence and strength of the belief in recurring inflation. In the heyday of the gold standard before World War I, price movements usually reversed themselves (as shown by a negative serial correlation) after a few years; but since it was abandoned, the movements have had a positive relation—that is, when prices rose, their subsequent change was more likely to be up than down.[34]

In this environment there is little assurance that prices will stay within any bounds, and considerable uncertainty surrounds the future. The implication for behavior is a dampening of the initial response to a shift in demand because its permanence seems uncertain, and, at the same time, a reinforcement of the expectation that inflationary surges like that of 1973 will not be reversed because policy is committed to avoid declines in output and employment. The problem of controlling inflation is thus exacerbated by a ready transmission of upswings through the price system and a laggard response of prices to a slowing of aggregate demand.

The Dilemma of Policy

Since World War II a central issue of policy has been whether price stability and full employment are compatible. With the explosion of prices in 1973 and 1974 after seven years of inflation, that issue gave way to the more frightening question of whether inflation could be controlled at all. Where debate once concerned the willingness and ability of the nation to live with permanent inflation of 3 to 4 percent per year in order to enjoy full employment, the public has had to cope with inflation at double or more those earlier rates and to worry about the possibility of ever higher rates. The inflation that began in 1965 followed three other postwar episodes, during which public dissatisfaction and concern was also manifest. An injunction to public officials to avoid inflation was not lacking.[35]

Part of the escalation of inflation in 1973, to be sure, reflected the closer ties to foreign countries inherent in expanding international trade and finance: the escalation was worldwide. The abandonment of fixed exchange rates in the early 1970s was supposed to loosen those ties, but whether it did is not clear. Nevertheless, inflation had become a major problem in the United States primarily as a result of domestic developments. Although similar developments had occurred in other countries, inflation has been handled in most countries as a domestic problem, linked worldwide by the ties of international trade and finance but not determined by them.

The Declining Effectiveness of Policy Restraints against Inflation

For U.S. policy in particular, the problem relates to the drawn-out process by which an inflationary impulse continues to work its way through the economy once the pressure of excess demand eases. To recapitulate briefly, the slow pace of the process can be traced to the sluggish response of most manufacturing prices to short-run shifts in demand. These prices are "administered" by individual sellers, as distinct from prices determined in the market from moment to moment by supply and demand, as on commodity exchanges. To be sure, administered prices are also determined ultimately by supply and demand conditions, but the determination is the outcome of a market process in which firms set their selling prices, not to clear the market at the moment, but to follow the perceived equilibrium path. Although the sluggish behavior of manufacturing prices has long been observed, its theoretical explanation has yet to be worked out. It appears to be the outcome of various methods to coordinate price changes among firms in the industry, with the purpose of avoiding the disarray and confusion of a group of competitors searching for an equilibrium price individually and at cross purposes. Price leadership is one method, and infrequent price changes are another. Coordination is also facilitated by basing selling prices on unit resource costs common to all firms in an industry. That accounts for the observed dependence of manufacturing prices on input costs and the apparent unresponsiveness of prices to short-run shifts in demand, which are absorbed instead by variations in inventories, unfilled orders, and output. As a consequence, inflationary surges in aggregate demand, which usually appear first in markets for final goods and services, are transmitted back to earlier stages of production via expansions in demand and output, affecting prices initially in basic commodity markets and then traveling forward from stage to stage in the form of increases in input costs. The tightening of labor markets occasioned by these expansions of output may lead to some immediate wage advances, but custom and union contracts make wage rates extremely sluggish, and delay the main effect on wages until renegotiation allows them to catch up to the rising cost of living. The higher wages then generate further increases in costs and prices which ripple up and down the price structure. Of course, as with most generalizations about the economy, this sequence has many exceptions; but experience shows that, after an inflationary movement subsides, the price system takes several years to complete all adjustments.

The dependence of prices on costs causes prices to continue to rise after market demand slackens, a puzzling phenomenon that, at first sight, fosters the view that such prices are impervious to policies to curb inflation. The sequence of cost-price responses also gives the appearance that costs initiate inflationary impulses, whereas excess demand is responsible in most cases. Prices in the more concentrated industries and of large corporations tend to increase more than other prices in the aftermath of inflationary upswings when demand slackens, because they lag behind at first and catch up later. These later price increases are criticized for spearheading a continuation of inflation when in fact they are bringing up the rear. Such lagged behavior slows and prolongs the transmission of inflation and, though a moderating influence, complicates the timing of policy restraints.

Labor unions are also falsely accused of initiating cost-push inflation, for they too generally lag and have to catch up later. But the complaint against unions has some merit, because catch-up wage demands of strong unions may interact to initiate a leapfrog sequence that brings about increases that go well beyond what market conditions would justify. The construction trades in the late 1960s offer the prime example. Under the pressure of this leapfrogging, cost push replaces demand pull in the later stages of inflation.

Wages and some prices also become less responsive to demand conditions to the extent that they are influenced by anticipations of the future rate of inflation. This becomes a serious problem should policymakers try to reduce the rate of inflation below the anticipated rate. Although a slow adjustment of the anticipated to the actual rate preserves a tradeoff between inflation and employment and therefore has been extolled, it is beneficial only for increases in inflation. For reductions, slowly adjusting anticipations are a problem for policy because they build a momentum into rising prices that can be halted only over an extended period. This is true whether anticipations of inflation partially or fully adjust to the actual trend rate in the long run and whether the tradeoff is permanent or temporary.

Thus, when restraint on aggregate demand takes hold, price increases will begin to decelerate, but the deceleration may take a long time to make much headway, and in the meantime the restraint appears to be largely ineffective. Wages and manufacturing prices have always been sluggish, of course, and inflationary movements, when not reversed sharply as in 1921 and 1951, have always taken years to work through the price system. But the process was clearly working more slowly in the recessions of the late 1950s and of 1970–71 than had been expected from earlier experience. As table 1.1 showed, prices became less and less responsive to business recessions over the postwar period, so that in the 1970 recession the rate of inflation actually rose slightly. The rise did not mean that restraint was not at work below the surface, for the inflation did begin to ease in 1971 even before the imposition of the freeze. Still, a mild recession like 1970 had less effect on prices than ever before.

Part of the smaller amplitude of cyclical fluctuation in prices reflects the reduced severity of business recessions since World War II, for which some credit goes to the contribution of economic research to improved stabilization techniques. Nevertheless, in addition to the smaller cyclical contractions in aggregate expenditures, the response of prices to a given amplitude of contraction has declined, so that now proportionately more of the contraction in expenditures falls on output.

What explains the diminishing response of prices? The anticipated rate of inflation has no doubt increased as actual inflation has progressed, but this by itself would not influence the magnitude of changes in *rates of price change*. Since the prices of nearly all products are less responsive (the main exceptions are raw materials), the phenomenon cannot be blamed on particular sectors characterized by union or corporate monopoly, or high concentration, though certainly unions impede the deceleration of costs in times of slack. Although strictly a postwar development, the phenomenon covers over two decades now and so qualifies as a trend. Such a broad and gradual change in price behavior seems to arise from a strengthened, general belief that inflationary movements will not be quickly subdued.

This belief has presumably been fostered by several developments: the upward trend of prices since World War II; the national commitment to stabilize economic activity and maintain high employment, as expressed in the Employment Act of 1946; and a growing suspicion that the nation's determination to fight inflation and endure the resulting economic slack may, when the chips are down, have weakened. Certainly, preoccupation with the extreme unemployment of the 1930s heightened sensitivity to *any* unemployment. Finally, a spreading awareness of the reduced effectiveness of the policy instruments, highlighted by the failure to avoid the spectacular burst of inflation in 1973, has no doubt further strengthened the belief that inflation is more likely to escalate than to slow down. This would explain a reduced response of prices to declines in demand.

Whatever the reasons, the declining effectiveness of policy restraints against inflation can be documented by postwar changes in the behavior of prices. It may seem paradoxical to attribute the problem of controlling inflation to the *sluggish* response of wages and manufacturing prices to shifts in demand, but the effect is to prolong the adjustment of prices to policy restraints, so that, whenever inflation gains a foothold, a restraint to be successful must be pursued with a vigor or persistence that the postwar sensitivity to unemployment no longer permits. Policymakers face a dilemma. Inflation can be stopped, but the traditional policies work less effectively, and the nation has become more reluctant to incur the costs of using them forcefully. Hence doubt of the nation's ability to control inflation deepens, thus weakening price responses and, in turn, the effectiveness of policy restraint. Thus does inflation feed on its own strength.

The Resort to Wage and Price Controls

In the search for a way around the policy dilemma, many people view direct controls on wages and prices as a natural step. Controls put a damper on inflation without seeming to require restraints on aggregate demand or any increase in unemployment. Aside from wartime, controls were loosely imposed as guideposts for wage and price increases in the early and middle 1960s and then were formally imposed in successive phases beginning in August 1971 and finally ended in April 1974. From the public's point of view, price increases serve only to augment unnecessary profits of sellers, so a remedy that makes increases unlawful seems natural. The fact that, in the vast majority of cases, price increases are necessary to cover costs of production is lost in the oversimplification of this view. There is never a right moment when an inflationary process can be frozen by decree without imposing hardships on many sellers who need to raise prices to cover recent cost increases. Price controls interrupt this continuous process without removing the pressure for increases and so blindly dislocate the price system and disrupt production.

Furthermore, controls are unlikely even to make the ultimate total rise in prices less than it would have been had they not been imposed, given the same path of aggregate demand. Prices gravitate toward an equilibrium determined by the interaction of demand and supply conditions. Constraints such as controls can delay the adjustment, but eventually prices will find their equilibrium through evasion or after the controls are lifted. If controls do not affect the final equilibrium position, their delay of price changes accomplishes nothing except to cater to the public's proclivity to find scapegoats for rising prices.

The common rationale for controls is that they prevent the exercise of union and corporate power to push up wages and prices. Hence enforcement usually focuses on the labor and corporate giants, even though the evidence shows that they do not initiate inflation but actually tend to lose ground as it progresses. When later they begin to catch up, controls penalize them for having fallen behind. Delaying their catch-up provides no permanent benefit. Controls are equally disruptive and ultimately ineffective whether price increases are an adjustment to higher costs, which maintains or restores a standard profit margin, or are pulled up by excess demand, which initially raises profits. Prices will eventually rise to the same equilibrium level. Controls are supposed to prevent "excess" profits, but the freezes imposed in 1971 and 1973 largely exempted agricultural commodities, for which demand pull was strong, and for ease of administration were mainly enforced against large corporations, whose profit margins had been and were further depressed.

What case can be made for controls? One rationale is that they prevent wage and price increases due to anticipations of inflation. According to this argument, the anticipated rate of inflation enters into wage negotiations and to some extent into the setting of prices. Anticipations appear to adjust slowly to the actual rate of inflation and in an upswing induce lagging behavior. As inflationary pressures subside, anticipations may cause some wages and prices to perpetuate rates of increase whose justification has disappeared with the onset of slack market conditions. If controls prevent those increases or actually help to reduce the anticipated rate of inflation, they bring actual wage and price increases into line with slower growth in aggregate expenditures. If the controls go no further, they may prevent the prolongation of inflationary movements due to incorrect anticipations. By preventing prices from overshooting their equilibrium level, the controls achieve a higher level of employment.[36]

There is evidence of this effect of controls on construction wages after March 1971. It may have also been at work in the first year of general controls after August 1971, though there is no confirming indication of much deceleration in wages during that period. The main impact was on profit margins[37] which had declined during the upswing of inflation from 1966 to 1969 and would sooner or later have to rise. The controls had no lasting benefit. When controls are most wanted by the public—in periods of rising demand-pull inflation—they collapse. This happened to the guideposts in the mid-1960s and to the freeze in June 1973.

To be effective and beneficial, controls must distinguish between those wage and price increases that represent catching up with past inflation and those that are anticipating future inflation. To prevent the former increases is futile; and such an attempt, if directed against union wages, creates strife. But at any moment the two kinds of increases are for all practical purposes indistinguishable. Furthermore, the anticipatory increases should not be repressed unless they are indeed mistaken, which implies that policy will in fact be successful in its intention to subdue inflation. In that event, controls may be marginally effective when they are least needed and demanded by the public. They cannot, moreover, rescue an unsuccessful policy. In view of their limited usefulness, their dislocations to the economy, and the danger they will mislead policymakers into believing that suppressed inflationary pressures are in fact subdued and thus into overstimulating the economy, as in 1972, their value as a placebo is not worth the costs. The bitter experience of 1973 and 1974 showed once again that controls do not help.

The Bumpy Road Ahead

If controls offer no solution, and if the effectiveness of aggregate-demand restraint has diminished and little determination exists to step it up and sustain heavier cutbacks in output and employment, the prospects of subduing inflation are bleak. Sporadic outbursts, as in

1973, are bound to occur from time to time—indeed, more often and vigorously now in an inflationary world than ever. A growing belief in the persistence of inflation and fear of its escalation work to reduce the response of prices to restraint and make policy even less effective. A fight against inflation under these conditions is all uphill.

Yet the public injunction to fight inflation remains in force and, at least in public, policymakers remain committed to the battle. But what can they do? So long as public concern over unemployment rules out severe restraint, the only feasible policy is to maintain mild restraint for a long haul. Since the zone of demand-pull inflation moves about and cannot be predicted with precision, a cautious trial-and-error procedure is unavoidable in maintaining mild restraint. Furthermore, the response of prices is affected by the speed at which the zone is approached. The economy has to be kept below the zone of demand-pull inflation, which means braking cyclical recoveries like that in 1972 before they attain top speed and go too far. We know now that quick remedies for inflation do not exist and that restraint almost surely requires at least a mini-recession at the beginning and slow growth thereafter—though the earlier it is imposed in an inflationary movement the faster the results, as the difference between the effect on prices of the 1967 and 1970 slowdowns proved.

The standard method of curtailing aggregate demand is monetary restraint. Its effect on economic activity occurs in part through a restriction of the volume of lending and related investment spending, in which financial markets tighten and interest rates rise. The hardships thus imposed on certain sectors—particularly housing, which is dependent on mortgage funds, and on small businesses, which are dependent on bank loans—generate vociferous complaint. The only palliative is a special federal program to aid the stricken sectors, such as government funds channeled into the mortgage market. These programs do not alleviate the total pressure on financial markets but merely shift it from one sector to another. Ideally, the federal government should run a substantial budget surplus during times of monetary restraint to alleviate much of the financial pressure. This would require a timely reduction of expenditures or increase in taxes, however, and so far has not proved politically feasible. In any event, there is no alternative to monetary restraint. If monetary growth is not reduced, no combination of other steps can have any lasting effect on inflation.

Galloping inflation had been held up as a danger to the U.S. economy since the early postwar years. When it did not materialize during the 1950s and early 1960s, the danger was dismissed. Now that it is coming true, recent experience hardly gives much ground for believing that policy can be more successful in preventing inflation in the future. But galloping inflation does carry one benefit—the impressive demonstration that it can indeed happen. We know now what mild inflation can eventually turn into, and how little to expect from a mild restraint on aggregate demand.

The traps that the process of inflation holds for policy are now evident: the slow response of prices to shifts in demand have led, on the up side, to a prolongation of stimulative policies, which increases the momentum behind rising prices, and, on the down side, to an impatience with restraints, because of the larger initial effects on output and employment than on prices, and to their premature reversal. The net outcome has been a policy on balance favoring stimulus and giving an upward tilt to the trend of prices. To subdue inflation, the nation has to redress this imbalance.

2

Monetary versus Cost-Push Theories of Inflation

Inflation has been the subject of much controversy and research in recent years. Since the mid-1930s, prices have generally followed an upward trend, with still no end in sight. Yet, in historical perspective such a movement is not unusual in extent or duration, except for the absence of major declines in prices which often interrupted earlier inflations. Historical accounts tell us that inflation frequently plagued the ancient world. Later on, records since the thirteenth century on consumer prices for England show a strong upward trend for almost 150 years from the early 1500s to the mid-1600s and again for over 50 years from about 1750 to the early 1800s. Those earlier episodes also touched off much discussion and controversy. Since the recent flow of articles on inflation seems to have expanded in proportion to the duration of inflation, one wonders how in the mid-1600s, after 150 years of inflation, they found time to publish and read about anything else. One answer may be that economics was not then a university discipline. If the present dictum to "publish or perish" continues in academic life and the attention paid to inflation accelerates, I shudder to calculate the distribution by subject matter of journal articles and university courses in another 100 years.

That assumes, of course, that inflation stays with us that

Adapted from a paper originally published in Stephen W. Rousseas, ed. *Inflation: Its Causes, Consequences, and Control,* Proceedings of a Symposium held at New York University, January 31, 1968, The Calvin K. Kazanjian Economics Foundation.

long—a hazardous prediction. Prices generally fell during the second half of the nineteenth century. By the end of that period economics had become a university subject, and academic opinion took the view that deflation was a natural state of affairs and desirable as a way to distribute the benefits of technological progress to people with fixed incomes. The twentieth century has mangled many ideas of the nineteenth, but none more thoroughly than that one. Prices in our century have nevertheless fallen at times, most notably in 1921 and the early 1930s.

Because of the preoccupation with unemployment and stagnation during and following the Great Depression of the 1930s, the postwar resurgence of inflation was not widely expected and caught many economists unprepared. But not for long, and since World War II numerous theories and views of inflation have been presented—some of them new, though many only a slightly altered version of old ones. Theories of inflation have never been in short supply—no less in earlier times than now. We understand better why certain theories are popular today if we see how they have developed in response to the deficiencies of earlier views. The first part of this chapter briefly examines these antecedents, before appraising the current favorite.

Earlier Theories of Inflation No Longer Popular

The Quantity of Money

Theories of inflation come and go, dating an era like an archaeological artifact. Since early modern times, however, one theory has enjoyed a persistent though sometimes limited popularity. It is that the quantity of money is an important determinant of the value of money, and that continuing inflation reflects an expanding money stock. The evidence is certainly consistent with this explanation, and it is correct to say, I believe, that the money stock has been the main contributor to price changes in the long run.[1] The money stock itself can be explained by other factors—gold production and the interplay of domestic monetary institutions. Changes in the money stock have usually been independent of secular price changes and therefore are a determinant of them, though there is some interdependence through the feedback of prices on gold production in the very long run.

The reasons for monetary expansion vary greatly among periods—from the debasement of coinage by monarchs in earlier times to the more sophisticated expansion of currencies and deposits by central banks today. For countries on the gold standard the principal long-run determinant of money supplies has been each nation's gold stock, which for all countries together can expand in physical amount only through gold production, but which has from time to time been increased in value by currency depreciation—the modern counterpart to the ancient debasement of coinage. Barring major gold discoveries or new methods of extracting gold from low-grade ore, periodic depreciations are a prerequisite under the gold standard to a continuation of inflation over the long run: since rising prices discourage gold production, there must be some means of issuing more money for a given physical stock of gold. Increasing the monetary value of gold through currency depreciation is one way; enlarging the drawing rights of each member nation through the International Monetary Fund has been proposed as another.

An explanation of inflation in terms primarily of growth in the money stock, and secondarily in terms of gold discoveries or currency depreciation, has never received universal acceptance. It is even less popular today with our complex and managed monetary systems.(And since 1971, of course, gold reserves no longer play a role.) One side effect of the 1930s depression was to foster a disbelief in the importance of the money stock in economic affairs, a viewpoint which influenced subsequent thinking on the causes of inflation. The reasons for rejecting this explanation, in whole or in part, have varied, but the main one is that it is incomplete—it does not explain why governments have been forced to depreciate their currencies and allow money supplies to expand. Some recent theories seek to remedy this deficiency of the traditional quantity theory. They developed out of earlier theories which were quite inconsistent with the quantity theory, but recent versions have removed nearly all the inconsistency while retaining much of their original character.

Production Costs of Individual Commodities

The main competitors to the quantity theory can all be classified as cost-of-production theories in one form or another. Such theories posit an increase in the cost of producing goods and services, forcing prices to rise. In its original form, now seldom heard, the theory simply asserted that inflation reflected increases in the cost of producing commodities, for various reasons all related to the particular supply conditions of each commodity. This is obviously inadequate, since individual supply (as well as demand) conditions would affect relative prices but not the general level of prices. Such an explanation was given for the inflation of the 1850s and 1860s, and I find Stanley Jevons' rebuttal[2] to be a convincing blend of economic logic and empirical inference. He pointed out that the falling prices before 1850 had been rightly attributed to expanding population and trade, though not perhaps for the right reasons. The rising prices since 1850, in the face of a continuing expansion of population and trade, must be attributed to some other special factor that was not present before. He contended that the only plausible explanation was to be found in the extraordinary gold discoveries of 1848–51 in California and Australia. When the new sources petered out, therefore, prices would resume their normal downward trend. Jevons wrote that in 1869, not long before world prices began a descent that continued for over two decades. Few forecasters have done as well.

Capital Costs

A special version of the cost-of-production theory is that rising interest rates add to the cost of manufactured goods and so cause prices to rise. It has long been noted that interest rates and the price level tend to move in the same direction over time—the phenomenon has come to be known as the Gibson Paradox. It is an old idea that the creation of new money through a banking system initially adds to the supply of loanable funds and lowers interest rates. If increases in the money stock also lead to higher prices, interest rates and prices should therefore move in opposite directions. Yet we observe prices and interest rates to rise and fall together, which appears to contradict the quantity-theory explanation. Some writers have attributed the positive association to an effect of interest rates on the cost of production of goods. Authorities such as David Ricardo and Knut Wicksell have pointed out the fallacies in this argument, but it keeps reappearing. Monetary restraint is often criticized in Congress and the press as inflationary because it raises interest rates.

Economists no longer subscribe to this theory. Their mathematical training makes them immediately suspicious of linking interest rates to prices. Rates are pure numbers with a time dimension and have no dollar dimension as prices do. If 4 percent per year is paid to borrow money instead of 3 percent, how is that translated into the dollar price of a TV set? The interest rate must first be expressed as a dollar cost of the capital goods used in producing TV sets. For capital already financed over its full life by a bond issue, the interest cost is fixed. Only newly financed capital is affected by a change in interest rates. The fallacy of viewing interest as a cost affecting prices lies in ignoring the cause of changes in interest rates and the effect on the marginal productivity of capital. Suppose that interest rates rise because of a shift in the demand or supply curves for loanable funds. Only capital goods which are expected to provide a return equal to the higher interest rates will be purchased. Consequently, the carrying cost of new capital is covered by receipts from selling the goods produced at prevailing prices. No increase in prices is required just because interest rates rise. To be sure, shifts in the demand or supply of loanable funds can alter the amount of capital purchased per time period, which sets in train a reallocation of resources between the capital and consumer goods industries, with temporary repercussions on employment, output, and prices. But those effects can result from a shift of resources in either direction. Such effects on prices cannot be attributed to changes in the cost of production due to interest rates.[3]

This conclusion holds as well for the interest-rate effects of monetary policies. Suppose that the Federal Reserve reduces the growth of the money stock by selling U.S. bonds and thus raises interest rates. Capital financing becomes, for the moment, more expensive. Only investment projects with a rate of return above or equal to the higher borrowing rate will be undertaken. If market conditions remain as expected, existing prices will provide sufficient receipts to cover the higher cost of this new capital. Since the higher interest rate produces less investment than would otherwise have occurred, aggregate demand is held down, which is of course the purpose of monetary restraint in a boom.

The Wage-Price Spiral Theory

Rapid Acceptance of the Theory since the 1930s

Up to the 1930s there was no serious competitor to the quantity theory of money as the framework for explaining secular inflation (or deflation as well). The 1930s brought great changes, in economic theory and opinion as well as everything else. We need take note of just two changes here. First, that greatest monetary catastrophe of modern times produced a climate of opinion in which, ironically, economic events were widely analyzed and interpreted without regard to monetary conditions. Second, the labor union movement spread and became much more effective. The jump in wages and prices in 1934 resulting from the provisions of the National Recovery Act helped focus attention on the importance of wages and other costs in determining prices. The idea gained ground that labor unions had acquired widespread power over wages and pushed up the cost of production, which forced sellers to raise prices. These price increases then eroded the wage gains in real terms and led unions to press for additional wage increases. The seesaw process became known as the wage-price spiral. No doubt antecedents can be found in earlier writings, but the theory took shape in the 1930s and first became a topic of serious discussion in the inflation following World War II.

Increases in prices by product monopolies have also been cited as a source of inflation, but wages have received the most attention. The public attitude toward trade unions has changed. In the early days they were favored by many people as a means of raising the real wages of downtrodden workers. Today unions must contend with an unsympathetic public which takes them at their word and holds them responsible for raising nominal wages and forcing up prices. Union propaganda skirts the issue by stressing the allegedly "excessive" level of profits and has not succeeded in convincing the public that efforts to raise real wages are not at bottom inflationary. Yet raising the level of *real* wages, which is the economic purpose of unions, is not the same thing as continually raising *nominal* wage rates, which the public condemns. The difference between real and nominal wages should not be blurred. Union monopolies can be expected to try to widen the spread between members' real wages and other wages, but they cannot be expected to succeed in widening it continually. To produce a continual rise in nominal wages, either union power must continually increase, which has not occurred, or wages must adjust to prices and prices adjust to costs both with a lag. Then there might be adjustments back and forth which give the effect of a continuing spiral. The lag is therefore essential to the theory of a spiral. If the mutual adjustments occurred together without a lag, the market would remain in equilibrium and there would be no reason for a spiral.

Many people inferred from the price increases posted during 1946 and 1947, following the removal of the wartime price and wage controls, that inflation was simply a matter of prices and wages chasing each other around a spiral staircase. It must have soon become evident to most people that the removal of controls merely allowed public disclosure of inflationary pressures created during the war, and that such sizable price increases as occurred in 1946–47 resulted from the comparable wartime increases in the quantity of money. Price increases moderated thereafter, except for the scare buying in response to the outbreak of the Korean War. It took several years, well into the 1950s, before the public became fully aware that prices were relentlessly creeping upward, albeit by small sporadic steps. Each step was unalarming, but over a period of time the increases far outweighed the declines, and the net accumulation unmistakably produced an inflationary trend. With this realization public discussion rapidly adopted the wage-price spiral as one of the facts of life like those that science has conditioned us to accept without our observing or understanding them, such as subatomic particles, viruses, and the transformation of matter into energy.

Wage Push and Monetary Velocity

In its early versions, the theory of a wage-price spiral was incomplete and unconvincing, because it did not explain how aggregate demand could sustain rising prices. If labor unions push up costs and force prices higher, there must also be an increase in aggregate expenditures in order to sell the same quantity of goods. Otherwise, the higher costs and prices would lead to an undesired accumulation of inventories, followed by production cutbacks and unemployment. The upward thrust of prices would then lose momentum and soon falter. If prices in some sectors somehow continued to rise, the resulting unemployed resources in those sectors would gradually shift to other sectors of the economy and reduce costs and prices there. The average level of prices throughout the economy would then not rise.

One of the first counterarguments offered to this criticism of the spiral theory was that businesses would not immediately reduce output when faced with higher labor costs. Rescheduling output takes time, and meanwhile companies would continue as before, paying higher wages and meeting the higher payroll cost by dipping into their money balances. The higher wage income of workers would provide them as consumers with the means of increasing expenditures, and businesses would find that they could sell their output at higher prices. Aggregate expenditures thus could rise, attributable to an increase in the velocity of circulation of the money stock. After all, it was argued, an important motive for holding money is to allow time to deal with contingencies; it is to be expected that businesses will reduce cash balances to meet a sudden increase in costs.

To carry the analysis a step further, however, businesses would eventually want to restore the original relation between their average cash holdings and the volume of sales or total transactions. The restoration would in the aggregate reduce velocity and be deflationary, thereby forcing the production cutbacks previously put off. To be sure, one can suppose that the spiral keeps going by arguing that the demand to hold money permanently falls, so that the initial increase in expenditures is not reversed. The only possible reason why money demand should fall permanently in this process, however, is that the initial price increase somehow engenders an expectation that prices will continue to rise. People would then want to hold lower real money balances to avoid some of the expected loss in purchasing power. Although expectations of some rate of inflation will produce a once-and-for-all reduction in desired real money balances, such expectations will not produce continually falling balances. Consequently, the first round of the spiral, if it threatens to be regularly repeated, might be financed by such a once-and-for-all reduction in real balances, raising monetary velocity. However, subsequent rounds of the spiral necessary to maintain the reduced level of real balances will not be financed by increases in velocity, unless the expected rate of change of prices increases—which implies an explosive process, not the moderate inflation we have had. A self-generating inflation, in which expectations of an increasing rate of price change themselves produce the result expected, is theoretically possible, but it is so far removed from usual patterns of behavior that even hyperinflations do not satisfy the required conditions.[4] Such an explanation is out of the question for our recent experience.

In the years following World War II, velocity, as measured by the ratio of GNP or national income to the money stock (however defined), did in fact rise for many years, in contrast to its falling or horizontal trend in earlier decades. This fostered the view that wage-push inflation somehow led to a faster circulation of money and in that way increased aggregate demand. However, recent research has found quite different reasons for this behavior of velocity. It was abnormally low during the wartime years, and part of its rise in the first few years after the war merely offset the wartime decline. Then, in the early 1950s, the Federal Reserve abandoned its support of bond prices, allowing interest rates to rise, as they did. That increased the cost of holding money and led to a fall in desired real money balances, which raised velocity. In addition, expectations of rising prices may have contributed in small part to the rise in velocity, but a growing public recognition of the unlikelihood of severe depressions probably was more important. The new availability of attractive alternatives to money, like Treasury bills and insured savings and loan shares, also contributed. For a variety of reasons, therefore, velocity rose during this period. None of them had any relation to union pressures on wages.

Wage Push and Bank Loans

All inflations covering an extended period have, so far as is known, been accompanied by an expanding money supply. Velocity movements often reinforce the monetary expansion, but they have never accounted for a major part of the increase in prices. Any theory of inflation, to be complete, must explain how and why the money supply expands. Such incompleteness in early versions of the spiral theory was soon recognized, and one of the first attempts at rectification brought in bank loans as the missing link between wage costs and the money stock. It was argued that businesses, when faced with higher costs, borrow more from banks, thus increasing the money supply and providing the purchasing power to sustain the higher prices charged to cover the increase in costs. Such a link may have some relevance to business cycles: banks often meet an increased demand for loans during business expansions by reducing their excess reserves and borrowing from Federal Reserve Banks.[5] Both steps increase the money stock. To explain secular inflation by this route, however, requires continual reductions in banks' excess reserve ratios and continual increases in borrowing to maintain growth of the money stock. Banks are simply unable to finance an expansion in that way for very long. Since the early 1950s, most banks have kept excess reserves close to minimum working levels, not a potential source of much increase in the money stock even if banks wanted to reduce reserves further. Furthermore, member-bank borrowing from

Federal Reserve Banks indicates temporary distress; it is seldom requested or allowed for extended periods in increasing amounts. Over the long run, it is true, the reserve ratio of U.S. banks has declined, but not because of the secular increase in the demand for loans. Reserve ratios have declined mainly when statutory requirements were lowered, though also when institutional developments, such as the founding of the Federal Reserve Banks, reduced the need of the banking system for excess reserves.

Wage Push and the Federal Reserve

In practice the money stock can grow faster over a number of years only if the Federal Reserve supplies reserves faster—that is, increases the growth rate of high-powered money.[6] This characteristic of our monetary system means that the Federal Reserve—or any central bank in a similar monetary system—plays a crucial role in any continuing inflation. As a matter of simple fact, increases in high-powered money and the money stock have accompanied and sustained a moderately rising price level since World War II, and the question is why this has happened, in view of the traditional attachment of central bankers to a stable price level and a sound currency.

The answer given by the latest version of the wage-price spiral is summed up in the contention that national priorities changed: in effect we abandoned the traditional gold standard in the early post-World War II years, despite all denials, in favor of the labor standard. Our monetary authorities bow in the end to public concern over unemployment and sustain inflationary wage demands by unions. The money supply is now determined, not by the Board of Governors of the Federal Reserve System, but by union bargainers.

I have stated this view in the crude form it is so often heard, but it can be expressed in a subtler form to portray the problem from the point of view of the monetary authorities. Suppose that, during cyclical upswings in economic activity, the expansion of aggregate demand raises prices and wages. In the subsequent downswing, aggregate demand and output decline, but wage rates are sticky due to unions or simply custom, and hardly fall at all, preventing a decline in production costs and prices. The Federal Reserve takes steps to buoy up the economy, which involves increases in the money supply, and continues to do so until employment achieves its previous peak level, or a little more to absorb growth in the labor force. The attainment of that goal requires that aggregate demand be brought up to equal or exceed its previous high point at wage and price levels largely unchanged from the previous peak. Each expansion in the economy therefore starts with prices and wages at their last high point, producing cyclical spurts of inflation. Since no deflation occurs inbetween, the result is a persistent rise in prices.

Of course, if monetary policy could prevent the cyclical spurts from ever occurring, by evening out expansions and contractions in aggregate demand, prices need never rise despite the fact that wages never decline. Such perfection in controlling business fluctuations seems out of reach, however, even during peacetime. On this view, persistent inflation can be attributed to our newly acquired unwillingness to allow deflationary pressures to last very long, together with our demonstrated inability to slow down the growth in business activity the moment prices on the average begin to rise.

There is some truth in this description of the problem facing monetary policy, but it is also an oversimplification. Although wages may be extremely slow to decline due to custom and institutional rigidities, prices are generally not so inflexible, as is amply demonstrated by the drop in actual prices paid for many products when inventories are excessive or established firms face competition from new producers. If money wage rates remained constant when there is less than full employment, it would be possible for prices to fall during that particular part of the business cycle by the amount of the long-run growth in labor productivity—about 2 percent per year—and by even more if prices had previously raced ahead of wages when the economy was at full employment. If prices declined to that extent during part of each full cycle, the economy would be able to achieve full employment following a recession each time at a price level much lower than has lately been our experience.

In the now popular version of the wage-push theory, the failure of recessions to produce a decline in prices which offsets the advance during expansions is attributed to the upward thrust of wage costs. Wages outpace labor productivity, and prices go along to preserve profit margins, allowing no room for a decline in prices during recessions or at any other time which did not erode profits. In this view, wages are not only sticky downward but constantly push up the labor cost of products. If the monetary authorities did not validate these increases through appropriate expansions of the money supply, unemployment would spread and might have to reach alarming proportions before the push let up completely.

Deficiencies of the Theory

Although this explanation is now well entrenched in popular thought and almost impervious to doubt or criticism, it is not self-evident. To begin with, the fact that nominal wage rates rise faster than indexes of labor productivity, so often cited in the press and pronouncements of management as evidence of wage push, is simply no evidence at all. Inflation stemming from any source will produce the same result. If prices rise, nominal wages must also rise to keep real wages at the same equilibrium level. Attempts to observe in time series whether wages lead prices or vice versa have so far proved fruitless, because one increase blends into the next over time, and none have an obvious starting or ending point. Even if we could establish that wages lead prices, it would prove little. An increase in output raises the demand for labor and thus wage rates, and might do so in many industries before producers decide to raise product prices. A shift in product demand affects quantity, price, and wages, and we have no tested theory as yet of the time sequence in which these variables respond to the shift. Unfortunately for an empirical study of economic dynamics, the existence of lagged responses means that observed time sequences seldom can establish causation, though they are admittedly not entirely irrelevant.

One need not deny that strong unions have effects on real wages to have serious doubts about the wage-push theory of inflation. To the extent that unions raise real wages, they tend to reduce the amount of labor demanded in unionized firms. This increases the supply of labor available elsewhere, putting a downward pressure on the relative wage rate in the nonunion sector. No doubt many unions successfully press for higher real wages at the risk of unemployment among members, and continually reexert the pressure because rising prices continually erode their gains. But how can union bargaining raise the average level of wages throughout the economy? A wage-push theory implies that wage gains in union industries are transmitted to other sectors, so that wages push up prices throughout the economy. If a substantial nonunion sector absorbed excess labor at declining real wages from the unionized sector, average wages and prices in the economy need not rise. This is an important point so far as the U.S. economy is concerned, since union membership constitutes only a fifth of our total labor force.

It might be argued that wage push in unionized industries alone is responsible for the unemployment that leads the monetary authorities to take steps which support secular inflation. But that seems unlikely. For one thing, such pressure, if exerted solely by unions, would tend to widen their wages relative to those of other workers. We do not observe, however, that the wage differential between union and nonunion workers is continually widening, or that most unemployment occurs among union members, or that during periods of unemployment the wages of union members continue rising while those of nonunion workers remain constant. Actually, a striking characteristic of our mild inflation is the widespread increase in wages across the economy.

According to the wage-push theory, union wage gains are rapidly and fully transmitted to nonunion sectors. How is this done? Proponents of the wage-push theory cite a certain "demonstration effect" whereby nonunion workers insist upon union wage gains as the standard for the entire economy, or employers grant them in order to avoid unionization or disgruntlement of their workers. Yet, this simply makes no sense as a general economic proposition. Why should many employers who have never been threatened with unionization, and in the near future are not going to be, agree to advance wages in order to match those of unionized workers, unless aggregate demand were rising and new workers could not be hired at the old wage rate?

No doubt many large firms, as a practical rule, pass union wage gains granted to production workers on to their nonunion clerical and supervisory personnel. Yet, if the available supply of such workers did not warrant an equal increase, it is hard to believe that a policy of fully matching union gains would continue for long. Moreover, most small firms in the service trades have no unionized workers and are not pressured to equalize wage levels. Why do these firms match union wage increases of the manufacturing sector? Small nonunionized firms raise wages because of the competition for labor or because of periodic increases in statutory minimum wages. Neither of these pressures reflects a market process in which union gains force up wages of all workers. Until these questions have been answered adequately, they pose difficulties for an economic theory of wage-push inflation in its present form.

Recent Statistical Studies on Wage-Push Inflation

The Tradeoff between Inflation and Unemployment

Recent statistical research on the inflation problem ignores these questions and forges ahead to quantify the rate of increase in wages and prices, by relating it to the level of unemployment. The theoretical approach assumes that wages tend to move toward an equilibrium level at a rate depending upon the amount of excess demand or supply. This applies the conventional theory of dynamic price adjustments to the labor market. If at the current price the amounts demanded and supplied are not equal, the price moves toward equilibrium at a speed depending upon the size of the discrepancy, where some markets adjust more rapidly than others. Such a relationship was first applied statistically to wages by A. W. Phillips on British data with some success, and has come to be known as the "Phillips curve."[7] He related wage changes to the percentage of the labor force unemployed, but this is deficient in not allowing for the effect of prices on wage rates and for changes in labor productivity. Equilibrium in the labor market means that real wages equal the marginal productivity of labor. In equilibrium, therefore, nominal wages would rise when prices and labor productivity increase. Other studies have attempted to account for these other influences.

Such equations purport to show the rate at which prices will rise at any level of unemployment; or, put differently, the average level of unemployment at which, given stable prices, nominal wages would rise no faster than the rate of productivity growth. The equations do not indicate whether wages push up prices or prices pull up wages. Since prices can affect nominal wages, the Phillips curve does not answer that question. If we assume that price increases are largely due to wage push, however, we can ask what level of unemployment would allow a constant price level. At that level, wages no longer push up on prices and the market is in equilibrium. Carrying the argument one step further, we may interpret such an equilibrium as a point of "full" employment, in the limited sense that the effective demand and supply are accommodated at prevailing real wage rates given the structure of the market.

The estimate of equilibrium unemployment so defined, however, is disturbingly high. Depending upon which study you consult, the U.S. data suggest a figure of 4 to 7 or 8 percent, when in the early 1950s 3 percent was considered uncomfortably high. The conclusion widely drawn from these estimates is that wages increase even when unemployment exceeds what might be considered a "normal" percentage of workers looking for jobs. The increase at such times is attributed primarily to unions, though their importance has not been established in the statistical studies and is far from proven. In any event, on this view, inflation reflects a public insistence on low unemployment, accomplished by raising prices with the grudging acquiescence of the monetary authorities.

The Role of Price Expectations

But that cannot be all there is to the problem. How can a monetary policy of allowing secular inflation lead to a lower level of unemployment than would a policy designed to keep the price level constant? One might at first answer that, if inflation results from trying to achieve full employment too closely, every appearance of "excess" unemployment elicits an expansionary monetary policy that overshoots into price increases. That goes back to the earlier version of the spiral theory. There the cyclical character of inflation is emphasized, whereby business expansions are carried too far by easy money policies. Such an explanation is deficient, however, in not explaining why wages and prices do not fall during recessions to offset the price increases which occur during expansions. To avoid that deficiency, the current version of the spiral theory, as said, sees a net upward push of wages occurring on the average from cycle to cycle. The average rate of unemployment does not continually increase from cycle to cycle, because prices rise and keep real wages from rising faster than productivity. Given that the demand for labor depends upon real wages, therefore, inflation can raise the amount of labor demanded only by keeping real wages lower than they would otherwise be, which is achieved through price increases that are always a step ahead of the push on nominal wages.

Yet surely that trick does not work for long. Sooner or later the equilibrium wage rate incorporates the new rate of inflation. At that point, continuation of the lower level of unemployment requires a step up in the rate of inflation, with subsequent adjustments in the rate of wage increase, and so on with an accelerating spiral of increases. Such interaction between wages and prices means that the definition of full employment as the level at which wages are constant is incomplete. It should be defined as the level at which *expected real* wages are constant (productivity growth aside), that is, when nominal wages are changing at the expected rate of price change. On this interpretation the *long-run* level of full employment can be affected by legislation affecting the structure of the labor market but not by monetary policy.

Unanticipated price increases reduce the real value of wages in the short run, because most wage rates are changed infrequently and adjust to price changes imperfectly. In that way wages lag behind prices and tend to reflect past changes in prices. The past has an additional effect on the determination of nominal rates of pay, however, through expectations. It is never clear which price changes are most relevant to particular wages, and expectations of the relevant changes will be vague and imprecise. Nevertheless, expectations of some kind are formed, based in part on the past, and they influence the setting of wages in an attempt to allow for and to anticipate price changes, though they do so imperfectly and sometimes quite inaccurately. Errors are not recognized immediately and are gradually corrected in future periods. Wages can continue rising for a while, therefore, at too fast or too slow a rate when judged solely in the light of concurrent price changes and market conditions.

Expectations are thus important in a way not usually stressed in monetary theory. Usually price expectations are brought in as a determinant of the demand to hold money, in which an increase in the expected rate of change of prices reduces desired real cash balances and raises spending, thus contributing to the expected inflation through effects on aggregate demand. Expectations also play a more direct role in the determination of wages and prices as described above, which sets up an additional link with the past. Frequent adjustments in most wages and many prices are inconvenient and costly and are when possible avoided. An expected rise in a general index of prices tends to be incorporated ahead of time into the setting of particular wages and prices. When inflation continues for some time, therefore, wages gradually make up for it and begin to anticipate it. Nominal wages then rise that much faster than they would have risen at any given level of unemployment without the inflation, which in turn affects production costs and feeds back on prices.

The theory of a wage push has developed in response to the

seeming paradox of inflation continuing when aggregate demand appears slack and unable to account for price increases. If inflation were not of the demand-pull variety, it was argued, it must reflect cost push. Expectations, however, provide an alternative—and more plausible—explanation of that paradox.[8]

The adjustment of wages to past price increases as well as to the expected rate of future increases can make the unemployment level necessary to hold wage increases down appear excessively high. The data for such periods seem to imply that price stability can be attained only at the cost of prohibitive unemployment. But if the stability were attained and widely expected to continue, the average level of unemployment would then be no higher than could be produced by an inflation at any rate which workers and employers came to anticipate.

Price Expectations and the Problems of Monetary Policy—Conclusion

The dilemma of monetary policy dramatized by events since World War II is that inflation, once it grips the economy, cannot be eradicated quickly or without repercussions on employment and output. A large body of opinion sees the problem as a continuing upward push on wages due to union activity and other forms of noncompetitive behavior. By implication, a stable price level can no longer be maintained without appreciable unemployment.

I do not believe the evidence supports such a conclusion. Wages tend to increase if the general price level has been rising or is expected to rise in the future, apart from the effects of current demand and supply conditions. Consequently, if prices continue rising long enough for expectations of inflation to take hold, wages develop a persistent upward thrust, which pushes up prices and continues for a time even if aggregate demand declines. To counteract and change expectations of inflation, aggregate demand must be curtailed enough to offset the increases in wages and prices due to expectations. Because expectations are based in part on past experience, monetary policy must restrain aggregate demand by more when inflation is in process than would otherwise be necessary. The additional restraint involves increased unemployment.

There is one important difference between this analysis based on lagged adjustments and expectations and the simple wage-push theory of inflation. The point neglected in the simple theory is that the expected rate of inflation gradually declines if prices rise less than they are expected to. Consequently, price stability once achieved and expected to continue can be maintained at full employment. The crucial step, so difficult in practice, is to eliminate the periodic cycles in aggregate demand which on the upswing raise prices, produce lagged adjustments in wages, and help to form expectations of further advances. Given such cycles, monetary policy faces the dilemma of increasing short-term unemployment if it tries to pull the economy back to price stability once an inflation has gained headway. Recent experience indicates that there is no easy or complete solution to the problem, in view of the social and political objections to restraining aggregate demand sufficiently to prevent inflation.

It is commonplace to observe that persistent social problems are at bottom complex and intractable, else they would have been remedied when they first appeared. So too with inflation. Yet nations will continue to struggle against inflation, simply because an escalation of price increases is not an acceptable alternative either. The various economic theories of inflation, now partly in agreement, still differ on the important question of whether or not price stability requires higher unemployment. Yet the evidence suggests that inflation alleviates unemployment only temporarily, and that the advantages of a stable price level, once attained, are *not* achieved at the continuing cost of a higher average level of unemployment.

3

Changes in the Cyclical Behavior of Prices

Although cyclical fluctuations in business activity have on the whole been milder since World War II than ever before and price increases during cyclical expansions (before 1973) have been correspondingly moderate, prices have declined less than they used to in periods of mild business recession, with the result that the price level has risen to higher and higher levels with no significant reversals. This change in the cyclical behavior of prices lies at the heart of the ''inflation problem'' in the postwar period.

The present chapter examines the recession behavior of wholesale prices since World War II and compares it with the mild recessions of the 1920s. The focus is on changes in recession behavior, possible bias in the data, and differences in behavior among various groups of wholesale prices. (Differences between wholesale and consumer prices, though important, are not examined here.) Evidence is also presented on various interpretations of the changes in price behavior.

The Reduction in Cyclical Amplitude of Aggregate Price Indexes

Table 1.1 in chapter 1 showed the cyclical behavior of the Bureau of Labor Statistics index of all wholesale prices. In the four business

Adapted from an article originally published in *Explorations in Economic Research* (winter 1975), 2:54–104.

Table 3.1 Rate of Change of Wholesale Prices over Business Cycles by Stage of Processing, 1913–1970 (percent per year)

Reference Cycles			*Basic Materials*			*Intermediate Materials*			*Finished Goods*		
Trough	*Peak*	*Trough*	*Expansions*	*Recessions*	*Rec. minus Exp.*	*Expansions*	*Recessions*	*Rec. minus Exp.*	*Expansions*	*Recessions*	*Rec. minus Exp.*
	Jan. 1913	Dec. 1914		−0.9			−6.5			−1.3	
Dec. 1914	Aug. 1918	Mar. 1919	30.2	2.1	−28.1	34.2	−20.1	−54.2	51.2	−3.5	−54.7
Mar. 1919	Jan. 1920	July 1921	12.4	−31.6	−44.0	83.5	−38.3	−121.8	21.2	−21.5	−42.7
July 1921	May 1923	July 1924	11.6	−3.3	−15.0	20.4	−13.6	−34.0	0.8	−5.5	−6.3
July 1924	Oct. 1926	Nov. 1927	1.0	0.5	−0.6	−2.4	−4.8	−2.4	2.2	−3.6	−5.8
Nov. 1927	Aug. 1929	Mar. 1933	−0.5	−13.7	−13.2	0.1	−10.9	−11.0	−0.1	−8.7	−8.6
Mar. 1933	May 1937	June 1938	18.5	−16.9	−35.4	13.0	−13.7	−26.7	8.0	−5.6	−13.6
June 1938	Feb. 1945	Oct. 1945	9.1	1.3	−7.8	3.8	4.1	0.3	3.5	0.6	−2.9
Oct. 1945	Nov. 1948	Oct. 1949	16.0	−8.8	−24.9	21.0	−9.4	−30.4	18.0	−6.7	−24.7
				−12.7			−7.9			−4.8	
Oct. 1949	July 1953	Aug. 1954	2.1	−2.0	−4.1	5.2	−0.5	−5.7	2.7	0.3	−2.4
Aug. 1954	July 1957	Apr. 1958	0.7	1.2	0.6	3.3	0.0	−3.3	2.2	3.1	1.0
Apr. 1958	May 1960	Feb. 1961	−0.2	−1.3	−1.1	0.9	−1.5	−2.3	0.1	1.1	1.0
Feb. 1961	Nov. 1969	Nov. 1970	1.3	−0.1	−1.4	1.3	3.5	2.2	1.6	2.5	0.9
Averages											
By period											
6 cycles 1921–49			9.3	−8.9	−16.2	9.3	−8.1	−17.4	5.4	−4.9	−10.3
4 cycles 1949–70			0.8	−0.6	−1.5	2.7	0.4	−2.3	1.6	1.8	0.1
By period and similar severity											
2 cycles 1921–27			6.3	−1.4	−7.8	9.0	−9.2	−18.2	1.5	−4.6	−6.0
2 cycles 1954–61			0.2	−0.0	−0.2	2.1	−0.8	−2.8	1.2	2.1	1.0

NOTE: "Raw materials" to 1948–49 overlap and "crude materials" thereafter; "semi-manufactured goods" to overlap and "intermediate materials" thereafter; "finished products" to overlap and "finished goods" thereafter; all seasonally adjusted except finished goods since 1949.

Method of computation and severity of business recessions are the same as for table 1.1.

recessions from 1954 to 1970 the aggregate index did not decline and in the last three it rose. In previous recessions this index had failed to decline only twice (in 1900 and the short recession following World War II in 1945).[1] In 1961 and 1970 it even rose slightly faster in the recessions than in the preceding expansions, a perverse cyclical behavior which it never exhibited before.

Table 3.1 shows the cyclical behavior of three major subgroups of wholesale prices available since 1912, basic materials, intermediate materials, and finished goods. (See figure 1.1 for the period since 1947.) A sharp decline in cyclical amplitude occurs for all three subgroups in the recessions following 1949, thus demonstrating that the decline for the aggregate index cannot be attributed to the decreasing weight of the volatile prices of basic materials.

The rates of price change during business expansions have also declined, though not uniformly. Some expansions in the 1920s and earlier had rates of price change as low as or below those of some postwar cycles. Although it was not unusual in the 1920s and earlier for the expansion rates to be low, it was rare for prices to fail to decline appreciably in recessions. Such a reduction in amplitude has occurred in other economic series as well, including the rate of growth of the money stock. It reflects in part better data but also the fact that cycles in business activity have been milder on the average since World War II than formerly. Still, a change in behavior of prices is evident even after allowing for differences in the cyclical amplitude of business activity. A pairing of two mild recessions in the 1950s with two in the 1920s at the bottom of tables 1.1 and 3.1 shows that the later price swings were considerably smaller, though less so for expansion rates alone. Although expansion rates have come down at the same time that recession rates have moved up toward and past zero, recession rates have moved farther.[2]

Changes in the Distribution of Cyclical Price Changes since the 1920s

Although the decline in measured price changes has been widely discussed, its statistical basis deserves reexamination. Because we want to distinguish broad changes in market behavior from changes in statistical composition of the data, there are several difficulties in relying exclusively on the aggregate indexes. They are disproportionately influenced by certain product groups, and the composition and weighting have shifted over time toward the less volatile prices of manufactured goods. Although the index of finished goods in table 3.1 shows the same change in cyclical behavior as that for basic and intermediate materials, the composition of each of these subindexes has also shifted over time; the substitution of new series for old and increases in the total number have given more weight to the highly fabricated products which characteristically exhibit less price fluctuation. A 1952 revision of the index reduced the recession rate of decline for intermediate materials and finished goods, though not for basic materials, as is shown by the overlap in table 3.1.

Figures 3.1 and 3.2 present cumulative frequency distributions of essentially the same set of wholesale prices in mild business cycles of the 1920s and the period after World War II. These distributions avoid weighting and compositional effects by not combining the components into one total and by not changing the coverage. Figure 3.1 covers seven mild recessions back to the 1920s, omitting the large cycles of the 1930s and World War II. There are 48 major component series of the wholesale price index which are available from 1926 to 1970, and 44 of these can be extended back to 1923. The 48 series make up 93 percent by weight of the 1926 aggregate index though only 50 percent of the 1970 index. (The 44 series make up 92 percent of the 1924 index.) These components include most of the major subsectors that span the full period without a significant revision and so pertain to essentially the same kinds of products, though the Bureau of Labor Statistics replaced individual items from time to time. Figure 3.2 is based on about 1,100 products of the wholesale price index that had no major change in specification over the postwar period. Since few of these series carry back before 1947, this figure depicts only the five postwar recessions. Because it covers more series, it provides smoother and probably more accurate distributions. The statistical measures of these distributions by major industries are given in appendix table A.

Each component of the distributions in figures 3.1 and 3.2 measures the change in the average rates of price change from the expansion period to the ensuing recession period.[3] The figures show the percentage of all the price series with changes in rates of change up to but not including the change shown on the bottom scale. All the

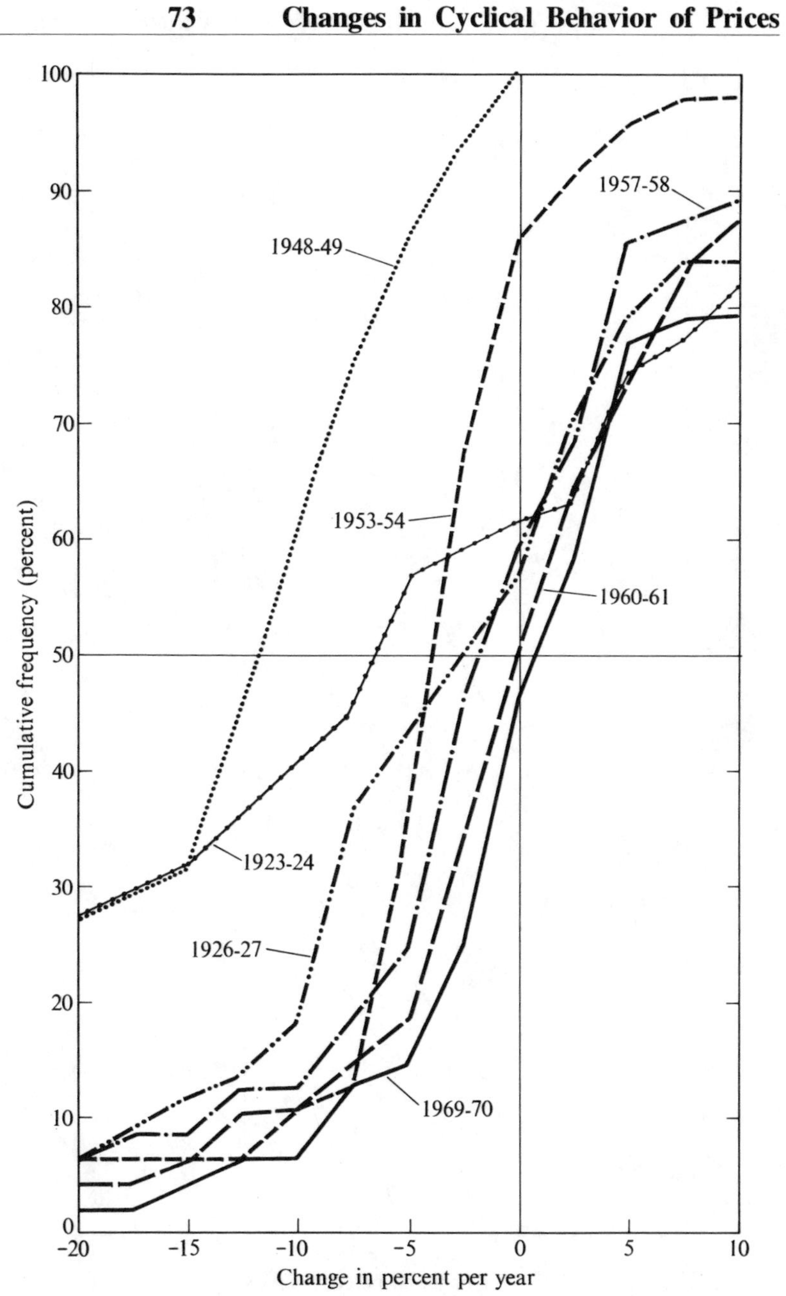

Figure 3.1 Cumulative Frequency Distributions of 48 Subindexes of Wholesale Prices in Mild Business Cycles, 1920s and after World War II[a] (change in rates of change from expansions to ensuing recessions)

[a] Forty-four subindexes for 1923–24.

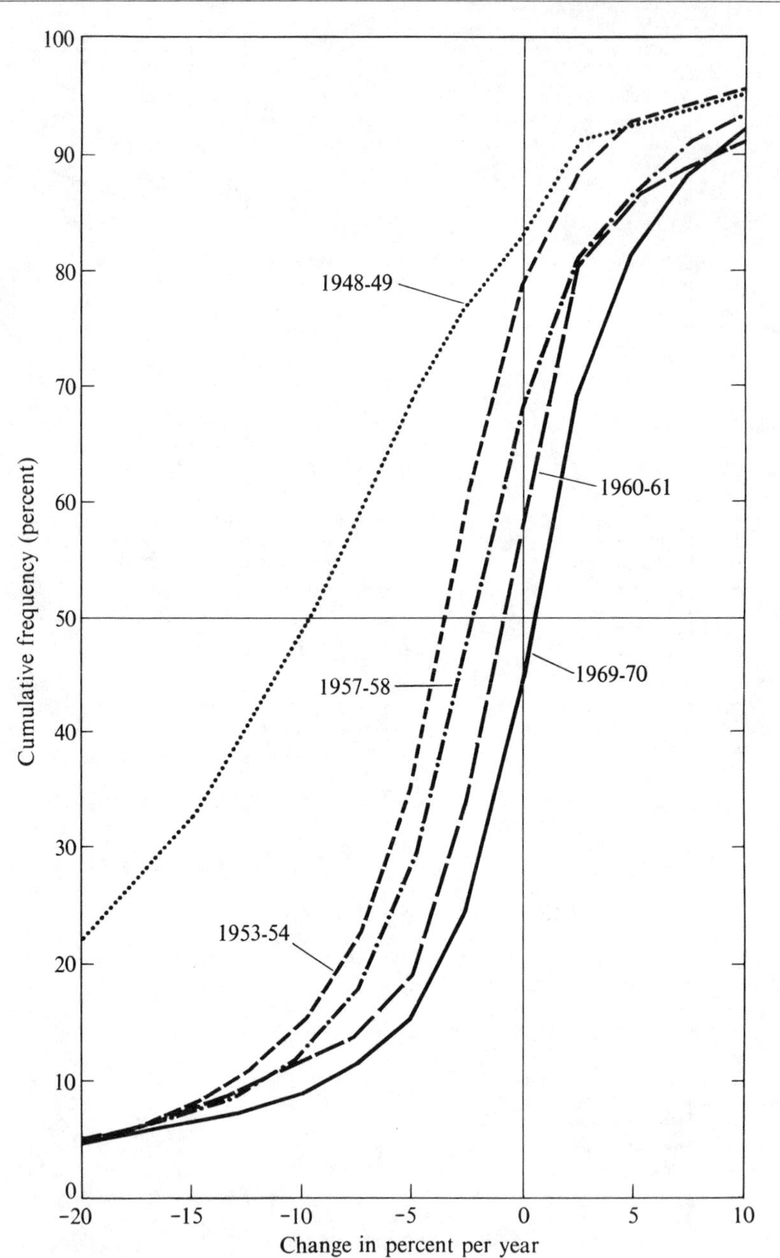

Figure 3.2 Cumulative Frequency Distributions of about 1,100 Wholesale Product Prices in Post-World War II Cycles[a] (change in rates of change from expansions to ensuing recessions)

[a] 1,138 price indexes for first four cycles and 1,106 for the last cycle.

rates for each recession were classified as being in one of 14 intervals from −20 to 10 percent per year; the width of each interior interval is 2.5 percentage points and the two extreme classes are open-ended. Zero was made the beginning of the first positive interval in order to distinguish price declines from no change. Thus, at the zero point on the bottom scale, the vertical scale shows the percentage of price series for which the change in rate of change fell (that is, was below zero) from the expansion to the recession.

This *change* in the rates from expansion to recession eliminates any trend in the rates over the full business cycle. Recessions generally work to reduce rates of price change, but the level of prices can continue rising until—if ever—the rate gradually declines to zero. Consequently, if a price has a high expansion rate, the ensuing recession rate may be lower but can still be a comparatively high positive rate. The postwar phenomenon of inflationary movements persisting in the face of slack markets reflects the carry-over of expansion rates, with only small reductions, on the average, into recessions.

Figure 3.1 shows that the dispersion of price changes across the economy has generally declined since the 1920s.[4] Apparently the responses of prices in different industries have become more uniform. The 1949 recession is exceptional and should perhaps be disregarded as not representing typical peacetime behavior, since prices in that recession declined from the inflated levels carried over from wartime.

Although the distributions for the recessions following 1949 display a similar dispersion, they shifted consecutively rightward to larger increases and smaller declines, which confirms the diminishing size of the change in the rates of change from expansions to recessions suggested by the aggregate indexes in table 3.1. This shift stands out more clearly for the comprehensive distributions in figure 3.2. These shifts are not a mechanical result of the method of computation. Even when the rates have an upward trend as was true in the 1960s, there is no arithmetical reason for the *change* in rates of change from expansions to succeeding recessions to be higher or lower than in previous cycles. Even allowing for escalating price trends, therefore, recession responses have attenuated. The changes in rates of price change have become progressively less negative fairly uniformly along the entire range of price changes except for the very large declines.

The decline in responses is summarized by the measures of the distributions in table 3.2. By the mean or median, the changes in the rates from expansions to recessions became less negative or more positive in sequence from one recession to the next. The 1966–67 mini-recession has been added to the table to provide a further test of the chronology of the shifts in price behavior. It falls in its chronological order for the median and is only slightly out of order with 1961 for the mean.

Table 3.2 Measures of the Distribution of Rates of Change of About 1,100 Wholesale Prices in Post-World War II Recessions (percent per year)

	Recession Rates minus Preceding Expansion Rates			
Recession	*Unweighted Mean*	*Median*	*Dispersion (Average Deviation from Mean)*	*Percent Declining*
1948–49	−11.7	−9.5	11.8	82.7
1953–54	−4.0	−3.5	6.2	78.0
1957–58	−2.2	−2.0	7.3	66.9
1960–61	−1.1	−0.7	7.0	56.9
1969–70	0.1	0.6	6.5	43.7
1966–67	−1.3	0.2	6.8	48.5

NOTE: Dates for the 1966–67 mini-recession are November 1966 to May 1967, and the preceding expansion period begins in February 1961. Other periods are given in table 3.1 and note 3.

Number of series is 1,138 for 1947–61, 1,106 for 1969–70, and 1,131 for 1966–67.

The severity of postwar business cycles has generally been decreasing in real terms, which conceivably might account for the declining response of prices. This cannot be said of the decline in response from the 1920s to the later postwar recessions, because that decline is too large to reflect the small differences in severity. But it is a possible reason for the declines following 1949. The evidence on this point has been assembled in figure 3.3. Various measures of the distributions of recession-minus-expansion rates are plotted for five postwar recessions and the 1966–67 mini-recession. The figure graphs the distributional measures of table 3.2, the change in rate of change of the weighted aggregate index, and the change from peak to trough rates of corresponding specific cycles in the industrial component of the aggregate. A ranking of the severity of the recessions in

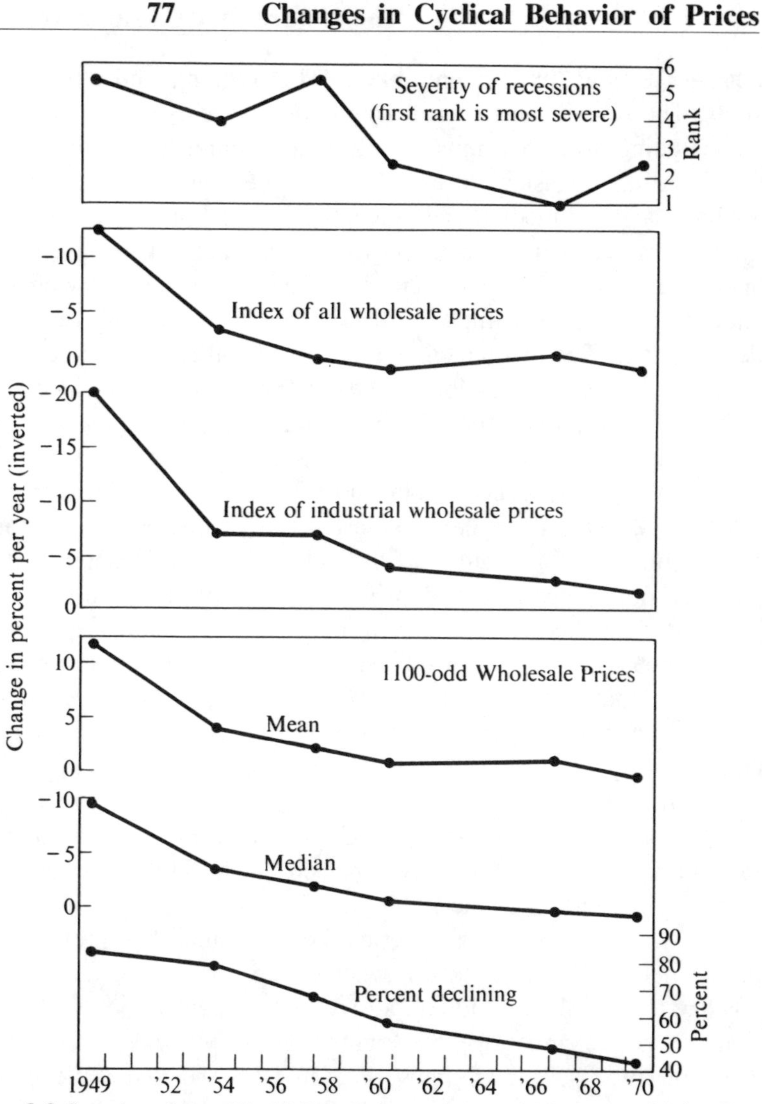

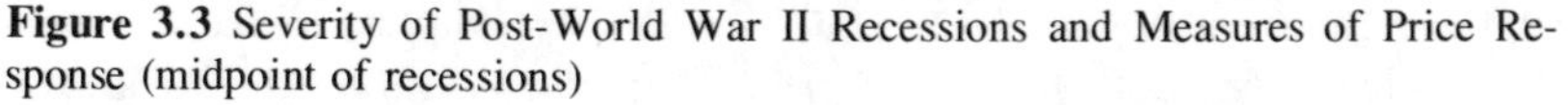

Figure 3.3 Severity of Post-World War II Recessions and Measures of Price Response (midpoint of recessions)

SOURCE: Rank of severity: Moore (1973), p. 18. Index of industrial wholesale prices: Moore (1974), p. 30, table 4. Index of all wholesale prices: table 1.1 except that expansion for first cycle is February 1947 to November 1948, for mini-recession of November 1966 to May 1967 is February 1961 to November 1966, and for last cycle is December 1965 to November 1969. Eleven-hundred-odd wholesale prices: table 3.2.

NOTE: Price responses are based on recession rates minus preceding expansion rates except for the index of industrial wholesale prices, which is based on the difference between the trough and preceding peak rates of change (centered six-month averages) for specific cycles in the rate of change of the index corresponding to business cycles.

business activity is also presented. (This ranking omits the expansions. The severity of the total amplitude of cycles in business activity including the expansions has also been diminishing, but by less.)

All the measures of price response decrease over the period as a whole, and the median and percentage of declining rates show significant decreases from each recession to the next. The startling failure of the 1970 recession to curb the inflation was not a new phenomenon, therefore, but simply a further step in a progressive postwar development. The median *change* in the annual rates of price change from expansion to recession in the 1949–54 cycle was a *decline* of 3.5 percentage points. In 1970 the median change was an *increase* of 0.6 percentage points. By contrast, the ranks of severity do not decrease in exact sequence: 1949 and 1958 tied for most severe and 1961 and 1970 tied for next to least severe. None of the price measures follow the time pattern of the ranks. The price responses in the 1966–67 mini-recession are conspicuously out of order with its severity. Based on this evidence, therefore, the diminishing response of prices apears to have occurred sequentially, due presumably to a set of institutional and expectational developments, and not due solely to the overall reduction in severity of recessions, though it no doubt contributed.

It also appears that the degree of inflation in the expansion is not crucial either, because the 1958 distribution in figure 3.2 followed upon a more inflationary expansion than did the 1961 distribution which is farther to the right.

Since the response of prices to recessions has progressively diminished, it is natural to ask whether the time lag of the response has lengthened. To provide an answer we may examine the distribution of price changes for the eight months following each trough. This span was selected because it terminates the first cycle in June 1950 as prices erupted at the outbreak of the Korean War, and the last cycle in August 1971 as a price freeze was imposed. To allow comparison between the cycles, eight months was used for the other recovery periods as well. To facilitate comparison with figure 3.2, the rate of change of each price in the preceding expansion phase was subtracted from these rates for the eight-month period following the trough. The cumulative distributions of these rate differences are shown in the accompanying figure 3.4.

Although the distributions in figure 3.4 are quite similar in shape to those in figure 3.2, they are closer together. Compared with the recession distributions in figure 3.2, there was a shift to the right in the recoveries following 1949 and 1954, almost no shift following 1958 and 1961, and a slight shift to the left following 1970. Thus, while the recoveries from the 1949 and 1954 recessions brought the usual acceleration of prices from the recession rates, the recession pressures on the rates of price change continued unabated after 1958 and 1961, and to some degree intensified after 1970. Figure 3.4 hints at a delay in the response of prices from the 1970 recession until the 1971 recovery period, but the shift in all these distributions relative to their positions in figure 3.2 is too slight to be of any significance. The amplitude of price responses has changed far more than can be accounted for by any minor changes in the lag time.

Rates of Change for Eight Months Following
Trough Minus Preceding Expansion Rates

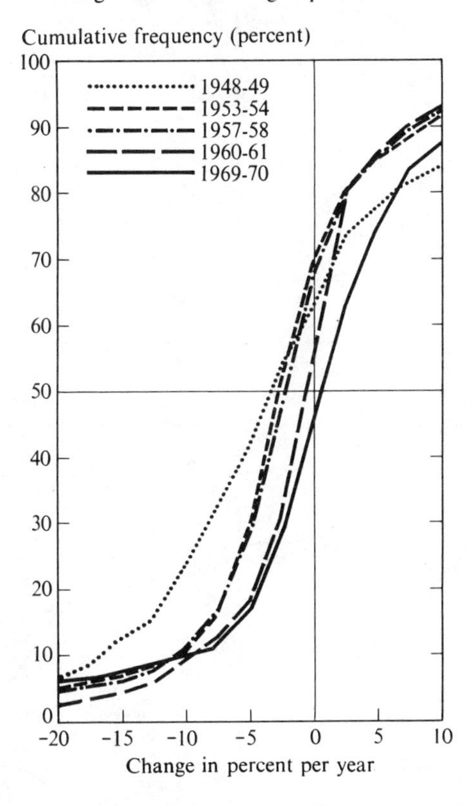

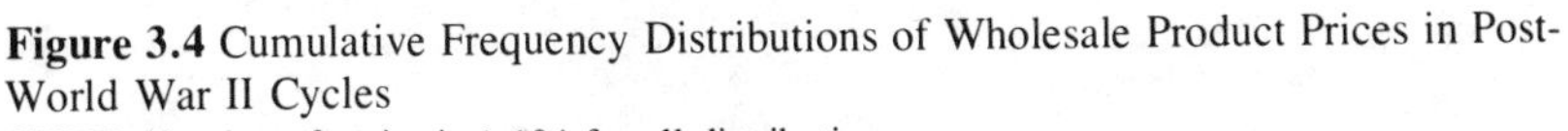

Figure 3.4 Cumulative Frequency Distributions of Wholesale Product Prices in Post-World War II Cycles

NOTE: Number of series is 1,104 for all distributions.

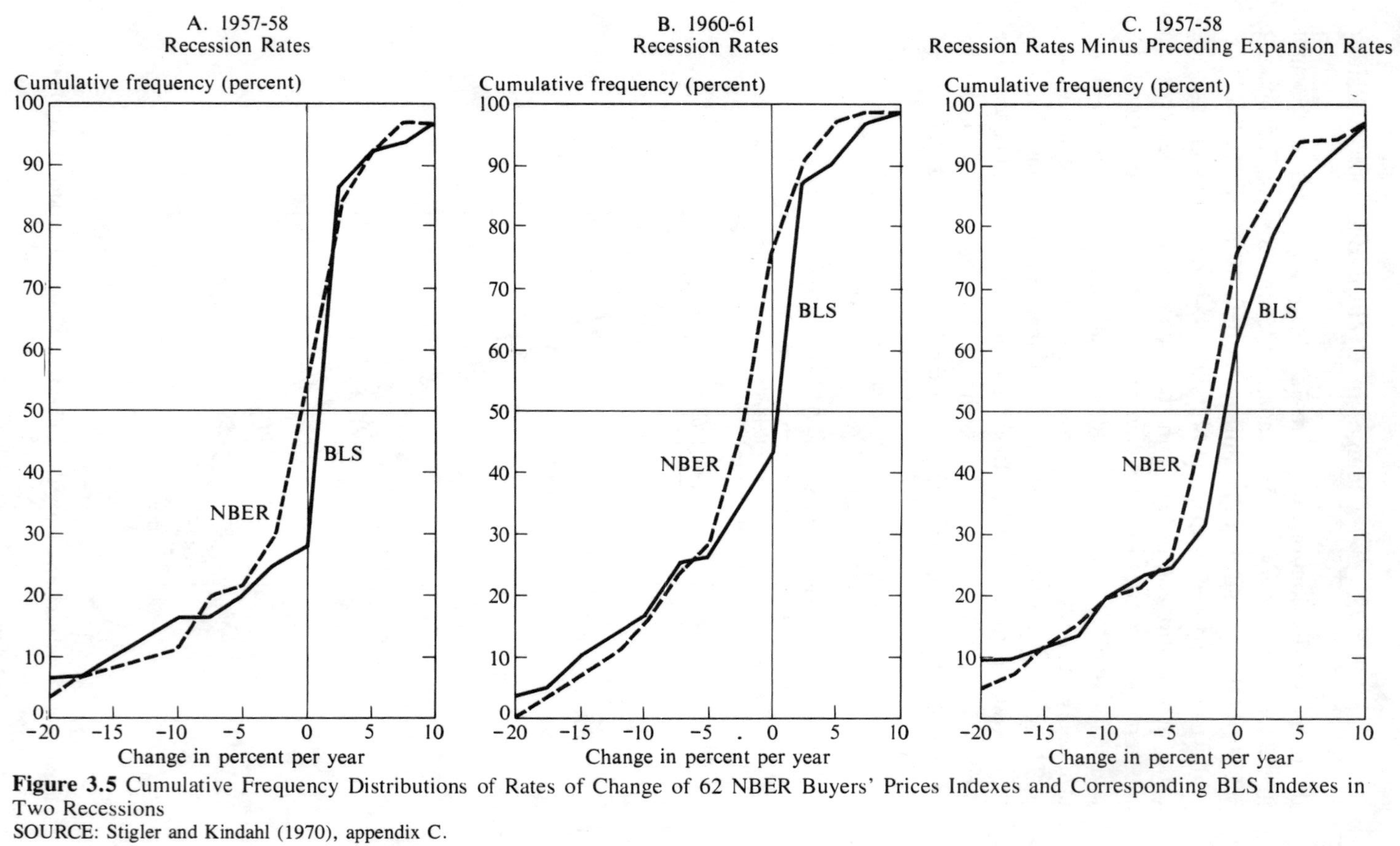

Figure 3.5 Cumulative Frequency Distributions of Rates of Change of 62 NBER Buyers' Prices Indexes and Corresponding BLS Indexes in Two Recessions

SOURCE: Stigler and Kindahl (1970), appendix C.

The Bias toward Rigidity in Reported Prices

The phenomenon of price inflexibility has received wide attention. It has been attributed to the rigidity of "administered" prices, which allegedly do not respond to short-run shifts in demand. Yet it is partly a statistical artifact of the data. For prices fixed by contract, for example, no change occurs until they are reset (assuming no prearranged escalation). Even for noncontract prices, the BLS compiles reports from sellers who may fail to report (though requested to do so) the unannounced discounting and shading of prices often made in actual transactions.

We may analyze this omission with the aid of the National Bureau collection of prices compiled from buyers, largely of products for which "administered pricing" was likely to be strong.[5] These data cover the 1958 and 1961 recessions only. Figure 3.5 presents three sets of cumulative frequency distributions of 62 National Bureau price groupings and the corresponding BLS indexes. Two panels show the 1958 and 1961 recession rates, and the third panel shows recession-minus-expansion rates for 1961.

It is apparent that the BLS series underreport price decreases, mainly small ones. The paired distributions are fairly close except between −5 and 2.5 or 5 percent per year. It is clear from the underlying data not shown here that the main exception occurs at zero. This result presumably reflects a tendency of the quoted or list prices reported to the BLS to omit market shading when no change in the list price has occurred, but to include them when the market strays too far from the list price and the list is changed. Thus the paired price series display the same cyclical behavior overall, as is indicated by a correlation coefficient between the two sets of price changes for 1958 of .81. (This correlation was not computed for 1961, but it would give similar results.)

The right-most panel of the chart which shows changes in the rates of price change reveals similar differences between these two sets of data. Although such changes in rates of change usually do not bunch at zero, the expansion rates for this cycle were fairly small and partially replicate the results for recession rates alone.

There may be other reasons, to be sure, for the difference between these two sources of price data. The NBER data involve some interpolation of price observations, which spreads a change occurring in one month over the intervening months back to the previous observation. This makes less difference for the 9 to 12 month recession periods covered here, however, than for individual months. Also, buyers who shift to lower-priced sellers when prices rise would report a price decline even though many sellers reported an increase. This causes the NBER data based on buyers to show price changes below those of the BLS indexes. On the other hand, the BLS apparently does not list contract prices except in the month they are set, while the NBER data list them in all months of the contract period as having no change. These differences in buyer and seller reports are difficult to evaluate, but the tentative conclusion seems valid that the greater zero bunching in the BLS series mainly reflects the omission of market discounting from list prices.

Prices Grouped by Durability, Value Added, and Concentration

To what extent does the reduced response of prices in successive business recessions following 1949 reflect the behavior of particular groups of prices? The answer will help identify which of various possible influences may underlie this development. Three classifications of prices were selected for examination. They pertain to the durability of the product, the ratio of value added in production to shipments, and the concentration of firms in the industry. The classification by durability follows the fourfold BLS grouping of wholesale prices as of 1967 into durable and nondurable manufactures, and durable and nondurable raw or slightly processed goods. While the durable nonmanufactures comprise very few series in our sample and have been omitted, the other three groups are large enough to allow comparison of the frequency distributions of their prices. Value added and concentration can be derived from the BLS assignment of each wholesale product price to a five-digit SIC industry, for which the 1963 census of manufactures provides data on value added and shipments[6] and concentration.[7] These data are not published for every five-digit industry, so that some manufacturing prices had to be omitted from these distributions in addition to the exclusion of all nonmanufacturing prices (farming and mining). However, to minimize exclusions, value added and shipments for unavailable five-digit product codes were approximated by the corresponding four-digit code where the five-digit product was the only one in the four-digit group, though this inadvertently incorporates other miscellaneous products of the four-digit industry. Individual price series were classified according to these ratios into low, middle, or high ratios of value added to shipments and similarly for concentration. Since these two classifications are based on 1963 data, they are less appropriate for other years, but these characteristics of the products and the industries are not likely to have changed greatly even over the two decades from 1948 to 1970; the task of reclassifying the prices using other survey years was not deemed worthwhile.

Although these classifications are quite different in concept, they may in fact overlap for many prices. Such interdependence of characteristics makes identification of influences on price behavior difficult. Still, with the large number of prices in our sample, there is sufficient diversification to allow some indication of differences in behavior.

Figures 3.6, 3.7, and 3.8 present cumulative frequency distributions for all the previous 1,100-odd product prices except those omitted from these classifications for the reasons noted.

Prices Classified by Degree of Processing and Durability of Product

The group of largely unprocessed goods isolates the raw materials, which characteristically undergo large price fluctuations. The raw materials aside, the durability of manufactured goods affects their price behavior because of differences between the rate of use and of purchase. Most durable finished goods have variable use lives, and replacement can be postponed. (The converse is not invariably true, of course, since users of some nonessential nondurables can also do without for temporary periods.) This classification also corresponds to degree of perishability, which determines the feasibility of sizable inventories. Inventories absorb short-run changes in demand and also dampen price fluctuations. Unfortunately, figure 3.6 corresponds to this classification only roughly. The durable manufactures are not all finished goods, and the demand for some of them may remain steady to maintain production schedules of nondurable products for which they are inputs. Furthermore, apart from perishable basic foods, the

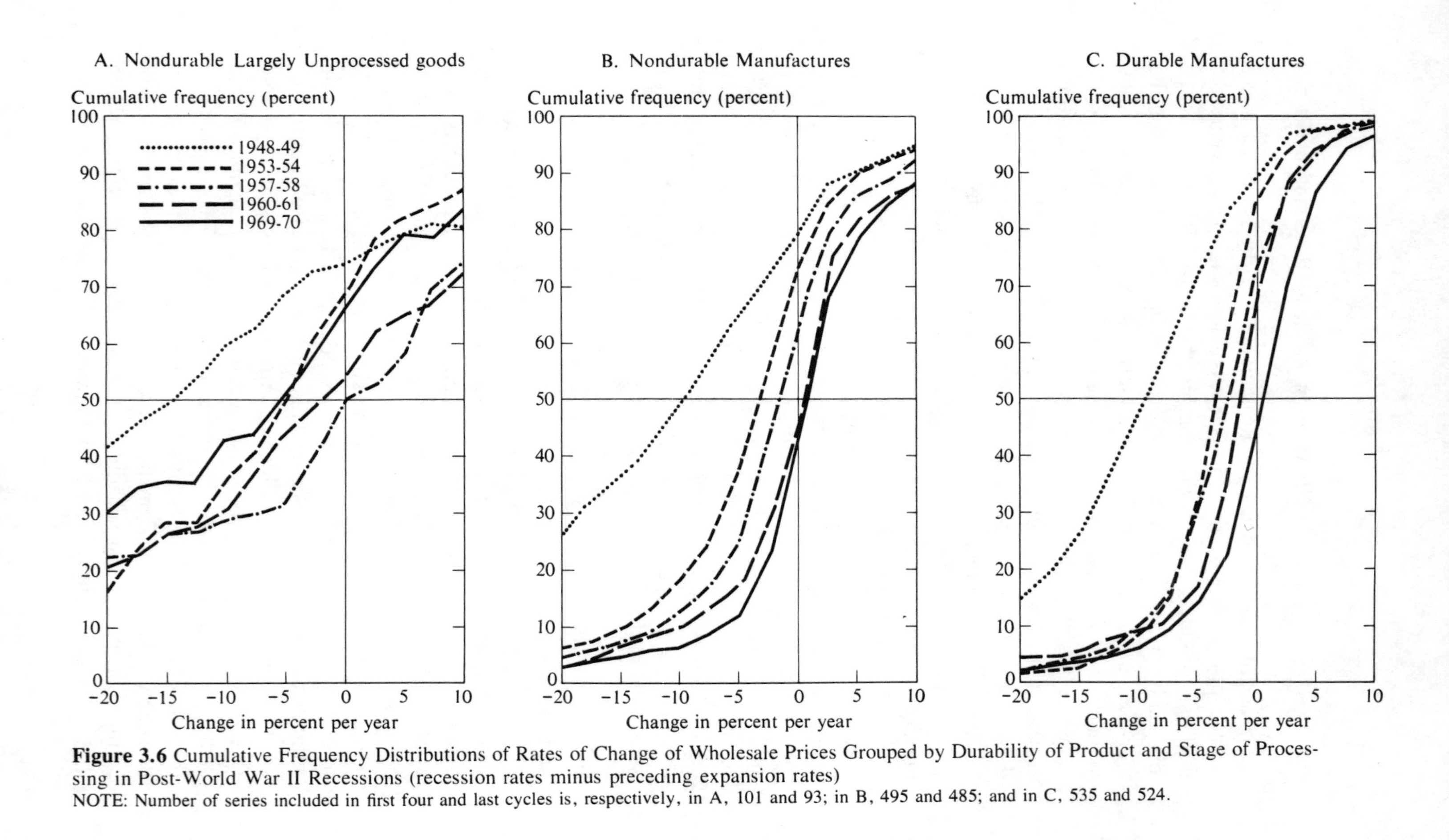

Figure 3.6 Cumulative Frequency Distributions of Rates of Change of Wholesale Prices Grouped by Durability of Product and Stage of Processing in Post-World War II Recessions (recession rates minus preceding expansion rates)

NOTE: Number of series included in first four and last cycles is, respectively, in A, 101 and 93; in B, 495 and 485; and in C, 535 and 524.

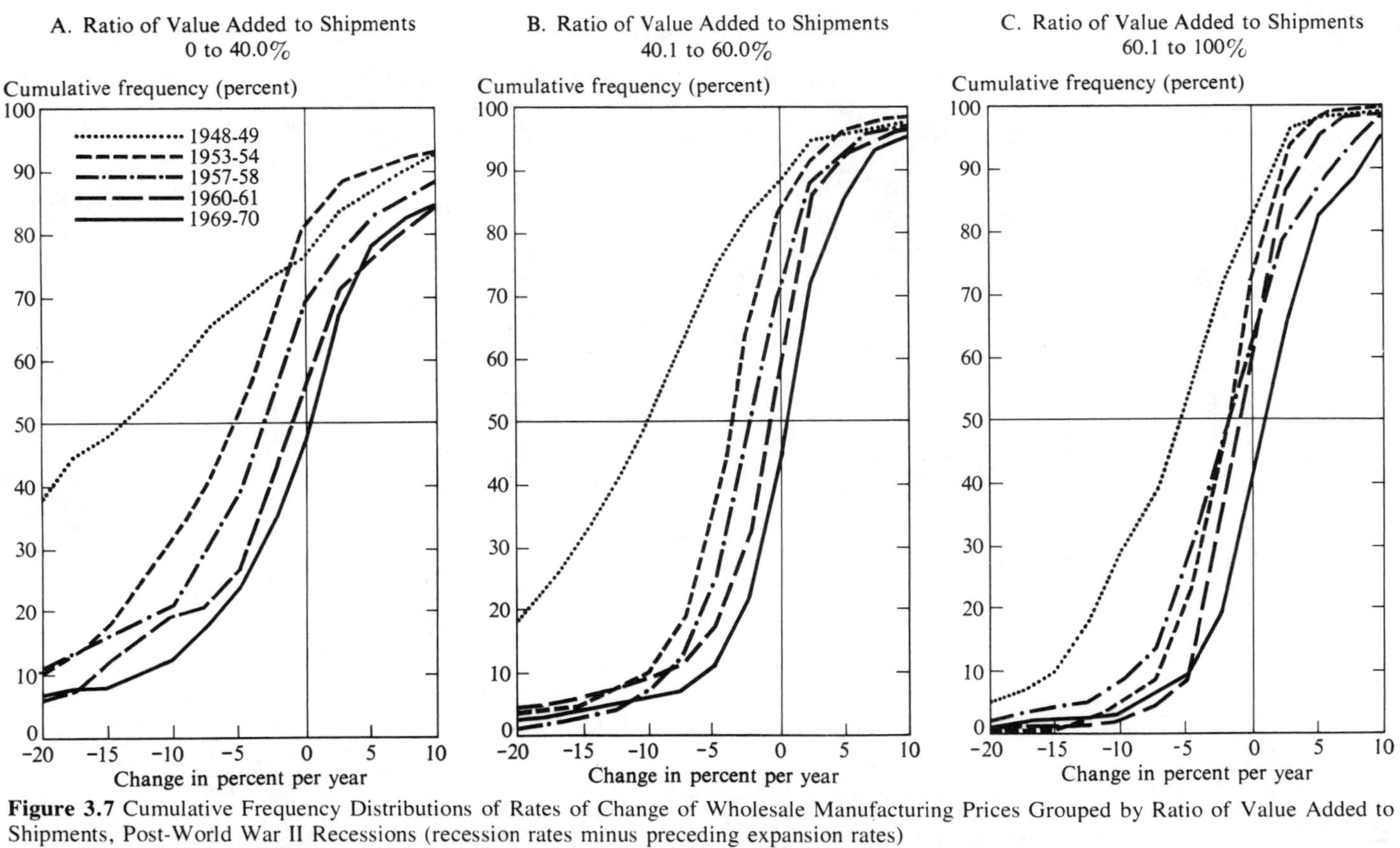

Figure 3.7 Cumulative Frequency Distributions of Rates of Change of Wholesale Manufacturing Prices Grouped by Ratio of Value Added to Shipments, Post-World War II Recessions (recession rates minus preceding expansion rates)

NOTE: Number of series included in first four and last cycles, respectively, is in A, 208 and 200; in B, 552 and 540; and in C, 174 and 173.

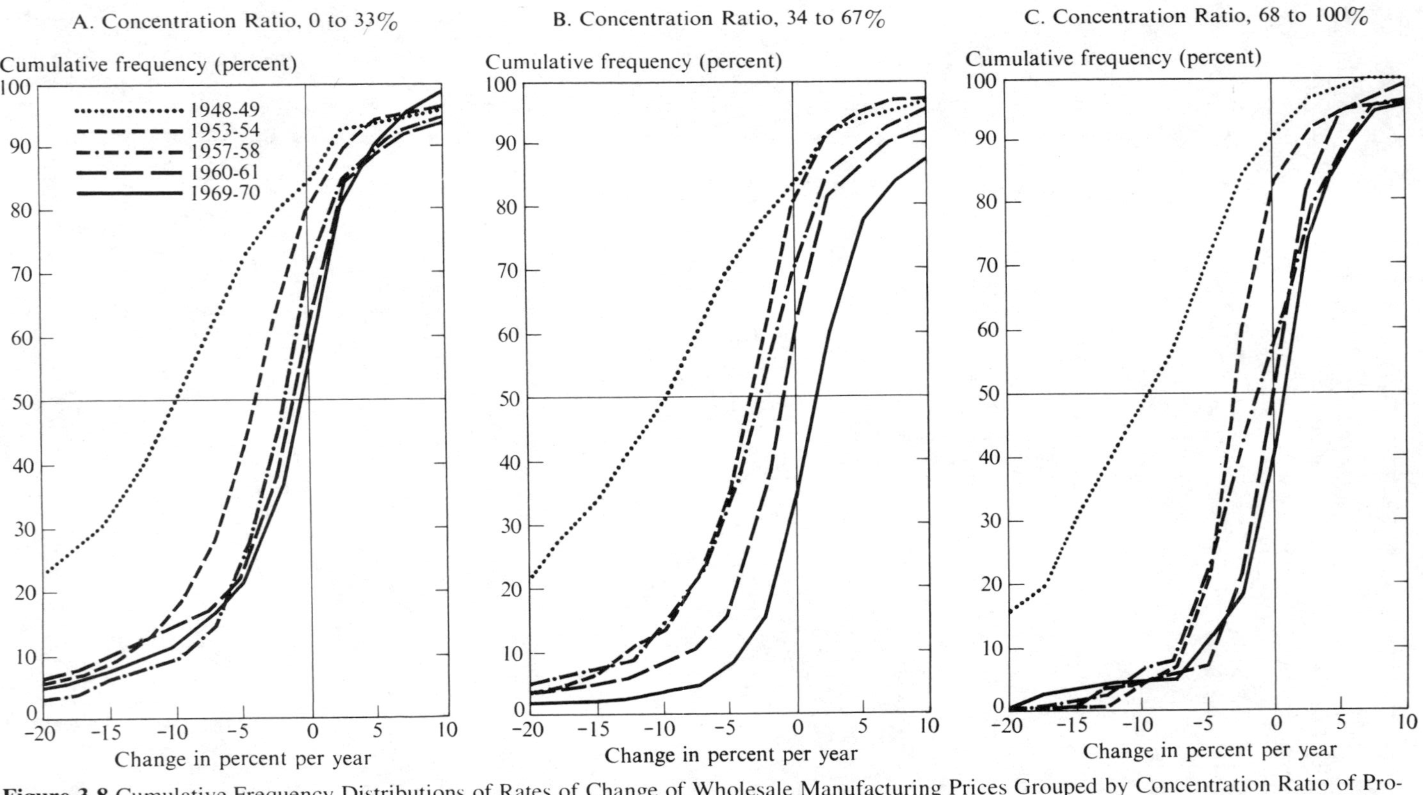

Figure 3.8 Cumulative Frequency Distributions of Rates of Change of Wholesale Manufacturing Prices Grouped by Concentration Ratio of Producers, Post-World War II Recessions (recession rates minus preceding expansion rates)

NOTE: Number of series included in first four and last cycles, respectively, is in A, 376 and 366; in B, 482 and 474; and in C, 126 and 123.

nondurable group includes textiles, leather, paper, petroleum, chemicals, and other such products classified as nondurable but regularly held in inventory. No attempt was made to alter the BLS classification for present purposes. Nevertheless, the classification helps to show whether the durability of products is related to the changes in cyclical behavior of prices.

Figure 3.6 reveals a sharp difference between the largely unprocessed nondurable goods and the two manufacturing groups. As expected, the distributions of the former are much flatter, indicating considerable dispersion of price responses to the recessions. The smaller number of series covered by this group (about one-fifth of the other two) makes these distributions more jagged but would not ordinarily affect their slope or median. The strong dependence of these prices on short-run market conditions apparently is the reason why these distributions do not shift progressively rightward for each recession, as do those for the two manufacturing groups and for the combined distributions in figure 3.2. Indeed, the distribution for 1970 in figure 3.6A is further to the left than that for 1958. In the 1970 recession basic commodity prices declined as usual, while in 1956–57 they weakened during the final stages of the business expansion and began to recover in the 1958 recession before it ended.

The distributions for the two manufacturing groups (figures 3.6B and 3.6C) are surprisingly similar, though as expected the durables exhibit somewhat less price dispersion. Both sets show successive rightward shifts from one recession to the next, but less for the durables than the nondurables except in 1970. Apart from the raw materials, therefore, the rightward shifts in successive recessions do not differ by durability and by inference are not related to inventories.

Prices Classified by Ratio of Value Added to Shipments

A higher value-added ratio means that materials and fuels are less important in the cost of production, and wages and salaries, which are less responsive to short-run shifts in demand, play the main role. Of course, labor costs are a component of materials too, but the proportion is generally lower than for manufactures. A higher ratio gives less importance to volatile prices of raw materials, and this explains why price dispersion declines as the ratio increases. The average ratios in the three groups are 28, 50, and 66 percent, respectively,

Table 3.3 Measures of the Distribution of Rates of Change of Wholesale Manufacturing Prices Grouped by Durability, Value Added, and Concentration, Post-World War II Recessions (recession rates minus preceding expansion rates in percent per year)

Classification		*Mean*					*Absolute Deviation from Mean*				
		1948–49	*1953–54*	*1957–58*	*1960–61*	*1969–70*	*1948–49*	*1953–54*	*1957–58*	*1960–61*	*1969–70*
Durability[a]											
Nondurable Manufactures		−12.1	−3.1	−1.1	1.2	2.1	13.6	7.7	8.0	7.5	6.8
Durable Manufactures		−11.1	−4.0	−3.1	−2.8	−0.3	7.9	3.5	4.5	4.6	4.5
Ratio of value added to shipments											
Interval	Average[b]										
0–.400	.284	−16.5	−6.8	−3.3	−0.4	1.6	17.3	9.2	10.8	9.6	9.3
.401–.600	.496	−9.5	−3.8	−1.9	−2.0	0.2	9.1	4.4	4.3	5.3	4.4
.601–1.00	.661	−6.6	−2.4	−1.9	−1.0	0.7	5.5	3.0	4.8	2.7	4.0
Concentration ratio											
0–.33	.218	−11.8	−4.2	−1.5	−2.2	−2.5	10.7	6.4	5.8	7.4	5.6
.34–.67	.484	−13.0	−4.2	−3.1	−0.5	3.3	11.9	5.3	6.3	5.7	6.0
.68–1.00	.789	−11.2	−2.7	−1.0	−0.2	0.6	7.6	3.2	4.6	3.4	3.9

[a] Not computed for nondurable unprocessed goods (figure 3.6A).

[b] For 1948–61. Averages for 1970 differ slightly because of a smaller number of series.

and the dispersion roughly declines commensurately between the first two groups, though by less between the second two (see table 3.3).

For each recession the medians of the distributions for each higher group of ratios tend to move rightward, though much less so for the later than the earlier recessions. Also, the distributions for the higher ratios cluster more around zero and exhibit a response to recession which is smaller overall and changes less over the postwar period.

Taken all together, these results support the view that the inflexibility of wage rates (due to custom as well as union bargaining) contributes to the lack of responsiveness of prices to recessions, whereas a high dependence in production on raw materials adds to price dispersion. Yet the tendency in successive recessions for the rate of change of prices to decline less or rise more in relation to expansion rates cannot be attributed directly to labor costs. These rightward shifts are largest for those prices having the greatest dispersion and least dependence on wages. In the 1949 and 1954 recessions at the beginning of the postwar period, the high value-added group displayed the least price response, but the subsequent rightward shifts in the distributions for this group were also the smallest. The rightward shifts in the total distributions of figure 3.2 reflect larger shifts by the lower value-added products. Therefore, while the well-known inflexibility of wage costs contributes to the inflexibility of prices, wage costs do not appear to explain the general reduction in price responsiveness to recessions.

Prices Classified by Concentration Ratio

Concentrated industries have long been linked to short-run price inflexibility, supposedly because they engage in oligopolistic price fixing or, even without overt collusion, set prices independently of short-run market conditions. Quite apart from pricing by oligopolies, various arguments can be devised why firms might prefer to avoid frequent price changes, and concentration may help them to exercise that preference. Market concentration ratios, however, may be a poor measure of the control exercised over market prices. The available industry data often exclude important substitutes and so do not follow the most relevant market boundary. Furthermore, the number of dominant firms in an industry is by no means always a good index of the degree of competition. Although profits are supposed to benefit from such control over prices, various studies have found concentration to be a poor indicator of profit rates among industries.[8] Despite these doubts and limitations, however, the concentration ratio is used here to approximate the degree to which firms can set prices independently of immediate market conditions. This use follows the common notion of "administered pricing," though that concept is sometimes used differently to signify a specific strategy of pricing, such as target-return or markup pricing. As originally used by Gardiner Means, administered pricing was defined by the frequency with which firms changed their prices.[9] For present purposes, however, this is not a satisfactory classification because it is not independent of the price series.

In figure 3.8 the distributions for the more concentrated industries generally show less price response—they have smaller dispersion and lie closer to zero, though this observation makes no allowance for the interrelation between concentration, durability, and high value added, all of which work in the same direction. To the extent that it is justified, this observation supports the contention that in concentrated industries price adjustments to a change in sales are weaker; this presumably reflects a greater ability to set prices independently of short-run market conditions.

Among the three groups, the smallest rightward shifts of the distributions in successive recessions occur in the lowest concentration group. The price response of these industries, which is sharp, has not changed much over the postwar period. Yet the rightward shifts are generally no smaller in the middle than in the high concentration group, and are somewhat larger in the middle group for the 1970 recession. It is hard to see here an important role for concentration in the postwar changes in price behavior, contrary to the attention often paid to concentration. The tendency of prices to respond less in successive recessions does not reflect the special behavior of highly concentrated industries, despite their weaker price response overall, but is a more general phenomenon.

Summary of Grouped Distributions

Certain groups of products reveal differences in the responsiveness of their prices to recessions. Table 3.3 provides summary measures of the distributions for durability, value added, and concentration. Larger declines in rates of price change are characteristic of low market concentration and high materials costs, and these prices exhibit greater dispersion. Such differences are borne out by product groups (see appendix table A), in which the farm, lumber, and leather industries with low concentration and value added exhibit these characteristics the most. Nondurable products display greater price dispersion but not in general larger declines in rates of price change.

Apart from basic commodity markets where prices closely follow short-run demand and supply conditions, wholesale prices exhibit a pervasive tendency to respond to recessions less and less over the postwar period. This tendency does not appear to be dominated by the behavior of any particular group, though it is strongest for manufactures with low value added and medium concentration.

Summary and Interpretation of Findings

The failure of the aggregate index of wholesale prices to decline in the recessions of 1954 and 1958 and then again in 1961, which contrasted with the sharp declines of previous recessions, was a new phenomenon. The change in behavior was attributed at the time to the emergence of downward rigidity in prices and a tendency of producers to "administer" their prices with less regard for short-run shifts in market demand. Why did this phenomenon emerge following the 1949 recession? One explanation given was the growth of market power of firms over prices and of labor unions over wages, but it is not clear that the changes in the structure of labor and product markets implied by this explanation have been sufficient to account for the change in price behavior. Another explanation was that price setting is strongly influenced by aggregate-demand policies. The Employment Act of 1946, which had committed the government to pursue high-employment policies, was followed in the postwar years by an upward trend of prices, and the two together reinforced a belief that any deflationary pressures would be brief. Presumably that gradually dissuaded firms from reducing prices in recessions. Given periodic cyclical expansions which increase prices, the failure of prices to undergo offsetting declines during the ensuing recessions seemed sufficient at that time to explain the upward trend of prices.

The findings above for wholesale product prices partly modify these views. First of all, rates of price change in recessions display a high diversity, reflecting both random variations and persistent differences in volatility between certain groups of prices. The dispersion of price changes was less in the recessions following 1949 in part because of greater bunching at zero, which was widely interpreted to imply a downward rigidity of prices. But such bunching results largely from a bias toward zero change in reported prices; the NBER data for transaction prices in 1958 and 1961 do decline moderately.

The emphasis on downward rigidity was not sufficient, in any event, to explain the continuing *rise* of most prices in 1970 when the recession had eliminated most excess demand pressures. Half of the prices in 1970 did not even rise less rapidly than in the preceding expansion. While lags in the system could be invoked to argue that prices continued rising to catch up with previous cost increases, such lags had not been equally significant in previous recessions. The new behavior required a revision of the theories.

An important revision brought in the anticipated rate of inflation as a basic determinant of price changes to which the effects of market demand and supply conditions are then added.[10] The anticipated rate supposedly depends upon anticipated trends in unit costs at standard levels of capacity utilization. Declines in demand reduce the rate of price change in relation to the anticipated rate. A high anticipated rate makes the actual rate high and, if demand subsequently declines, prices continue rising, albeit less rapidly. Rising prices in 1970 could thus be explained by anticipated rates of inflation higher than those in earlier recessions.

From this point of view the response of prices to recessions should be measured by a decline in rates of change below the anticipated rates. In the absence of an acceptable measure of anticipated rates, the preceding expansion rates were used as rough proxies, though admittedly they are far from perfect. The frequency distributions of changes in rates of price change from expansions to ensuing recessions indicate how prices respond to cyclical downturns. They also allow for differences in the trends of prices and are equivalent to measures of overall cyclical amplitude.

There is no doubt that this amplitude has diminished since the 1920s and has continued to diminish in successive recessions. Expansion and recession rates have both helped to reduce the cyclical amplitude, but the attenuation of recession rates has been greater. A decrease of the severity of recessions in business activity has contributed, but it does not provide a full explanation, because the severity of five postwar recessions in real terms has not decreased chronologically. The 1966–67 mini-recession was examined as an additional test case, and the size of its response to prices fell chronologically between that of the recessions of 1961 and 1970 even though in terms of business activity it was less severe than those two.

Furthermore, although the dispersion of recession price changes among products has decreased sharply between the 1920s and 1949, it has remained the same since 1949. Developments in market structure and mix which could stabilize price fluctuations would show up in the dispersion of price changes. Since dispersion has not decreased since 1949, we may conclude that the continued decline in response to recessions has occurred along the entire distribution of price changes and does not reflect any alteration in market structure which also affects dispersion.

Why have declines from expansions to recessions in the rates of price change progressively diminished over the postwar period? The answer cannot be that anticipated rates of inflation rose. Although that was probably true, rising anticipated rates would not account for diminishing declines in the rates of change. Part of the answer appears to be that a reduction has occurred in the magnitude of price responses to excess capacity because of a growing general belief that inflationary movements will not be reversed. If declines in demand growth have been brief, the price response to the next one will be less. Certainly the postwar history of government failures to curb inflation must have affected price responses significantly. In addition, a decline in demand is likely to reduce the rate of price change mainly to the extent that the rate has risen above the anticipated rate during the business expansion. Thus price increases would presumably be reversed faster in a subsequent recession if they had recently accelerated than if they had been rising at a fairly constant rate for some time, though an offset to this faster reversal is the persistence of a higher rate of inflation while its lagged effects on costs work through the economy. The anticipated rate of inflation at the beginning of the 1970 recession may have been closer to the actual rate than had been true at previous cyclical peaks because the rate of inflation at the end of 1969 had been about the same for a year or two. This would help explain why the average price response was so slight in 1970.

Have structural changes occurred in product markets to account for the decline in price responses? There has, for example, been a steady growth in the relative importance of highly specialized and fabricated products, which characteristically fluctuate less in price than do raw materials. But this cannot account for the rightward shifts of the distributions, which are composed of the same set of prices. In a related classification of the prices into durable and nondurable manufactures, the latter exhibited somewhat larger rightward shifts than the former. The exception to successive shifts of the distributions is shown by prices of raw materials, which continue to exhibit their characteristic sharp and variable responses to market developments. Other classifications of prices which might be thought to reveal structural changes are the concentration of markets and the ratio of value added to shipments of producers. It is true that dispersion of price changes is lower in more concentrated markets and for firms with high value-added ratios. And the more concentrated markets exhibit fewer and smaller price declines in the recessions. But these differences between groups of prices have remained the same over the postwar period. The price response to recessions of the high value-added and concentration groups has declined the same or perhaps less than the others have. Therefore, even if they had increased in relative importance, which is not generally true, they cannot account for the general decline in price response.

The decisive influence on price response appears to have been a general adaptation of economic units to inflationary prospects rather than structural developments, in which prices respond less to short-run fluctuations in demand. The attenuation of price responses appears to have moderated cyclical accelerations as well as decelerations of price changes similarly across industries. The change in price behavior appears to be long range and therefore not likely to change much either way within a few years.

Part II

The Escalation of Inflation since 1965

4

From the Beginning of Inflation in 1965 to the Imposition of Price Controls in 1971

In 1965, after having experienced relative price stability since the late 1950s, the U.S. economy entered a period of increasing inflation. The recovery from the business contraction of 1961 had been slow and the economy did not approach full employment until 1965. At that point, when restraint would have been in order, no change in policy was made, and the economic expansion continued into the zone of increasing prices. The GNP price deflator rose 22 percent from 1965 to 1970.

As with other major inflations in U.S. history, this one started with an expansion of war expenditures. But it differed from other wartime inflations in that nonmonetary influences had a smaller effect on prices. Armament expenditures did not require the gigantic diversion of resources that had been necessary in World Wars I and II, and consumers did not go on a buying spree in anticipation of shortages as they had after the outbreak of war in Korea. While the conjuncture of war and inflation supported the popular view that inflation follows inevitably from an increase in war expenditures, the sequence was certainly not inevitable in this instance. The start of inflation conformed to a classic example of overexpansion of the money supply. The growth rate of the money supply gradually increased from its low

Adapted from a pamphlet originally published as *Recent Monetary Policy and the Inflation*, American Enterprise Institute, Special Analysis No. 9, September 1971.

point in the 1961 recession, and continued to increase until 1966, instead of becoming restrictive during 1965 when the first signs of inflation appeared. Without continued monetary support, the inflation would have withered.

Monetary policy lives in controversy. This was true of its role in the slow recovery of the economy during the early 1960s and in the beginning of inflation in 1965. Controversy also surrounded the question of whether monetary restraint would be effective in combating the growing inflation. Monetary restraint was nevertheless applied in 1966 and again in 1969, producing two revealing experiments in its powers and problems. In each of those years the monetary authorities undertook to curb the inflation by contracting the growth in the money supply for two to three quarters. There can be no doubt that these contractions of monetary growth were deliberate steps of policy, rather than the feedback from a slowdown in the economy, which in past mild cyclical contractions had obscured the direction of influence between money and economic activity.

This chapter recounts the story of the inflation and the policies to combat it up to the imposition of the wage-price freeze in August 1971. The first section describes the purposes and steps of policy, leaving to the remaining two sections an analysis of the results and problems. A final section surveys the lessons to be learned from this experience.

Formulation of Policy

Background of Price Stability: The Years up to 1965

During the second Eisenhower administration 1956–60, economic policy fought and finally conquered inflation. Following the sharp price increases of the Korean War, prices advanced broadly in the business boom of 1955–56. The deterioration of the balance of payments after 1957 and the continuing outflow of gold made it appear imperative that price stability be quickly achieved and maintained. Inflationary tendencies subsided during the second half of the 1950s, but slowly. By the late 1950s pressures to increase prices had finally been eradicated from the economy, as evidenced by the virtual stability in the wholesale price index and an average rise in consumer prices of only 1.2 percent per year from 1958 through 1964. The cost of achieving stability was several bouts of monetary restraint, which kept the economy below full employment and led to several recessions. The fourth of these since World War II occurred in 1961, during which unemployment reached 7 percent.

In the presidential campaign of 1960, John F. Kennedy promised "to get this country moving again." Ironical as it appears today, the overriding domestic concern of his administration was to speed up economic growth. Public opinion then ignored, as today it overplays, the problems of pollution aggravated by growth. Slogans are very much a sign of the times and, in 1961, sluggish business activity and high unemployment headed the list of public issues. To dramatize the issue, many critics of the performance of the U.S. economy pointed to the alleged rapid growth and technological advances of the Russian economy. The first Sputnik had startled the world in 1957. There were alarming charges that the U.S. was losing its technological and military superiority. The earlier concern with inflation faded, and the nation set its sights on growing as fast as possible.

The Kennedy administration's goals, however, were not immediately translated into a fundamental change in macroeconomic policy. The economy recovered from the 1961 recession at a steady pace, which was moderate rather than rapid, and unemployment did not reach the interim target set by the administration at 4 percent until the end of 1965. Both fiscal and monetary policy were blamed for the slowness of the expansion.

Fiscal policy was faulted because the expansion in federal expenditures did not keep pace with the natural growth in tax revenues. The government tended to absorb more of expanding incomes through taxes than it replaced by increased expenditures. This drain slowed down the expansion and kept the economy from catching up with the natural growth in the labor force and thus from attaining full employment. The Treasury was running a deficit, to be sure, but this reflected the less than full-employment level of income. To reduce this "fiscal drag," as it was called, tax rates had to be lowered, or federal expenditures raised, continually along with growth in the economy at large. This extended the theory of a stable full-employment budget, discussed in the 1940s, to the idea that without changes the budget could also hold back economic growth. The objective was to maintain tax rates and expenditures in such a relation to each other that the budget would be balanced only when the economy was at full employment. At lower levels of employment, income and tax revenues would be lower and the budget would be in deficit, thus contributing to a needed increase in aggregate demand.

Newspaper accounts of the effects of fiscal policy usually assume that a change in government expenditures has a dollar for dollar effect on aggregate expenditures, and give no consideration to the offsetting effects on private expenditures. When the government runs a larger deficit and has to borrow more, however, it absorbs credit which might otherwise have gone into private investment. With the offsetting reduction in private investment, there will be a net increase in aggregate demand only to the extent that higher interest rates produced by government borrowing reduce the public's demand for money balances. This is equivalent to an increase in the supply of money and will increase aggregate expenditures.

The multiplier effects of a budget deficit are much greater if the money stock expands at the same time. Then the deficit is indirectly financed by new money, and there is no tightening of credit supplies to offset the deficit's expansionary effects. In such a combined monetary and fiscal operation, the results cannot be attributed to fiscal policy alone. The proposals in the early 1960s to cut taxes generally did not specify a cooperative expansion of the money supply, but the sizable effects often claimed for fiscal actions suggest that an accommodating monetary policy was implicitly assumed.

At the urging of his economic advisers, President Kennedy proposed a tax cut in June 1962 to take effect at the beginning of 1963. The proposal languished in Congress, in part because it was packaged with tax reform but also because many congressmen were opposed to reducing taxes at a time when the budget was in deficit. The theory of "fiscal drag" had not yet made much impression on the public. When the tax cut was finally enacted under President Johnson in early 1964, the economy had recovered considerably from the 1961 recession, though unemployment still remained around 5.5 percent. Following the tax cut, unemployment fell—to 5 percent by the end of 1964 and to 4 percent in another year. The tax cut was acclaimed a great success. However, since monetary policy had become more expansive in 1963 and 1964, this did not demonstrate the power of fiscal policy acting by itself.

In the early 1960s, administration economists did not pay much attention to monetary policy, but it too, like fiscal policy, was open to criticism for holding back economic growth. On average, the money supply (excluding time deposits) grew slowly during that period (see figure 4.1). Its annual growth rate did not exceed 3 percent for any six-month period during 1961–62 and even declined to zero in mid-1962. It rose to an annual rate of 4 percent for the six months centered at the end of 1962 and fluctuated narrowly around that rate during 1963. GNP grew during those years, but by barely more, after allowing for increases in prices, than the growth in potential output of 3.5 percent per year. Consequently, even though unemployment had recovered from the 1961 recession in short order, it remained around 5.5 percent during 1962 and 1963.

The low monetary growth of those years was not viewed by the monetary authorities as overly tight or inappropriate. The reason was that they did not attach special significance to the money supply at that time and therefore were not trying to produce any particular rate of monetary growth. Their main attention was directed to "credit market conditions," such as interest rates and the availability of credit. These indicators seemed to suggest that credit was readily available, and that monetary policy was therefore providing the conditions for economic expansion and should attempt no more: First, high-grade corporate bond yields trended downward during 1960–62 from a peak of over 5 percent at the end of 1959 and, although they rose in 1963–64, remained around 4.5 percent until mid-1965. Second, free reserves of member banks (excess reserves minus borrowings from the Federal Reserve), though falling during 1961–63, remained substantially positive during those years. This, in the Federal Reserve's view, was indicative of easy conditions. And third, total bank credit was growing much more rapidly in the early 1960s than demand deposits, because of more rapid growth in time deposits. Another reason for not easing credit further was the adverse balance of foreign payments. The U.S. payments deficit had not improved since deteriorating in 1958, and it continued to cause great concern in financial circles.

A slack economy and a large deficit in the balance of payments posed a dilemma for policymakers and led to consideration of sophisticated methods of improving the balance of payments and domestic business simultaneously. One scheme was to raise short-term interest rates, as a means of attracting capital inflows from abroad, and to lower long-term rates, as a means of stimulating

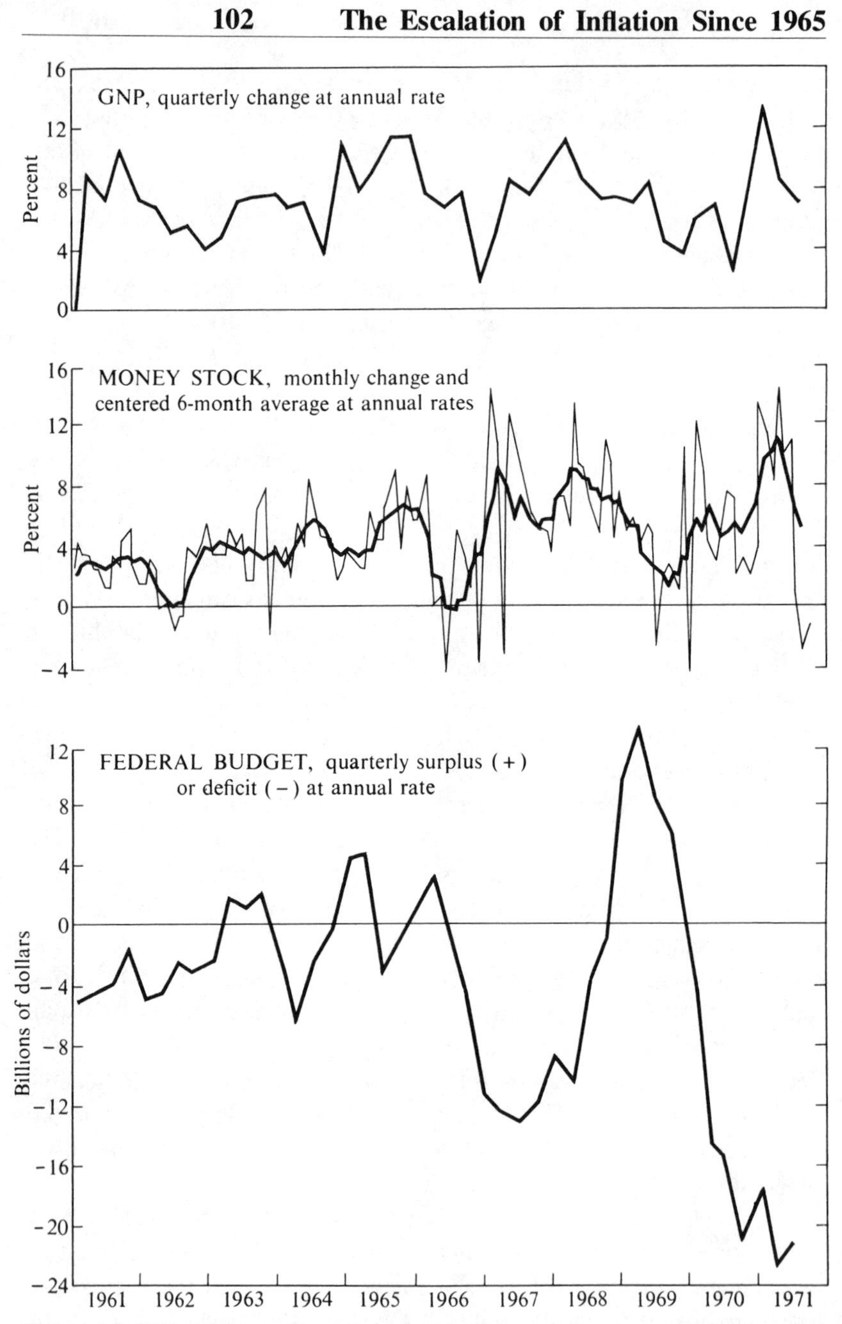

Figure 4.1 GNP, Monetary Growth, and Federal Budget Surplus or Deficit, 1961–71
NOTE: Money stock is demand deposits and currency. Federal budget is national income concept. All series are seasonally adjusted.

domestic activity. A proposal to accomplish this so-called "twist of the yield curve" by selling Treasury bills and buying bonds was discussed in early 1961. Under prodding from the new administration, the Federal Reserve gave lip service to it. But the purchase of bonds went against the Federal Reserve's "bills preferably" policy of the time, and they did not in fact attempt this twist aggressively. Yields did move in the desired direction, but largely because of market developments rather than Federal Reserve actions.

The summary of meetings of the Federal Reserve Open Market Committee, as reported in each *Annual Report of the Federal Reserve System,* does not disclose a sharp change in view during 1962 and the first half of 1963. Some members of the committee continued to be concerned over the deficit in the balance of payments, and others were equally concerned over the failure of unemployment to decline. The committee was clearly in a quandary over the appropriate policy. After each discussion a majority opted for a compromise of moderate expansion in activity. So long as the balance of payments did not deteriorate further, policy was directed toward producing a slow decline in unemployment. The committee was boxed into this decision during 1962 and the first half of 1963, as no basic change occurred either in the balance of payments or the level of unemployment. The lack of change despite the appearance of easy money markets fostered the view that monetary policy was not very important and that the unemployment problem required a fiscal stimulus.

Despite the absence of change in the Open Market Committee's directives, monetary policy was not in fact static over this period. Growth of the money stock, either including or excluding time deposits, declined during the first half of 1962. Business indicators weakened in the second quarter, and the year-old recovery from the 1961 recession faltered. (The accompanying decline in common stocks was dubbed the "Kennedy bear market" because the administration's angry attack on a rise in steel prices was widely interpreted as revealing an antibusiness bias and precipitated a wave of selling. But the faltering pace of the business expansion produced a basic weakness in stocks and underlay the decline.) Then, in September 1962, monetary growth spurted sharply and maintained an average rate of growth of about 4 percent through the first half of 1964. The spurt coincided with a general improvement in business conditions.

Business loans expanded and the monetary authorities allowed the expansion of bank credit to increase monetary growth. The increase in turn supported the renewed business expansion.[1]

During the second half of 1963 policy directives continued unchanged, but the committee viewed the money market as taking on a "firmer" tone, and members were not dissatisfied with that development. They approved the sharp rise in Treasury bill rates and the decline in free reserves of member banks. Nevertheless, policy had in fact become easier; the market was firmer owing to the rise in business activity.

An important reason for not taking steps toward restraint at this time was that the balance of payments improved markedly in the second half of 1963 and first quarter of 1964, due partly to introduction of an interest equalization tax and partly to an increase in the payments balance on goods and services. Though the improvements did not last, they made the balance of payments a less imperative issue for a while. Moreover, there was a growing conviction that the balance would be adverse on average for some time and could not be allowed to override domestic economic goals. This view was reinforced by a widely publicized report of the Brookings Institution[2] in 1963 which forecast that a gradual attainment of balance in U.S. payments was under way but would not be fully achieved for five years.

The year 1964 was the economic turning point of the decade. After two years of little change, the unemployment rate (seasonally adjusted) fell fairly steadily during the year, from 5.5 percent at the beginning to around 5 percent in the fourth quarter. This was evidence of a pickup in the rate of expansion of economic activity. Sentiment grew in the Federal Reserve Open Market Committee for imposing restraint. Nothing was done during the first half, however, since the economy, though expanding, gave little cause for alarm. The tax cut, which began to take effect in the first quarter of 1964, was immediately reflected in increased consumer expenditures (though it was partly absorbed by a higher personal saving rate in the last three quarters of the year). While the balance of payments began to deteriorate again during 1964, this was due to capital outflows; the balance on goods and services remained strong. Scattered price increases broke the calm surface of general price stability, but they were moderate during the first half and did not at first seem to be spreading.

By August 1964, with the economy continuing to expand and with capital outflows rising rapidly, a majority of the committee finally voted for a ''firmer'' money market, though not without strong dissents. The growth rate of the money stock, which had risen during the first half from 3 to above 5 percent per year, now began to decline and, from December 1964 through May 1965, averaged only 2.5 percent, despite a willingness by the Federal Reserve to accommodate Treasury financing in January and February. This tightening of policy appears to have been an appropriate response to the prevailing conditions, though perhaps too severe to be maintained very long. In any event, unemployment continued to decline, and the reduction in monetary growth promised to restrain the expansion without immediately halting it.

Outbreak of Inflation: 1965

In June 1965, the monetary growth rate suddenly doubled and for the next eleven months averaged more than 6 percent per year. Why was restraint abandoned in the midst of a vigorous business expansion and numerous signs of spreading inflation?

Surprisingly, the Open Market Committee issued no directive for easier monetary conditions during 1965. Several directives early in the year called for ''firmer'' conditions, and one, on October 12, called ambiguously for achieving a ''firm tone.'' The increase in the rate of monetary growth was simply not viewed by the committee as indicative of a shift to an easier policy. Here was a classic conflict between monetary growth and credit market conditions as indicators of the direction of policy. Free reserves of member banks turned negative in early 1965, after being positive for many years, and remained negative for most of the year. Interest rates of all maturities rose substantially during the second half. These were indications, in the Federal Reserve's view, of a tighter money market and a ''firmer'' monetary policy.

But the demand for credit was increasing, and the higher monetary growth helped fuel an expansion of aggregate expenditures. In that sense monetary policy was expansionary and not ''firm'' as directed.

This was not a case of monetary policy being forced by circumstances to underwrite heavy Treasury borrowing. As Vietnam expenditures rose, federal receipts initially rose just as fast. Budget deficits did not get out of hand until the end of 1966. Interest rates rose sharply in 1965, in response to expanded business activity and anticipations of heavy Treasury borrowing to come. Monetary growth increased because the Federal Reserve was trying to moderate the rise in interest rates, which required them to supply part of the expanding demand for credit. The President and top administration officials were adamantly opposed to a tightening of credit until "full employment" was reached. An indication of administration and congressional attitude toward restraint at this time was the reaction in December when the Federal Reserve felt compelled to raise the discount rate from 4 to 4.5 percent. This modest step touched off a furor of criticism, marked by barely concealed indications of presidential outrage and congressional hearings on the breach between the administration and Federal Reserve.

Inflation did not suddenly emerge in 1965 as a surprise. Wholesale prices of crude materials rose all during 1964, while other wholesale prices began to rise in late 1964. Their rise during 1965 was unmistakable and gave no sign of slackening as the year wore on. This did not go unnoticed; many people outside the government called for restraint.

Because it was gradual, however, the emergence of inflation did not suddenly demand the attention of policymakers in contrast to the Korean and 1955 episodes. Most of the accelerated increase in consumer prices during 1965 was due to foods, which reflected short-run supply conditions and which government economists dismissed as temporary. Labor costs per unit of output did not rise significantly until 1966. The human inclination of policymakers here, preoccupied for over half a decade with unemployment and now in sight of the cherished goal of 4 percent, was to ignore minor price increases as not justifying the imposition of restraint. They no doubt thought that a slow rise in prices could be easily stopped later by adjustments of policy—a judgment not widely criticized until later experience revealed the momentum which was developing behind the price increases.

In hindsight, the major mistake of policy was to disregard the first stage of inflation and to drive the economy full speed toward full employment in 1965 with a foot on the accelerator rather than the brake.

First Attempt at Curbing the Inflation: 1966

By early 1966 it was clear that the prevailing Federal Reserve policy of fostering "firm" monetary conditions was failing to curb rising prices. More drastic steps had to be taken. The authorities now slammed on the brakes and produced a rare experiment in the efficacy of severe monetary restraint. Seldom have the monetary authorities deliberately produced so sharp a break in monetary growth. In the past such breaks usually accompanied panics or speculative collapses, and cause and effect were hard to distinguish. Here the Federal Reserve clearly engineered the whole episode.

On February 8 the Open Market Committee unanimously called for a gradual reduction in bank reserves. (An important constraint on monetary policy was removed in the preceding month when the seasonally adjusted unemployment rate reached the administration's interim target of 4 percent for the first time since early 1957.) This directive to restrain credit was unchanged during March and April. While free reserves became increasingly negative, however, the effect on monetary growth was initially moderate. The annual growth rate of the money stock excluding time deposits remained above 5 percent in February and March and then jumped to almost 10 percent in April. Time deposits also continued to grow, though less rapidly, because the maximum interest rate allowed on large denomination certificates of deposit had been raised from 4.5 to 5.5 percent the preceding December and exceeded the offering rate until July.

The money market appeared to tighten in early 1966 as judged by the sharp rise in most interest rates, particularly bond yields. In the largest movement in many years, high-grade corporate bond yields rose from 5 to almost 6 percent in the first half and municipal bond yields, which started the year at 3.5, rose to 4 percent by August (see figure 4.2). But bank reserves did not decline as policy had prescribed. On a seasonally adjusted basis, member-bank reserves available for private demand deposits were virtually unchanged in January and February and even rose in March and April.

Accordingly, on May 10 the committee called again for gradual reduction in bank reserves and added, for the first time, a proviso that further restraint should be imposed if growth in required reserves (hence also net deposits) did not moderate substantially. The results were dramatic. The seasonally adjusted money stock excluding time

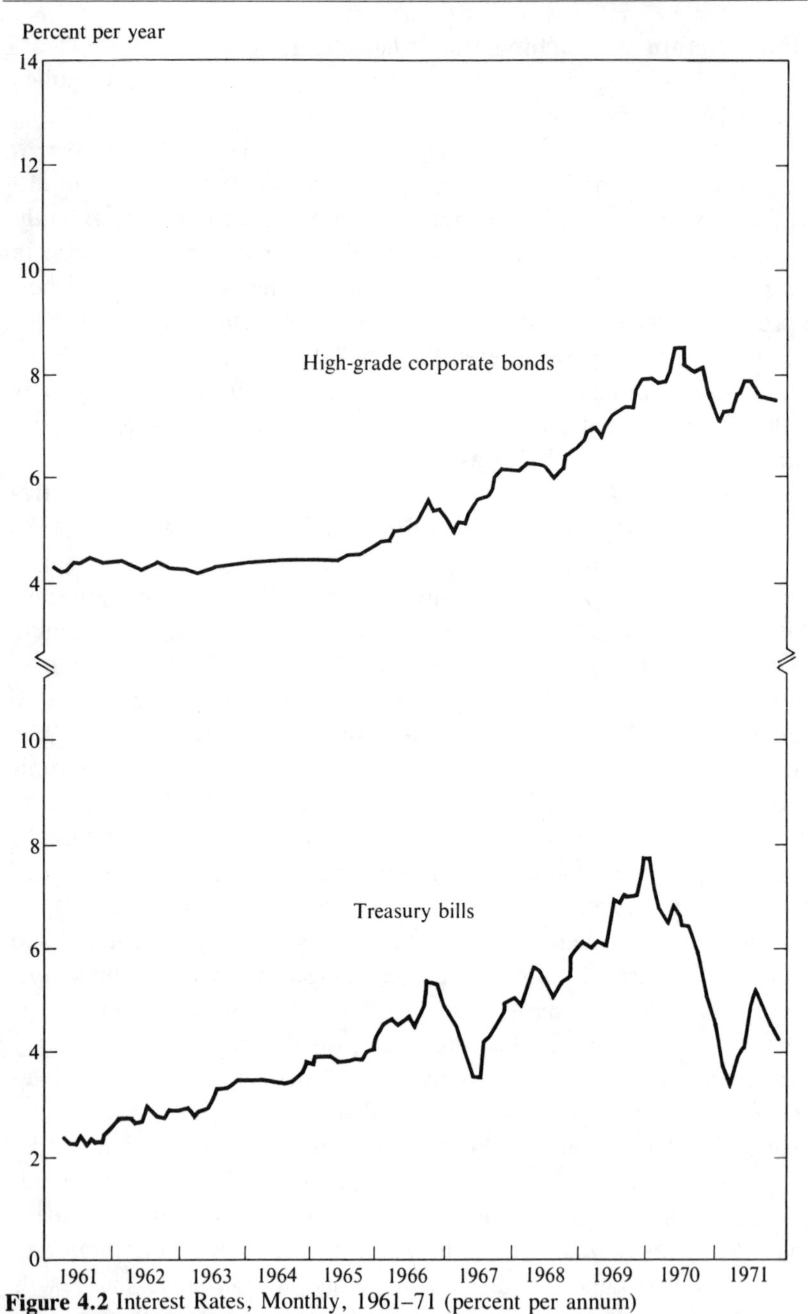

Figure 4.2 Interest Rates, Monthly, 1961–71 (percent per annum)
NOTE: Top series is Moody's index of yields on corporate Aaa bonds. Bottom series is market yields (bank discount basis) on 3-month bills.

deposits actually declined in May and, apart from monthly fluctuations, did not expand for the rest of the year.

There can be no doubt that this policy slowly curtailed economic activity. Although the growth of aggregate expenditures did not decrease until the first quarter of 1967, when real GNP actually declined slightly, the seasonally adjusted index of industrial production gradually leveled off during 1966 and then declined through the first half of 1967. In general, however, the slowdown in the economy was quite mild. It does not qualify as a conventional business recession, even though home building contracted severely.

The federal budget on a national income basis had run a surplus in the first half of 1966. The surplus was too small and occurred too far beforehand to account for the slowdown in the economy in the fourth quarter. In the second half of the year federal expenditures continued to rise fairly steadily while the growth of receipts began to level off, and the budget began a steep descent into deficit. This was also true of the full-employment budget. Despite the easing of the budget, the economy slowed down at the end of 1966. Fiscal changes, therefore, reflected the slowdown and did not produce it.

The deficits did add strain to the money market, coming as they did on top of severe monetary restraint. But Treasury borrowing was to be much higher during 1967 than it was in 1966, while a tightening of financial markets became severe in August of 1966, reached its peak in September, and subsided appreciably by the end of the year. The supply of credit slowly contracted and could not satisfy the growing demand. Increasingly, normally acceptable borrowers had to be disappointed, even though banks stretched their resources. During these months interest rates soared, and many corporations that borrow short-term funds on a regular basis began to doubt whether they would be able to meet upcoming financial commitments. The financial and business community developed a severe case of the jitters. Few had ever experienced a general financial stringency.

Many people felt that the Federal Reserve was carrying restraint too far and might blunder into a liquidity crisis. This would involve the wholesale dumping of securities on the market by businesses short of cash and cause widespread bankruptcies. Such a crisis did not occur, but the "credit crunch" imposed hardship on many, particularly small businesses and home building. The credit crunch is discussed further below.

The widespread complaints produced by monetary restraint alerted the Open Market Committee in September to the desirability of easing the pressure. This followed by one week a presidential announcement of a planned reduction in the rate of growth of federal expenditures and a suspension of tax incentives for corporate investment. The anticipated effects of thus reducing credit demands helped relieve financial markets. After the September tax and dividend payments were out of the way, financial strains subsided. In October new bond offerings fell. Signs of declining growth in business activity also began to appear. By November, weakness in the economy had spread, wholesale prices appeared to be stabilizing, and the committee voted for easier monetary conditions.

Renewal of Monetary Expansion and Inflation: 1967–1968

For a while, the seven months of no monetary growth during 1966 appeared to have been successful. It slowed the economic expansion and brought the rate of change of wholesale industrial prices down appreciably, while unemployment remained below 4 percent. A milder restraint might have accomplished just as much and jolted money markets less, but, overall, the policy achieved its purpose. The change to ease at the end of 1966 was also appropriate, though it probably should have come sooner.

The fault of policy was in the magnitude of the turnaround. In the first three quarters of 1967 the money stock excluding time deposits grew at an average annual rate of 8.2 percent, faster than in the three quarters preceding the second quarter of 1966. A comparable increase in growth rate occurred for money including time deposits. Why so sharp a reversal?

The major reason was a failure to foresee the strong recovery that high monetary growth during 1967 would provide for the mild slowdown in the economy. Real GNP was practically unchanged in the first quarter, but then jumped to a 3 percent annual rate of growth in the second quarter. The strength of this recovery was not sensed by the committee until May, and then uncertainly. Clear signs of the recovery were slow to appear. The index of industrial production declined until midyear, and the index of twelve leading indicators, a barometer of economic change, did not begin to rise until the second quarter. Moreover, it must be remembered that these indexes only become available with a lag of a month or more, and even then cyclical changes of direction often cannot be discerned for several more months. The Federal Reserve Board has a good record of recognizing economic developments once they occur, but it has done no better than most forecasters in foreseeing changes in direction of the economy. The period since 1965 has had its full share of forecasting blunders.

Despite the recognition by midyear of a resumption of economic expansion in the second quarter of 1967, no change in policy was made until November. The reports of the Open Market Committee indicate several reasons for the delay. Uncertainty continued to exist over the strength of the upturn in activity. And in August the President repeated his January proposal to add a surcharge to the income tax, now to be 10 percent, to begin in October for individuals and retroactively in July for corporations. This tax was expected, if enacted soon, to obviate the need for further monetary restraint. The proposal induced a wait-and-see attitude on the part of the monetary authorities. Finally, bond yields rose sharply during most of 1967 to levels much higher than the peaks of 1966, which had exceeded yields experienced since the early 1930s. Such high yields created the impression that somehow monetary policy must be tight. More tightening would raise interest rates even higher and complicate further the financing of the coming Treasury deficits and the revival of home building.

The second two reasons were related. The high and rising interest rates were not welcome to the populist-minded President Johnson, and he must have suggested to the Federal Reserve that it forgo further monetary restraint and instead let the tax surcharge dampen the economic expansion and the rise in interest rates. The Open Market Committee could in good conscience go along with this suggestion, because most forecasters in and out of government expected the surcharge when enacted to be very effective. Later on many even shuddered at the possibility of "overkill."

Unfortunately for this strategy, the committee had to wait until the middle of 1968 for the passage of the tax surcharge, and then more months to discover that this fiscal bomb was a dud. Meanwhile, the economy continued to expand and interest rates continued to rise. There was practically no recognition at this time that interest rates were high because of anticipated inflation and that, in real terms, they were not unusually high. To that extent the inflation—and not solely tight money—was contributing to financial disintermediation and the difficulties of mortgage financing.

As it became clear during 1967 that Congress would not pass the tax surcharge that year, sentiment in the committee gradually swung in favor of greater monetary restraint. A significant change in policy could not be made in November because of negotiations to provide assistance to Britain to shore up the pound—though the turbulence in international exchange markets following devaluation of the pound on November 18 led to an increase in the discount rate on the 19th. Finally, in December, with a menacing increase in speculation against the dollar in foreign gold markets, the committee called for "slightly firmer" monetary conditions on the 12th and voted on the 27th to increase reserve requirements effective the middle of January.

Actually, monetary growth had declined the preceding August. From a 7.25 percent average annual rate during the first eight months of the year, it fluctuated narrowly around a 5.5 percent rate until April 1968. Then for the rest of the year the growth rate became volatile again and grew on average at the higher annual rate of 8.5 percent, despite another directive on March 5, unchanged until December, calling for firmer conditions. This discrepancy between stated policy and actual monetary growth again illustrates the contrast between "credit market conditions" and monetary growth as indicators of policy. The failure of credit market conditions to indicate the true degree of monetary restraint during 1968 gradually became evident, and the Open Market Committee started to pay more attention to "monetary aggregates," meaning the money supply and bank credit. Nevertheless, while the May 28 report of the Open Market Committee notes that "the money supply continued to grow rapidly in May . . ." it concluded that

> a considerable degree of monetary restraint had . . . been achieved; the banking system was being subject to increasing liquidity pressures; over-all expansion of bank credit appeared to have halted in April and May; and market rates of interest had advanced sharply to levels that could give rise to a substantial amount of disintermediation.

The disinclination to tighten further was supported, after mid-year, by the turn in fiscal policy. With the new tax surcharge in effect, the budget deficit on a national income basis fell from an $11 billion annual rate in the second quarter of 1968 to $3.5 billion in the third quarter. Yet economic activity did not slow down during the third quarter, and inflationary forces even gained strength. By autumn the evidence of these developments would normally have led the committee to conclude that monetary restraint should be intensified no matter how "firm" it was thought to be. But faith in the power of the surcharge died slowly, and the majority still hesitated, expecting the surcharge eventually to provide all the restraint necessary. The report of September 10 concluded that:

> greater restraint was not considered desirable in view of the outlook for slowing in over-all economic activity, although it was noted that firm evidence was lacking thus far on the amount of slowing in prospect.

In preceding years the Federal Reserve Board had often lectured the administration and the Congress on the necessity of fiscal restraint to avoid overburdening the "limited" powers of monetary policy. In 1968 the request was granted, but ironically the monetary authorities paid dearly. Monetary policy was disastrously expansionary at a time of rising inflation for seventeen months from mid-1967, when the need for effective restraint was first recognized, to December 1968.

Second Attempt at Curbing the Inflation: 1969

The Nixon administration took office in early 1969 with the announced objective of curbing the inflation, though as gently as possible. The concept of a tradeoff between inflation and employment had been widely discussed and was very much in the minds of policymakers. There was general agreement that any success in slowing inflation would produce a higher rate of unemployment. The unemployment would reflect a gap between potential and actual output, and this pressure of excess capacity in commodity and labor markets would bring down the rate of inflation. The policymakers thus had a choice: larger excess capacity would bring inflation under control faster, but would also require a higher peak level of unemployment. The challenge to policy was to follow a thin line, bringing about reasonable if not spectacular reductions in inflation at the cost of moderate unemployment in the short run.

The new administration therefore faced the politically unappealing prospect of temporarily condoning unemployment in order to curb inflation. Yet it saw no choice; continued inflation was unacceptable. This distasteful necessity was sweetened by the hope that the short-run tradeoff would not be too harsh and would allow a reduction in inflation without raising unemployment too high in the process and that, in any event, the worst would be over before the congressional elections of November 1970.

The election of the new administration was promptly reflected in the posture of the Open Market Committee. At its meeting on December 17, 1968, the members were "unanimously of the view that greater monetary restraint was required at this time in light of the unexpected strength of current economic activity." The reported shift to restraint was left basically unchanged in the directives during 1969. There ensued a precipitous decline in the growth of the money stock including time deposits. From a rate of growth over the two preceding years of 11 percent per year, this stock actually declined 1 percent during 1969 because of a $10 billion reduction in time deposits. The reduction reflected mainly a runoff of certificates of deposit; their ceiling interest rates remained at 5.5 to 6.5 percent depending upon maturity, while the competitive commercial paper and Eurodollar rates soared.

The money stock excluding time deposits told a different story. Revised figures available a year later showed a moderate decline in the annual growth rate of this stock to 5 percent from January to July 1969 compared with a rate of over 8 percent in the preceding nine months (April–December 1968). But the figures available at the time showed a 2 percent rate of growth for the January–July period, down from 6.5 percent during 1968. (This revision in the money data was unusually large, because a heavy volume of Eurodollar borrowing by banks considerably overstated cash items in the process of collection in the unrevised figures.) While monetary policy was viewed at the time as becoming increasingly tight during the first half of 1969, the degree of tightening as noted was moderate. According to the revised figures, commercial banks managed to keep expanding demand deposits until July. Monetary policy appeared at the time to be tightening severely because interest rates were rising sharply and free reserves and time deposits were declining. But the shift by time depositors to commercial paper and Eurodollars did not reduce the total supply of credit; one asset was simply substituted for the other because of the change in relative rates of return.

The standard economic forecast made at the beginning of 1969 was for a slowdown in the first half of the year and an acceleration in the second half. This revealed an optimistic confidence in the ability of fiscal and monetary policy to attain their stated objectives. In large part these forecasts were wishful thinking, and they soon had to be revised. The new Council of Economic Advisers, testifying in February 1969, expressed doubt that the economy would slow down much before the end of the year. On that schedule, the acceleration previously slated for the second half could not be expected until early 1970.

Further indication of a stronger-than-expected first half of 1969 came from the Commerce-SEC survey taken in February. The survey indicated a planned increase in expenditures on plant and equipment of 14 percent in 1969 (a projection that was subsequently scaled down to 12.5 percent in the April–May survey).[3] This led many to doubt whether the economy would ever slow down, given the tendency to view corporate investment as the key to changes in GNP.

At the meeting of the Open Market Committee on April 1, its staff's previous GNP projections of a slowdown in 1969 were accordingly revised upward. The staff noted that the recent declines in bank credit gave a misleading picture of monetary tightness, because banks had developed unconventional means of raising and supplying credit in response to the runoff of their certificates of deposit. The magnitude of these new sources of financing had not previously been fully recognized. Moreover, funds that normally traveled through banks were finding their way to ultimate borrowers through an expansion of the commercial paper market and other channels, so that total credit was not declining despite the decline in bank credit.

The committee decided that the tightening effect of two coming policy steps—an increase in the discount rate in early April and an increase in reserve requirements in mid-April—should not be offset by open market operations. The language of this policy change reads like a minor adjustment. Combined with the policy directives issued since mid-December, however, the effect was dramatic. The growth in the monetary base slowed sharply after May, and the money stock excluding time deposits grew hardly at all from July to December. The shift in monetary growth provides a second revealing test, along with 1966, of the power of monetary policy.

Unlike 1966, fiscal policy was not wholly passive in 1969. As noted, the tax surcharge of mid-1968 reduced the federal deficit sharply. The new administration also put a lid on the expansion in federal expenditures and produced a surplus, on a national income basis, of $9.5 billion (annual rate) in the first quarter of 1969 and $13.5 billion in the second quarter. Thereafter, the budget eased. The surplus slid to $6 billion (annual rate) by the fourth quarter, and then the budget fell into deficit. As with the tax surcharge in 1968, the effect on aggregate activity of the 1969 swing to a budget surplus is difficult to detect. The growth in GNP (in both dollar and real terms) remained fairly steady through the third quarter of 1969 and fell sharply only in the fourth quarter, three quarters after the shift of the budget to surplus. We expect a lag of that length for monetary policy but not for federal expenditures. What happened in this case was that private expenditures took up the slack in the growth of federal expenditures. Although the 7 percent investment tax credit was repealed in April 1969, business investment continued to expand. With the budget shift from deficit to surplus, the Treasury no longer raised funds in financial markets but became a net supplier of funds. The strong private demand for credit absorbed these funds and channeled them back into the stream of expenditures. The Treasury surplus in 1969 no doubt helped to moderate the rise in interest rates and to that extent made monetary velocity lower than it otherwise would have been. But that contribution to dampening the boom was inconsequential, and the economy finally slowed down only after monetary restraint began to contract aggregate spending.

The continued expansion of the economy in the first three quarters of 1969, which contradicted the earlier forecasts of a slowdown, confused the public as well as many professional forecasters. The switch to a budget surplus had failed to produce the expected effects, and monetary restraint appeared to have failed too. It was, of course, not known at the time, as later data revealed, that the rate of growth in the money supply (excluding time deposits) had declined only moderately during the first half. A belief that no downturn was coming, or that if it came it would be extremely mild, gained wide currency in the business community during the summer and autumn and hardened the anticipations of continuing inflation. A survey of corporations by the Federal Reserve Bank of Philadelphia[4] in October 1969 found that 80 percent expected their after-tax profits in 1970 to increase over 1969, in the aggregate, by 8.5 percent. (Actually, corporate after-tax profits *declined* 8.5 percent in 1970!)

Financial markets tightened severely in the second half of 1969, and the public expectations of strong business activity were not considered inconsistent with widespread fears of another "credit crunch" as in 1966. Interest rates rose at a speed and to such high levels as to recall the financial panics of pre-1914 days. Funds by-passed or flowed out of savings institutions—which were no longer competitive due to deposit-rate ceilings—to be invested directly in security markets, thus drying up a major source of mortgage financing. Municipal bond yields rose above statutory rate ceilings in many states and prevented new issues. The growth of bank loans declined during the year despite the strong demand for credit. Many borrowers, especially many small businesses dependent upon bank loans, could not be accommodated. These developments are discussed further below.

Despite the turmoil, financial markets continued to handle a heavy volume of new security issues at rising interest rates during 1969. Many in Wall Street feared that monetary restraint would make credit tighter and tighter without ever restraining business activity. While the Open Market Committee was confident that business activity would eventually slacken, it shared the general uncertainty as to when this would occur. Around midyear the Federal Reserve staff began to report signs of slower economic activity, but the committee insisted upon waiting for concrete results before allowing policy to ease.

This flagrant disregard of the much-discussed lag in monetary policy can be explained by the committee's fear of repeating the policy mistake of 1966–67. At that time, the inflation was weakened by monetary restraint, only to resurge as soon as policy relaxed. Another such failure would surely harden public anticipations of inflation and magnify the degree of restraint which would then be required in the next attempt. There was some sentiment for waiting until inflation was completely under control. But evidence of such control remained scanty, whereas multiplying signs of a downturn in general activity by year-end made the urgency of easing policy increasingly clear.

The consequence of such a "hardline" monetary policy was that restraint was maintained too long, thus leading to a larger decline in economic activity than was originally contemplated or intended.

This raised the danger that the Federal Reserve might later overreact to the larger-than-expected decline in the economy with a rapid monetary stimulation which would refuel the inflation. Policy in 1966–67 was pointed to as having mistakenly fallen into such a stop-go pattern.

While both the Federal Reserve and its critics (which included some high in the administration) could accuse the other of interpreting the lesson of 1966–67 incorrectly, the events of 1969–70 disappointed both sides. The downturn in activity was considerably greater than that in 1967, despite not much more monetary restraint, but then took far longer to affect prices.

Economic Slowdown and Easing of Monetary Policy: 1970

By the start of 1970 the earlier buoyant optimism of the business community had swung around to pessimism, and sentiment in the Open Market Committee for a change in policy had grown. The January 15 directive called for moderate growth in money and bank credit, but ambiguously specified that the growth should be consistent with the continuation of the prevailing conditions of firm credit. In February, Arthur F. Burns replaced William McChesney Martin as chairman of the Board of Governors and, at the first meeting in February, the new policy was modified, though not without dissents. The directive called for less restraint "implemented cautiously." At the next meeting on March 10, the qualification was dropped and the directive called simply for "moderate growth in money and bank credit."

The money stock (excluding time deposits) had spurted in the last week of December 1969, but most of this reflected the unexpected effects of international transactions. The spurt largely disappeared during January, and not until the stock increased in March was it clear that monetary growth had resumed. For 1970 as a whole the stock grew 5.5 percent, though less in the latter than in the earlier part of the year.

Statements of policy now gave full recognition to the lag in monetary effects. Real GNP had declined slightly in the fourth quarter of 1969, and was expected to show no growth in the first quarter because of the past monetary restraint. The resumption of monetary growth in the first quarter was expected to initiate an upturn in activity in the second and subsequent quarters.

The chairman of the Council of Economic Advisers testified to the Joint Economic Committee in February 1970 that the administration foresaw a rise and then a decline in unemployment during the year, with a maximum of less than 5 percent of the labor force. This proved to be optimistic. Real GNP declined 3 percent (annual rate) in the first quarter, considerably more than expected, and increased only slightly in the ''recovery'' of the second and third quarters. The fourth quarter registered a 4 percent (annual rate) decline because of a major labor strike at General Motors. (Without the strike there would have been little or no decline.) Industrial production continued on a contractionary course throughout the year and reached a trough in November. The unemployment rate climbed steadily to a peak of 6.2 percent by December.

Both the administration and the Federal Reserve stressed monetary policy as the key to economic developments during 1970, but differed on the appropriate rate of growth of the money supply. Administration officials wanted a growth rate higher than the 5 to 6 percent rate implied by Federal Reserve pronouncements of its intentions. They reasoned that a 5 to 6 percent rate would not permit real output to expand fast enough to keep unemployment around 5 percent, an unemployment rate that was considered sufficient to maintain pressure on prices and slowly unwind the inflation. Monetary growth of 5 to 6 percent might be adequate to hold the economy on the desired growth path once attained, but not to get back to it. Curbing inflation was going to take a long time, and little could be gained in the short run by accepting an excessively high unemployment rate. If the fight against inflation became too unpopular, political forces might force its abandonment. This was underscored by the November elections in which the Republican Party suffered setbacks partly because of unemployment.

On its part the Federal Reserve was reluctant to pursue such a policy for fear of the effect on anticipations. A vigorous expansion in the economy, even though only for a few quarters, might convince the public that the fight against inflation had been abandoned, no matter how the policy might be explained publicly. In that event, anticipations of inflation would intensify and the long labor of policy to slow down economic activity and to begin controlling inflation would have been lost, as had happened in 1967. The adverse balance of payments also counseled restraint. To be sure, tight money had brought capital inflows which produced temporary surpluses on a liquidity basis during 1969, and abandonment of support of the private gold market in 1969 took pressure off the gold stock. But the Federal Reserve continued to be concerned over the persistent deterioration in the balance on goods and services.

Although Federal Reserve officials were dismayed at the continued weakness in the economy as the year unfolded, they maintained monetary growth at an average rate of 5.5 percent, as noted. This represented a standoff between those who wanted more growth and those who wanted less. The argument for less was based mainly on three developments during 1970: the large decline in short-term interest rates mainly in the second half of the year; the phenomenal growth in certificates of deposit following the February increase in the ceiling rates and the June removal of any ceiling on the large denomination, short maturities; and the meager progress in curbing inflation. The first two developments had uncertain significance, however. The decline in interest rates reflected in large part a fall in demand for credit, and did not indicate that monetary policy was overly easy. Moreover, such a decline might tend to raise the demand for money balances and, if the supply did not rise commensurately, would work to reduce aggregate expenditures. The growth of CDs, like their runoff in 1969, reflected a switching among similar financial assets; at the time the large growth seemed likely to subside after several months. A much stronger argument against further easing was the third development—the meager progress in curbing inflation.

While the administration had looked forward to a significant reduction of inflation in 1970, little improvement could be detected during the year. By hindsight price increases did indeed reach a peak during 1970. But skeptical opinion at the time could not be convinced without dramatic signs of a decline, and they were not in evidence. The widely publicized consumer price index rose less rapidly during the middle months of 1970 but, by the end of the year, it again went above an annual rate of 5 percent and showed little overall deceleration from 1969. Thus a full year of business recession had yielded no clear-cut reduction in the inflation of consumer prices. Public exasperation with this situation was heightened by the fact that, while food prices rose very little during the second half of 1970, increases in the more stable nonfood prices accelerated. The more comprehensive index of prices for the private component of GNP told the same story: it continued rising at an annual rate of almost 5 percent, practically unchanged from 1969 (table 4.1). The index of wholesale industrial prices fluctuated during 1970, but over the year as a whole showed no tendency to decelerate. Its annual rate was 3.5 percent for the second half of 1970, somewhat lower than earlier in the year but above the corresponding rates of mid-1969. One encouraging sign was the behavior of consumer service prices, which had a rising rate of increase in early 1970 but a decreasing rate during the second half of the year. This was due only in part to declining mortgage interest rates (included in the services component). Nevertheless, its annual rate of increase in December was still more than 7 percent, and its downward trend had not gone far enough to be apparent by the end of 1970. Union wage settlements and nonunion wage adjustments were

Table 4.1 GNP, Prices, Costs, Productivity, and Compensation, 1968–1973 (percent change from preceding quarter, seasonally adjusted annual rate)

	All Sectors		*Private Sector*	*Private Nonfarm Sector*		
	GNP	*Real GNP*	*Price Deflator (Chain Index)*	*Unit Labor Cost*	*Output per Hour of Labor*	*Compensation per Hour of Labor*
1968 I	9.2	5.4	3.6	4.9	4.7	9.9
II	11.7	7.5	4.3	2.0	4.1	6.2
III	8.6	4.0	4.0	6.3	1.0	7.4
IV	7.1	2.4	4.3	7.5	1.3	8.8
1969 I	7.7	3.4	3.8	7.4	−1.6	5.7
II	7.5	1.9	4.9	7.7	−0.8	6.9
III	8.2	1.9	5.5	7.1	−0.6	6.5
IV	3.1	−2.3	5.3	10.6	−1.6	8.8
1970 I	3.9	−2.5	4.6	8.4	−1.8	6.5
II	5.9	1.5	4.6	2.4	4.7	7.2
III	6.1	2.0	3.2	2.0	6.9	9.0
IV	1.4	−4.8	5.6	8.0	−3.1	4.6
1971 I	14.3	8.0	5.5	1.5	7.4	9.1
II	7.9	3.4	4.4	4.2	3.2	7.5
III	5.4	2.5	3.4	2.5	2.5	5.2
IV	8.3	6.7	1.4	.3	4.7	4.9
1972 I	12.0	6.5	4.4	3.8	5.2	9.1
II	11.4	9.4	2.3	−.5	5.1	4.6
III	8.9	6.3	2.9	−.4	6.6	6.1
IV	11.0	8.0	2.9	3.6	3.6	7.6
1973 I	15.2	8.0	6.8	5.8	4.3	10.4

higher in 1970 than in 1969 and showed little tendency to moderate. Inflation was cooling at an excruciatingly slow pace.

Even if a recession does not stop inflation immediately, it initiates a deceleration in unit labor costs, which is the first stage in the process of reducing inflation and which can continue even after business begins to recover. Indeed, the business recovery contributes to the deceleration in unit labor costs—up to a point—because an expansion of production brings a greater utilization of fixed resources; this shows up as increases in output per hour of labor. The lack of progress in curbing inflation during the 1970 recession did not, therefore, preclude a policy designed to foster a strong recovery in 1971. Of course, a recovery in demand would exert an upward pull on many wholesale prices, particularly on those of basic commodities. But most of these increases were expected to taper off if aggregate demand did not rise so much as to strain productive capacity and if unit labor costs continued to decelerate. The hoped-for business recovery was not viewed as foreclosing further progress in curbing inflation.

The Business Recovery of 1971

All sights were therefore set on the business recovery forecast for 1971. Early in the year the Council of Economic Advisers set a GNP target for 1971 at 9.1 percent over 1970. This would have amounted to an unusually rapid recovery from a recession as mild as that of 1970. It represented a policy target as much as a forecast, since a vigorous recovery was very much desired to reduce unemployment.

Disagreement arose over how vigorously monetary policy should push the recovery. The Council's target of a 9 percent increase in GNP for 1971 seemed to call for 7 to 8 percent or more growth in the money supply excluding time deposits. In his testimony to the Joint Economic Committee at the beginning of the year, Federal Reserve Chairman Burns viewed such a policy as too ambitious and stated that the Federal Reserve would pursue a more moderate growth target. This implied continuation of the 6 percent average monetary growth that had prevailed during most of 1970 and through January 1971. By taking a middle-of-the-road position, the Federal Reserve was again seeking—as it had in 1970—a compromise in the tradeoff between inflation and unemployment.

From February until July, however, the annual growth rate

spurted to 10.8 percent, once again confounding the prognosticators of monetary policy (figure 4.3). For the first few months the spurt compensated for slow growth in the latter part of 1970, but that deficiency was made up by the beginning of the second quarter. What happened then was that the Federal Reserve resisted the cyclical recovery in interest rates, which began to climb sharply in March and continued rising until midyear. The yield on Treasury bills rose from 3.5 to 5.5 percent, and most long-term bond yields rose a half to three-quarters of a percentage point. The monetary spurt was justified by the Federal Reserve staff as necessary to supply an increased demand by the public to hold money balances. The staff's econometric estimates of the demand suggested that it had shifted upward in the second quarter. Another estimate later, however, questioned that interpretation.[5] If no shift had occurred, the sharp rise in interest rates could be attributed to the usual recovery of credit demand in the first stage of a cyclical expansion. The Federal Reserve sought to

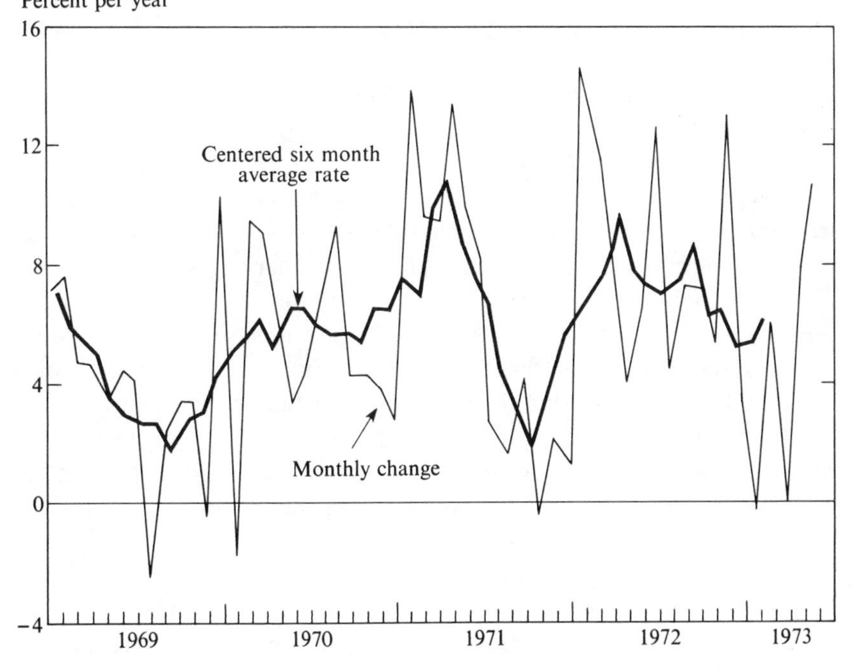

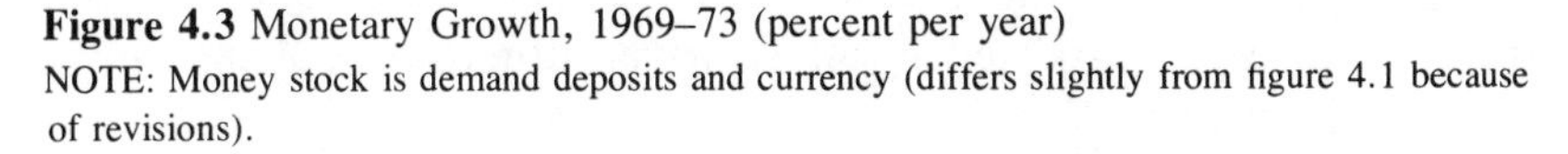
Figure 4.3 Monetary Growth, 1969–73 (percent per year)
NOTE: Money stock is demand deposits and currency (differs slightly from figure 4.1 because of revisions).

slow the rise in interest rates for fear that it might go too far and impede the business recovery. But the high monetary growth resulting from this policy choice raised fears of its own for the inflation. By summer, interest rates stopped rising, mercifully in view of the Federal Reserve's continuing dilemma whether to restrain monetary growth or interest rates, and monetary growth was reduced to a 1 percent annual rate for the remainder of the year, resulting in 6.5 percent growth for all of 1971.

Despite the increase in monetary growth during 1970 and the further spurt in the first half of 1971, the business recovery started off weakly. Shallow business contractions tend to be followed by slow recoveries; even then, this one was unusually slow. Forecasts for the first year of a business upturn often underpredict the strength of a recovery, but in this case it was the private forecasts for 1971, which had been much less optimistic than the Council of Economic Adviser's figure, that turned out to be correct. Except for the first quarter, which was pushed up by the ending of the General Motors strike, the quarterly increases in output were low (table 4.1). For the year as a whole, GNP rose 7.6 percent in dollar terms and only 2.7 percent in real terms. Home building accounted for much of the increase. It had fallen behind the growth of households owing to the dearth of mortgage funds during the credit crunch of 1969 and early 1970. With funds now readily available, the dollar amount of residential construction rose 44 percent from 1970 to 1971. The accompanying high rate of house purchases meant that consumer expenditures would spread to home furnishings in due course, but that did not happen until 1972. Even a flurry of new automobile purchases in August, due to the removal of the excise tax, faltered after several months. Consumers were consolidating their financial position: personal saving for the year rose to the unusually high rate of 8.2 percent of disposable income, and surveys of households revealed a general disposition to spend cautiously. Nonresidential business-fixed investment declined slightly. Since productive capacity remained ample to meet the increases in demand and sales trends showed little strength, businesses felt no need to expand facilities. Growth in the labor force offset the modest increases in employment, and unemployment remained around 6 percent. It did not decline even the modest one-half of a percentage point projected by most private forecasters at the beginning of the year.

Yet, productivity gained nicely during the slow recovery. The improvement was not recognized at first because, with a low fourth quarter due to the General Motors strike, output per hour of labor (private nonfarm sector) grew only 1.6 percent for the calendar year. But, from the first quarter of 1970 to the second quarter of 1971, it rose 3.8 percent at an annual rate compared with a decline for 1969 (table 4.1). Unit labor costs for the private nonfarm sector consequently rose only 3.6 percent per year for that period compared with 8.2 percent in 1969—even though compensation per hour rose 7.5 percent per year, up slightly from 6.9 percent in 1969. Because profit margins were depressed and now were being raised, however, the deceleration in unit labor costs had little discernible effect on most prices. From the first quarter of 1970 to the second quarter of 1971, the private GNP deflator (chain index) rose 4.7 percent per year compared with 4.9 percent for 1969. The slower growth in unit labor costs was bound to affect the inflation rate sooner or later, and a delay was not unusual. But prices appeared to be decelerating more slowly than ever before.

Nevertheless, the inflation was subsiding, as was most clearly apparent in the consumer price index. The rate of increase in this index (excluding foods) declined during the first half of 1971 from over 6 percent per year to 3.5 percent (six-month periods, figure 4.4). Part of this decline, however, reflected a fall in mortgage interest, which is a cost of living for borrowers but not an indication of the purchasing power of money vis-à-vis goods and services. If mortgage interest is excluded from the index (table 4.2), the peak rate of about 6 percent per year in late summer 1970 declined to 4.3 percent in the second quarter of 1971. This was a reduction of over 1.5 percentage points.

The lack of uniformity in the various price indexes, however, was confusing. It was noted that the personal consumption component of the GNP deflator differed from the CPI, although the two covered the same general group of expenditures. The explanation was that the GNP deflator had a different weighting scheme than the CPI and used many additional series.[6] Neither one was clearly preferable. While the CPI gave a closer approximation to the purchasing power of a dollar spent by certain consumer households, the GNP deflator gave a more comprehensive measure of the dollar's purchasing power for all goods and services. The conflict between the CPI and the GNP

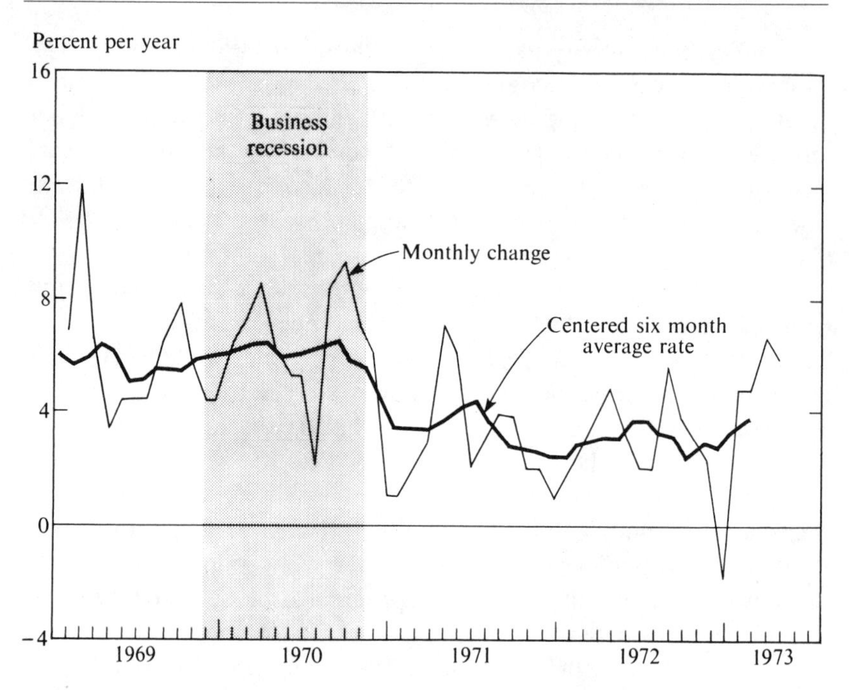

Figure 4.4 Rate of Change of Consumer Price Index (Excluding Foods), 1969–73 (percent per year)

deflator made the direction of inflation uncertain and created doubt that deceleration of the CPI was giving an accurate picture.

The suspicion that little lasting headway was being made against inflation found reinforcement in the wholesale price index. The industrial commodities component of this index showed no deceleration from early in 1970 to mid-1971. From March 1970 to June 1971, six-month average rates of increase deviated very little from 3.75 percent per year. In the third quarter of 1971 the index even accelerated.

The confusion over prices, the weak business recovery, and the lack of dramatic improvement in unemployment created a gloomy economic condition, and prospects for a sluggish second half pointed to more of the same. The median forecast for the second half by the experts reporting to the American Statistical Association in its early August survey[7] was for a 7.8 percent increase in dollar GNP and only a 3 percent increase in real GNP (annual rates). (As it turned

Table 4.2 Rate of Change in Consumer Price Index and Contribution of Mortgage Interest, 1969–1972 (centered six-month average at annual percentage rate)

	Total, Excluding Food	*Contri-bution of Interest*	*Total, Excluding Food and Interest*		*Total, Excluding Food*	*Contri-bution of Interest*	*Total, Excluding Food and Interest*
1969				*1970*			
Mar.	5.7	.5	5.2	Oct.	5.6	−.2	5.7
Apr.	6.3	.6	5.7	Nov.	5.4	−.4	5.7
May	5.9	.6	5.2	Dec.	4.4	−.7	5.0
June	4.9	.5	4.4	*1971*			
July	5.1	.3	4.8	Jan.	3.3	−.9	4.2
Aug.	5.4	.3	5.1	Feb.	3.3	−.9	4.3
Sep.	5.4	.3	5.1	Mar.	3.3	−1.0	4.2
Oct.	5.4	.2	5.1	Apr.	3.5	−.8	4.3
Nov.	5.7	.4	5.3	May	3.8	−.6	4.4
Dec.	5.8	.6	5.2	June	4.1	−.2	4.3
1970				July	4.3	.0	4.2
Jan.	6.0	.6	5.4	Aug.	3.4	.1	3.3
Feb.	6.1	.6	5.6	Sep.	2.8	.1	2.7
Mar.	6.3	.5	5.8	Oct.	2.6	.1	2.5
Apr.	6.4	.5	5.9	Nov.	2.4	.0	2.4
May	5.7	.3	5.4	Dec.	2.3	−.1	2.3
June	5.8	.0	5.8	*1972*			
July	6.0	.0	6.0	Jan.	2.2	−.1	2.4
Aug.	6.1	.0	6.1	Feb.	2.7	−.1	2.8
Sep.	6.2	.0	6.2	Mar.	2.9	−.1	3.0

NOTES: Total index is all items excluding food (same as series plotted in figure 4.4). Contribution of mortgage interest is the rate of change of this component times each December's weight in the total index, applied from June to June of the fiscal year.

Difference between columns 1 and 2 may not exactly equal column 3 because of rounding.

out, dollar GNP rose 6.8 percent per year in the second half, while real GNP rose 4.5 percent.)

At midyear 1971, given the appearance of little progress in reducing unemployment after a year and a half of sizable growth in money, a growing number of commentators supported nonmonetary proposals to add some zip to the recovery. Proposals for price controls received the widest attention. Such controls were thought relevant to both the inflation and unemployment problem, on the assumption that the growth in dollar GNP was determined by monetary and fiscal policy and hence any reduction in inflation would allow more growth in real terms. Since 1970 Federal Reserve Chairman Burns had been pressing the Congress and the administration for direct governmental influence in wage and price setting. Like many others in the middle range of opinion, he advocated an "incomes" policy, that is, the imposition of limits on wage and price increases. Impatience with the slow progress against inflation and unemployment was building up within the administration as well.

Around midyear the recovery sagged for a few months and seemed to many to be about to expire. Industrial production, which had regained about half of its recession decline by May 1971, leveled off in June and fell slightly in July and August. Such a long pause was unsettling because it was unusual for the first stage of a cyclical recovery. Then, during the summer, foreign exchange markets acted up, forcing the administration to take action to stem speculation against the dollar. The U.S. balance of payments (as measured by the net liquidity balance) had been in deficit since the late 1950s and deteriorated further during the Vietnam War. Holders of liquid international balances were alert to the possibility of a dollar devaluation. When the traditional U.S. surplus on goods and services declined further in the second quarter of 1971—this time practically to zero—the speculative outflow became a tidal wave. In the first half of 1971, U.S. liabilities to official foreign institutions (as recorded by the U.S.) rose by $10.2 billion.

The administration might have tried the simple ploy of reasserting its determination not to seek a devaluation of the dollar but, without steps to back it up, the announcement would not have been credible. Instead it decided to institute a full-scale activist policy in order to disarm the critics who charged the anti-inflation program with failure and who called for strong medicine. Thus the administration took its first step into the thicket of direct controls which it had once vowed never to enter.

Effects of Monetary Restraint on Financial Markets and Housing

The monetary experiments of 1966 and 1969 unsettled financial markets and produced deep contractions in residential construction. These effects raised anew the complaint that monetary restraint falls unfairly upon particular sectors of the economy. To achieve broad effects on the economy, it was widely proposed—after the experience of 1966—that major reliance be placed on fiscal policy. However, this strategy was undercut by the failure of the 1968 tax surcharge to restrain the economy. Therefore, at the start of 1969, monetary restraint was generally accepted as bitter but necessary medicine which had been tested and certified by an initial success in 1966, but then too quickly reversed.

As 1969 progressed, however, the afflicted sectors did not quietly accept the treatment. Financial markets experienced a ferocious competition for credit, and widespread sentiment developed behind proposals to distribute credit "more equitably" (which usually meant more for small businesses and home buyers) by putting credit controls on some other form of borrowing. Some congressional and public opinion favored restraining installment loans. That consumer loans should be asked to shoulder the main burden of restraint was ironical. It is true that they had been controlled during previous wars and were somewhat easier to restrict by regulation than other kinds of loans. But consumer durable purchases were a weak spot in the economy during 1969, and consumer credit controls would, in effect, have the shoe of monetary restraint pinch a lame foot. The strong demand for credit came from business fixed investment, and controls on corporate borrowing made more sense and were proposed by the Joint Economic Committee.[8] But corporate credit controls involve difficult problems of enforcement. Although the Congress authorized the president to control credit, this authorization was not used.

The pressure that monetary restraint inflicts upon financial markets can be explained in part by the fact that it has a lagged effect on aggregate expenditures. Reductions in monetary growth in 1966 and 1969 worked to reduce the supply of credit, but for a while business activity remained strong and the demand for credit continued to expand. The resulting rise in interest rates attracted funds from existing money balances, which were pared down in relation to the volume of transactions. The process of paring balances occurred in one form through the purchase of newly issued financial assets, but this addition to the supply of credit could not be maintained without continual increases in interest rates which took them beyond the reach of more and more borrowers. The so-called "credit crunches" of 1966 and 1969–70 largely represented a pricing of many borrowers out of the market. And many of those who were still willing and able to pay the high price found regular sources of funds no longer available, because financial institutions rationed credit in favor of long-standing, low-risk customers.

These crunches differed from the financial panics of an earlier era in which there were runs on banks and "bank holidays." In those cases, depositors rushed to exchange deposits for currency because of the risk of bank failures. In 1966 and 1969–70, by contrast, the banks were relatively safe, thanks to federal deposit insurance and to their ability to obtain large amounts of currency from the Federal Reserve. A crunch developed because the supply of credit did not expand as fast as the demand for it, reflecting in turn the curtailed growth in the total stock of money. This led to a squeeze on business liquidity.

The strain on financial markets was most severe during two periods, the third quarter of 1966 and again during the first half of 1970. In each case, when credit demand weakened after a quarter or two, the markets eased considerably and short-term rates fell sharply. At the height of the pressure while demand was strong, the amount of credit supplied actually declined, sending interest rates up sharply. Total funds raised in credit markets fell in the second half of 1966 and in the second half of 1969 and first quarter of 1970 (see table 4.3). The decline was more severe in 1966, when it affected all borrowing sectors. Although the cutback in monetary growth was as great in 1969 as it had been in 1966, the decline in loanable funds was smaller, in part because credit demand was apparently stronger, and interest rates temporarily rose much farther in order to induce holders of money balances to purchase more securities. The 1969 rise in interest rates lifted rates above statutory ceilings in many states and hampered the borrowing of state and local governments,[9] while business corporations borrowed heavily and obtained an unusually large share of the available funds.

Many businesses nevertheless suffered delay or loss of investment opportunities, with hardship or even bankruptcy for some. Especially hard hit were the borrowers of depository institutions. Not only did the growth of demand deposits (seasonally adjusted) stop in the second half of 1969, but so did the growth of time and savings deposits as market interest rates rose far above the ceiling rates allowed on those deposits (see figure 4.5). These funds flowed into se-

Table 4.3 Total Funds Raised by Nonfinancial Sectors, 1966–1967 and 1969–1970, Seasonally Adjusted Annual Rates (billions of dollars)

	1966				*1967*			
	I	*II*	*III*	*IV*	*I*	*II*	*III*	*IV*
Total	84.1	83.2	62.6	49.9	74.3	44.3	104.6	108.9
U.S. gov't.	10.8	6.7	4.9	2.9	8.0	−21.3	34.7	29.2
State & local gov't.	6.6	7.5	6.1	6.9	10.5	11.8	8.1	11.4
Business	38.7	43.3	30.9	21.1	34.7	35.8	36.9	41.4
Households	25.1	23.1	21.0	17.7	15.6	14.2	21.1	24.1
Foreigners	2.7	2.5	−.4	1.2	5.5	3.7	3.9	2.8
	1969				*1970*			
	I	*II*	*III*	*IV*	*I*	*II*	*III*	*IV*
Total	92.5	93.6	88.4	86.8	80.9	102.9	92.2	105.7
U.S. gov't.	−5.4	−9.5	−.7	1.2	2.7	16.2	12.3	19.6
State & local gov't.	13.4	9.7	5.8	5.1	9.4	10.4	9.2	19.7
Business	47.4	51.3	49.4	49.9	41.6	54.1	45.4	44.4
Households	33.0	36.0	31.5	28.2	24.5	20.6	22.7	17.5
Foreigners	4.0	6.0	2.3	2.4	2.6	1.7	2.6	4.5

SOURCE: *Federal Reserve Bulletin,* May 1968; "Flow of Funds, Revised Data for 1967–70," Board of Governors of the Federal Reserve System, February 22, 1971.
NOTE: Figures may not add to totals because of rounding.

curity markets to absorb the heavy issue of corporate bonds. Noncorporate businesses and small corporations normally cannot market bonds, however, and for a time equity issues of small risky enterprises could not be sold. Banks could not satisfy the heavy demand of these customers for loans. Dollar liabilities of business failures rose sharply in the closing months of 1969 and the first half of 1970. This all added to the anguish instilled by the severe decline in prices of common stocks during 1969 and the first half of 1970, which also created severe financial difficulties for many brokerage firms. Despair and anger shook the public's earlier staunch support for monetary restraint.

Then the collapse of the giant Penn Central Railroad in June 1970 precipitated a crisis of several weeks duration in the commercial paper market. That troubled company had seemed bound to go under sooner or later, but tight money hastened the debacle. Because of the large losses to holders of its commercial paper, lenders now held back from that market, and many regular borrowers could not raise funds there. The Federal Reserve rushed to reinstate banks in their

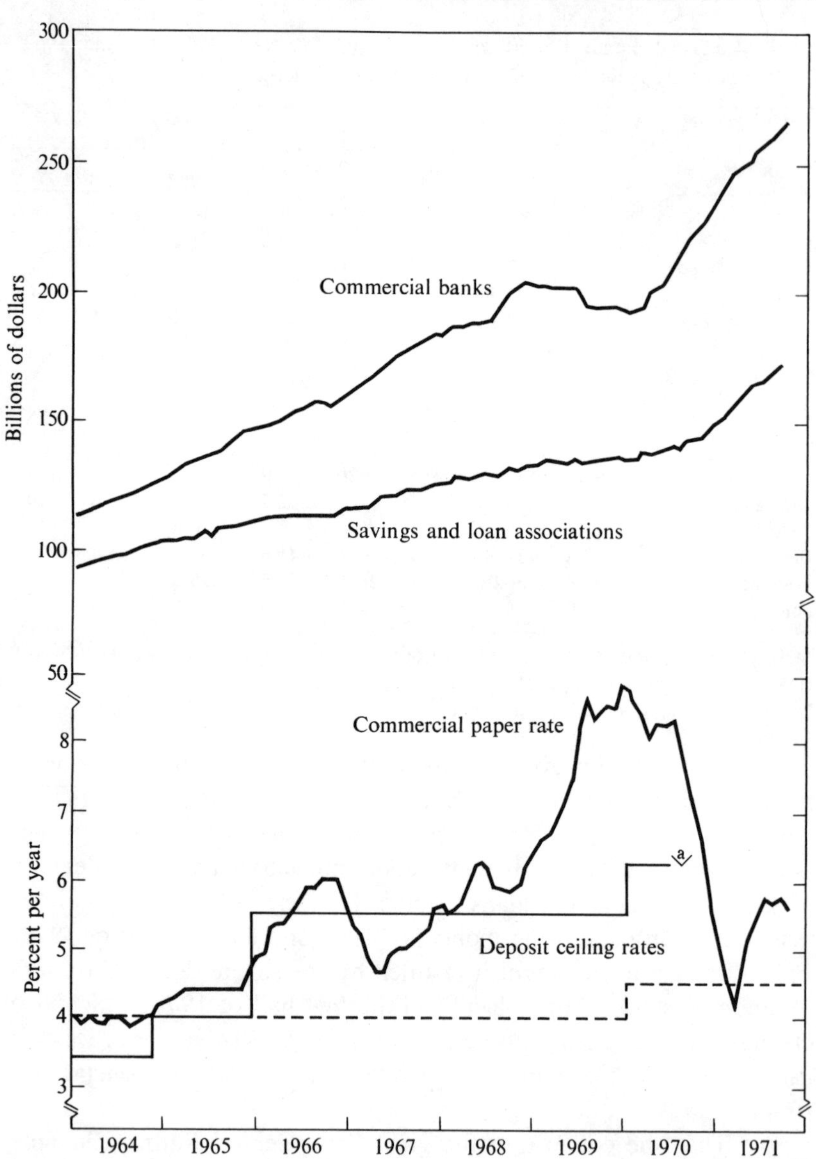

Figure 4.5 Time and Savings Deposits and Interest Rates, Monthly, 1964–71

NOTE: Deposit ceiling rates: dotted line, commercial bank savings deposits; solid line, 30–89 day certificates of deposit \$100,000 or over beginning July 1966; maximum rate on other time deposits up to 12 months for earlier months.

Commercial bank time deposits are seasonally adjusted; other series are not. Commercial paper rate is for dealers' 4–6 month prime paper.

[a] Ceiling suspended June 24, 1970.

traditional role as the major suppliers of commercial credit. This was done by the simple step of removing the rate ceiling from large denomination certificates of deposit of short maturity, which allowed banks to increase the rate paid on such CDs to competitive levels and raise funds again in large volume. Also, during the first weeks of this crisis in the commercial paper market, the Federal Reserve lent freely to banks with the understanding that they should lend freely to companies in need of short-term funds. This they did, preventing further serious difficulties.

In 1966 and 1969, when the rates available on Treasury bills and commercial paper rose sharply, the authorities kept deposit rate ceilings down, despite the temporary but disturbing decline in savings deposit flows and mortgage financing. One reason was to prevent banks and savings institutions from competing with each other for deposits. But this reason does not explain the maintenance of lower ceilings for large denomination CDs in 1966 and 1969. These are purchased by large corporations and do not compete with savings deposits. The main explanation is that the authorities also wanted to restrict bank credit. Yet the ceilings served mainly to redistribute credit rather than reduce the total. If such interferences with the flow of funds had been avoided, monetary restraint would not have disrupted financial markets so severely.

There is another reason why monetary restraint may not produce financial "crunches" in the future. Businesses reduced their liquidity to low levels in 1966 and 1969, partly in the belief that monetary restraint would not be carried so far. An examination of "Corporate Liquidity in 1969 and 1970" in the 1971 *Annual Report of the Council of Economic Advisers* reveals that most large manufacturing corporations had a decline in liquidity by standard measures during 1969 and 1970. Few corporations reached a dangerously low level of liquidity. The general decline appears to have reflected planned responses to market incentives rather than involuntary adjustments to a deterioration in financial position. Nevertheless, the large issue of bonds in the first half of 1970, which kept bond yields from declining despite the contraction in economic activity, was required to refund previous short-term borrowing and to rebuild liquidity. This reversed actions taken during 1969 to avoid the high cost of long-term funds then mistakenly expected to decline in early 1970. Thus, gross private domestic investment fell $4 billion in 1970 while the net issue of securities by nonfinancial businesses rose $11.5 billion. These businesses raised $22.8 billion net in 1969 from bank and other loans, compared with $15.4 billion in 1968, but in 1970 they raised only $7.8 billion, indicating that many firms were reducing short-term borrowing. The costly heavy borrowing and investment in 1969, when financial markets were extremely tight, was a miscalculation based on anticipations of continued economic expansion and of a reduction in interest rates. The experience would not be soon forgotten.

But a dose of monetary restraint comparable to that administered in 1969, no matter how smoothly the economy adjusts to it, will always produce large fluctuations in interest rates. The steep rise in nominal bond yields in 1969 partly reflected heightened anticipations of inflation. However, the rise in short-term rates and the equally steep decline later in 1970 and early 1971 are typical responses to changes in monetary growth, though in magnitude they are more characteristic of the pre-1914 period than recent decades.

Because of this accompanying large rise in interest rates, monetary restraint will continue to have a sizable effect on housing in the future, as it did in 1966 and 1969. From the first to the second half of 1966, housing starts declined 28 percent. For 1969 the first- to second-half decline was only 14 percent due to federal mortgage loans discussed below. Complaints of "discrimination" against housing failed to mention that curtailment of long-term investments like housing is natural when financial markets are tight. The rise in interest rates was a signal to postpone some investment in view of the excessive demand on total resources; long-term investments like housing would ordinarily be postponed, even without market disruptions, since part of the rise in interest rates appeared to be temporary. While the sharp contraction of mortgage credit during 1969 had elicited dire warnings of the collapse of the home-building industry, they proved totally inaccurate. The industry revived dramatically after monetary policy eased in 1970. Housing starts, after hitting a low in January 1970 of 1.1 million units at a seasonally adjusted annual rate, recovered by July to the 1.5 million rate of 1968 and then rose to 2 million units by December.

The dependence of mortgage financing on savings and loan associations helps explain why the decline in housing was so sharp while commercial construction remained about the same. The associations have financed about half of home mortgages in recent decades. Since their deposits can be withdrawn on demand, they can attract a steady inflow of funds only by paying an interest rate on deposits competitive with other short-term financial assets. They are unable to do so, however, when interest rates rise rapidly. The average return on association portfolios rises slowly, despite higher yields on new mortgages, because most home mortgages, though extinguished long before maturity, still remain outstanding over five years.

Indeed, the associations avoided a disastrous outflow of funds in 1966 and 1969 only because the government, concerned for their solvency, maintained the ceilings on deposit rates paid by commercial and mutual savings banks (as noted above), refrained from paying a competitive return on U.S. savings bonds, and (in March 1970) upped the minimum denomination of Treasury bills after they started to become popular with small savers. The small saver has benefited over the years from government protection of savings and loan associations, but he paid a price in terms of restricted investment options during these periods of financial tightness.

Although the savings and loan associations avoided widespread failures in 1966 and 1969, their sudden decline in growth was transmitted to the residential mortgage market. Their deposit growth of $8.1 billion in the fourth quarter of 1965 at a seasonally adjusted annual rate fell to $1.4 billion by the third quarter of 1966. The net annual rate of increase in their home mortgages fell from $7.6 to $0.1 billion in the same period (seasonally adjusted). In 1969, on a comparable basis, deposit growth of $8.0 billion in the first quarter fell to $0.7 billion in the fourth quarter, and the net annual rate of increase in their home mortgages declined from $9.1 billion in the first quarter of 1969 to $3.0 billion in the first quarter of 1970. These were drastic reductions.

The basic problem here was the use of short-term funds to finance long-term mortgages, a development which public policy had long fostered. The federal government has taken various steps over the years to make sure that housing can be financed on easy terms. Among other actions it enhanced the attractiveness of savings and loan deposits in federal associations in 1950 by providing insurance virtually identical to that for commercial and mutual savings banks. The charters of the associations required that they invest the bulk of their funds in mortgages. Since mortgage yields generally exceeded short-term interest rates during the 1950s and early 1960s, the associations paid an attractive rate of interest, and their growth was phenomenal. In the period from mid-1950 to mid-1965 their savings capital (deposits) increased from $13 to $105 billion, an average rate of growth of 15 percent per year.

At first, little thought was given to the weaknesses of such an arrangement. Even during the 1950s, however, cyclical swings in home building became more and more pronounced as fluctuations in interest rates grew larger and affected the differential return on savings deposits and their rate of growth. Deposit-rate ceilings on commercial and mutual savings banks protected associations from severe competition, however, and the industry prospered without making important structural changes. Finally, in 1966 and again in 1969, as interest rates rose steeply, the flaw in this regulated cartel arrangement came to the fore: open-market securities became extremely attractive to small savers, and major outflows from depository institutions could not be prevented.

The Housing Act of 1968 had set an ambitious goal of 26 million new dwelling units by 1978. With the 1966 and 1969 declines in construction, that goal began to slip out of reach, though the rapid growth in mobile homes (413,000 were produced in 1969) brightened the prospects. Among the government's myriad programs to help housing, the largest contribution in dollar terms during these years came from the Federal National Mortgage Association, which finances purchases of mortgages by selling bonds guaranteed by the Treasury. The net increase in its mortgage holdings was $1.9 billion in 1966 and $3.8 billion in 1969. All together the federal government and federally sponsored agencies poured $3.6 billion into the residential mortgage market in 1966 and $8.6 billion in 1969 (including the borrowing of savings and loan associations from Federal Home Loan Banks). This was one-third of total home mortgage loans in 1966 and over one-half in 1969.

Since these programs prevented mortgage yields from rising even higher and thus encouraged some private funds to go elsewhere, the net increase in mortgage financing so produced is unclear. The effect probably was not inconsequential, however, because housing declined much less in 1969 than in 1966 as noted, consistent with the larger government support.

Despite the assistance of federal programs, the fluctuations in the availability of mortgage funds in 1966 and 1969 have made financial reforms imperative. A Presidential Commission on Financial Institutions, appointed in 1970, endorsed many previously made proposals to reverse the proliferation of financial regulations and allow the institutions to adapt more freely to changing market conditions. It is also desirable to relax deposit-rate ceilings, in order to remove the more severe distortions which hamper the operation of monetary policy. Some proposals have been adopted, but Congress has not so far found the consensus to initiate basic reforms.

Mistakes and Problems of Policy

The inflation that began in 1965 can be attributed largely to the mistakes of monetary policy. Excessive expansion of the money supply allowed inflation to gain a foothold in 1965 and to gather momentum in 1967–68. The accompanying expansion of war expenditures contributed to the inflation indirectly through an influence on monetary growth and on the speed with which new money affected the economy. By themselves federal expenditures were not critical, however. For example, monetary restraint still slowed the economy in 1966 at a time when those expenditures were rising rapidly.

Errors of forecasting will always occur, but errors of judgment based on a faulty analysis of events can be avoided by learning from past mistakes. This section discusses the lag in monetary policy, the role of bank credit, the effect of fiscal policy, the behavior of interest rates, and the behavior of prices.

Lag in Monetary Policy

During 1969, monetary restraint appeared to most of the public to be pushing up interest rates—creating havoc for residential construction and small business—but not to be working to curtail aggregate activity. And it is true that the anti-inflationary monetary policy that was announced in early 1969 took almost a year before a perceptible slackening in general business activity occurred. But a change in monetary growth impinges on the public's money balances and induces adjustments in lending and spending which affect aggregate activity, all with a lag. Furthermore, several months can elapse before a stated shift in policy takes hold of monetary growth, because the Federal Reserve has trouble controlling the money supply in the short run and, until 1970, did not even view the money supply as a major indicator of policy. Finally, it takes a few months to recognize a change in business activity.

Even so, by historical experience the lags in 1966 and 1969 were not of unusual length.

1966 peak. The Open Market Committee voted to impose restraint in February 1966. A sharp reduction in monetary growth occurred in May, and economic activity turned down in November. The lag from the monetary step peak in April to November was seven months.

1967 trough. The committee voted to lift the restraint in November 1966, and monetary growth resumed the following February. Economic activity recovered in May 1967. From the January monetary step trough to May was four months.

1969 peak. The committee voted for a second round of restraint in December 1968. Monetary growth declined moderately during the first half of 1969 and then sharply around midyear. The accuracy of the money series for this period is questionable because of a large volume of foreign bank transactions which falsified the figures for cash items in the process of collection.

If we rely on the 1970 revision of the series, a step peak occurred in July. The peak in activity occurred in November 1969. The lag from July to November was four months.

1970 trough. The committee voted in January 1970 to ease monetary restraint. Monetary growth spurted in March according to the data then available (or in January, according to a later revision). November was the trough in activity. The lag was therefore eleven months measured by the revised series. (The General Motors strike in the fourth quarter may have made this downturn longer than it would otherwise have been; the second and third quarters showed a slight recovery before the strike brought a slump in the fourth quarter.)

These lags seemed longer at the time, because the turning points in activity became apparent only several months after they had occurred.

How do these lags compare with previous experience? Milton

Friedman and Anna J. Schwartz examined the monetary lag in 21 cyclical movements from 1870 to 1961 and reported their findings in the *45th Annual Report of the National Bureau of Economic Research*. One of their measures of the lag corresponds to that used above, namely, a comparison between the date of a step in monetary growth to a higher or lower average rate for at least several months and the corresponding peak or trough in the level of economic activity.[10] (Using the rate of change of economic activity gives much shorter lags.) They found a median lag at peaks of seven months with an interquartile range from zero to thirteen months. The median lag at troughs was four months with an interquartile range from zero to nine months. The wide range indicates that the lags have varied appreciably in length.

The 1966–67 lags equaled the historical medians exactly. The 1969–70 lags differed from the medians but the peak fell within the interquartile range. The trough exceeded the range, probably because of the General Motors strike. At the 1969 peak, the lag was three months shorter than the median, and at the 1970 trough, seven months longer.

The short lag at the 1969 peak is full of irony, because the elapsed time from the announced change in monetary policy in January 1969 to the peak of activity in November was ten months, which overran the public's expectation based on the 1966 episode and proved exasperating to administration officials anxious for some tangible effect of their unpopular anti-inflation policy. According to the revised money figures, however, most of this lag was the inside lag of changing the policy; for many months, the talk of restraint exceeded the bite.

There was considerable confusion during 1969, not only over how long it would take monetary policy to work, but also over where its effects would fall. Ordinarily monetary restraint curtails investment expenditures. But surveys of business investment plans showed surprising strength all during 1969, notwithstanding the highest interest rates in a century. This did not mean, as was widely thought, that monetary restraint would not affect aggregate expenditures. A reduction in monetary growth forces some money-using sectors of the economy to make adjustments which require holding down expenditures. In reality, not all the plans for business investment could be financed, and actual expenditures were less than anticipated in the surveys. Even so, business investment was still high, which forced restraint upon other expenditures, not only for residential construction but also for consumer durable goods, state and local capital projects, and business inventory investment.

The lesson of this experience is that the sectoral effects of monetary restraint are hard to foresee. A strong demand for funds in one sector transmits the pressure of a limited supply to other sectors which are hard to identify ahead of time. Forecasts of GNP made in mid-1969 and based on elaborate models specifying fixed channels of monetary effects generally underestimated the decline in growth of GNP in the fourth quarter of 1969 and the first quarter of 1970. Thus, the regular panel of forecasters surveyed by the American Statistical Association[11] in August 1969 missed the decline in growth in those quarters. The median forecast was for a rise in nominal GNP of $13 billion in the third quarter of 1969 and of $12 billion in each of the next two quarters, whereas the actual pattern of increases was $19, $9, and $8 billion, respectively. Predictions in mid-1969 by the Federal Reserve Bank of St. Louis, which were based on conditional forecasts of changes in the money stock, caught the slowdown more accurately—though one had to correctly assume little change in the money stock for the rest of the year. Even then, the St. Louis predictions erred by anticipating a slight slowdown in the third quarter of 1969 when actually GNP continued expanding until the fourth quarter.

Whether fiscal policy had much effect on the length of the lag at the 1969 peak is unclear. The full-employment federal budget (NIA basis) ran a deficit of $6 billion in 1968 and a surplus of $11.7 billion in 1969, a change of $18 billion, largely through a slowing in expenditure growth. In terms of quarterly budget figures, all of the increase in the surplus occurred in the first two quarters of the year. This cannot account for the downturn in activity in the fourth quarter of 1969 unless fiscal policy has a longer lag than monetary policy does, which—for a change largely on the expenditure side, such as here—is implausible on theoretical grounds. But the continuing budget surplus during the second half of 1969 could have reinforced the monetary restraint which came at that time and thus may help explain the fairly short lag observed for monetary policy.

The long lag in monetary policy in producing the upturn in economic activity in 1970 cannot be explained by perverse fiscal policy; the full-employment surplus declined moderately in 1970. The contraction in activity was both longer and deeper than that in 1967, though the decline in the average rate of monetary growth was about the same, roughly five percentage points. However, the six-month moving average of monetary growth (figure 4.1) brings out two differences: compared with 1966–67, the period of declining monetary growth in 1968–69 lasted twice as long, and the subsequent easing in 1970 was not as sharp. After allowance for the General Motors strike at the end of 1970, these differences appear to account for the greater effect on the economy of the second round of monetary restraint.

Role of Bank Credit

Much evidence, including the 1969–70 episode, indicates that monetary restraint initially affects postponable spending, which means a decline, not only in housing and capital equipment, but also in consumer durables and luxury items. This evidence is consistent with the theory that changes in monetary growth disturb the desired distribution of assets in portfolios, thus producing adjustments which in the first instance affect purchases of assets and their prices. A popular—and narrow—view of this process stresses the first-round effect of monetary change via bank credit. In this view monetary restraint curtails investment because it affects the supply of bank credit (that is, loans and investments of commercial banks). The Federal Reserve has traditionally framed its policy directives in terms of bank credit rather than the money supply, though the emphasis shifted to include money for the first time in 1970. Sometimes the rates of growth of bank credit and the money supply (excluding time deposits) are approximately equal, but generally not.

The important difference between money and bank credit was dramatically highlighted by the events of 1969 noted earlier. Interest rates climbed, but the maximum rates that banks could pay on time deposits were not raised during the year, and these deposits declined drastically. Deposits were withdrawn to purchase commercial paper and corporate bonds, thus supplying funds directly to the market that had previously been channeled through banks. The decline in credit supplied by banks did not reduce the total supply of credit but resulted in a different distribution among potential borrowers—home and municipal financing suffered while corporate investment benefited (see table 4.3). When banks began to tap nondeposit sources of funds in large volume during 1969 as a substitute for the loss of time deposits, the Federal Reserve took steps to block these too. For example, the Eurodollar borrowing of commercial banks was made prohibitively expensive in September 1969 when the amounts in excess of May levels were made subject to reserve requirements. Before that, this borrowing tapped foreign as well as U.S. funds, thereby increasing the supply of money and credit to the U.S. market—which ironically required the Federal Reserve to tighten even further to offset the inflow from abroad.

These restrictions on banks reflected a basic confusion over the appropriate indicator of monetary policy. The Federal Reserve was intent upon restricting the growth of bank credit. But bank credit gives a misleading picture of monetary effects on aggregate demand, because radical shifts in the channels of credit flows do not necessarily imply anything about the total supply of credit. For example, while total bank credit grew less rapidly during 1969, it nevertheless continued to grow through most of the year, which seemed to suggest that policy was not achieving the intense restraint desired; but the lack of growth in the money stock after midyear meant that the policy was in fact succeeding. During the second half of 1970, on the other hand, bank credit expanded at an annual rate of 13 percent due to the explosive growth of CDs, whereas the money stock excluding time deposits grew at 5 percent per year. The poor performance of the economy in the second half of 1970 was a clear indication that the rapid expansion in bank credit was not producing a comparable expansion in the aggregate use of credit.

Fluctuations of time deposits and of financial intermediation in general hamper the interpretation of monetary policy and make growth of the money supply a less than perfect indicator of policy. But bank credit has much more serious conceptual drawbacks as an indicator and has declined in favor.

Effect of Fiscal Policy

Misjudgments of policy also occurred with respect to fiscal policy, especially the tax surcharge of 1968. The effect of government deficits and surpluses is often exaggerated because of the implicit assumption of a cooperative monetary policy. Little was said about monetary policy when the tax surcharge was enacted in mid-1968. The surcharge was supposed to restrain the economy by itself, but it did not do the job. Although the rate of expansion of current dollar

GNP fell from 11.5 percent per year in the second quarter of 1968 to around 8 percent in the third and fourth quarters, the reduced rate still almost matched the fastest growing quarters of 1966–67.

No government estimates of the expected effect of the tax surcharge at the time of its enactment were published, but the textbook theory of fiscal effects suggested that the surcharge would reduce GNP by at least $20 billion. This can be derived as follows: The actual increase in annual federal revenues from the surcharge, as reported in the 1969 *Annual Report of the Council of Economic Advisers,* was $10.5 billion. The surcharge legislation also required a $6 billion cut in federal expenditures—though the cut pertained to the budgeted level for fiscal year 1969 rather than the actual level of spending at the time of enactment. When signing the new tax measure in June 1968, President Johnson boasted that it would reduce the federal deficit by $20 billion. While that was an exaggeration, the $10.5 billion figure given by the CEA was probably less than the total effect on the deficit from the change in fiscal policy. Although the actual budget deficit in the national income accounts fell only $9 billion from the second to the fourth quarter of 1968, the high-employment budget deficit, as estimated by the Federal Reserve Bank of St. Louis, fell $15 billion.

According to the standard procedure, the decline in the deficit should be multiplied by the fiscal multiplier to give the sum of the initial and all subsequent effects on aggregate expenditures. A typical estimate of this multiplier at the time was about two.[12] Using a range of $10 to $15 billion for the effect of the tax measure on the deficit, this multiplier gives a range of $20 to $30 billion for the reduction in GNP. Little wonder that fears of "overkill" arose, leading the Federal Reserve to hold back in imposing monetary restraint.

It is difficult to measure the actual effect of the surcharge on GNP, since we do not know for sure what would have happened without it. One estimate is provided by comparing the increase in GNP in the second half of 1968 with that in the first half. GNP at an annual rate rose $42 billion in the first half of 1968 and $33 billion in the second half, or $9 billion less. This suggests that fiscal restraint had just about half the minimum effect of $20 billion it was expected to have. (Probably even less, because monetary growth slightly declined on average during the second half of 1968, which contributed to the lower GNP growth.)

An estimate more favorable to the power of fiscal restraint in

1968 can be obtained by projecting the second quarter increase in GNP rather than the increase for the entire first half. The second quarter increase was $23 billion and, if continued, would have raised GNP by $46 billion in the second half, or $13 billion more than it actually rose. If all this is attributed to fiscal restraint, the shortfall is 65 percent of the anticipated minimum effect of $20 billion derived above.

The surcharge of 1968 was supposed to repeat the policy success—in the other direction—of the tax cut of 1964, which was given credit for the subsequent decline in unemployment. In dollar effect on tax revenues, the 1968 surcharge was the larger of the two. But a comparison of effects on revenues is misleading. While the economy expanded following the 1964 tax cut, credit for the expansion must be shared with the accompanying increase in monetary growth. In 1968, although monetary growth declined over the second half, the money stock continued to grow rapidly and to be very stimulative, counteracting the surcharge. Even aside from the differing role of monetary policy in 1964 and 1968, however, other explanations have been offered as to why the surcharge appeared weaker than the tax cut.

The first explanation starts from the fact that the economy was at virtual full employment in 1968, with a strong demand for credit straining financial markets. This was quite unlike the situation in 1964 when the economy was below full employment. The funds not borrowed by the Treasury in 1968 found other eager borrowers, whereas in 1964 the Treasury borrowed funds not all of which would have found other takers right away. Therefore, in 1964 aggregate expenditures increased because Treasury borrowing raised interest rates and induced a rise in monetary velocity, while in 1968 the Treasury surplus did not have a comparable effect on monetary velocity. The reason given for this difference is that the effect on velocity of a given change in interest rates was large in 1964 at low interest rates and low in 1968 at high rates.[13] That the relation between monetary velocity and interest rates has this particular form is an old idea, but the statistical evidence is unclear.

A second explanation for overestimating the power of the tax surcharge is that it was originally scheduled to expire in six months and, even though later extended, was viewed as temporary. As a result, households simply saved less and kept spending at near previous levels, at least for a while, in the expectation that an undesired temporary reduction of consumption could be avoided. Personal saving as a fraction of disposable income fell from an average of 7.3 percent in the first half of 1968 to 6.5 percent in the second half. As a fraction of prevailing income levels, this reduction in saving amounted to $6 billion at an annual rate. The increased federal revenue due to the tax surcharge on individuals was a comparable $6.5 billion in the second half of 1968 and rose to a maximum of $11 billion in the second quarter of 1969.[14] The saving ratio did not return to the high levels of early 1968 until the second quarter of 1970. Other influences also helped determine saving during this period, of course, and the effect of the surcharge is hard to isolate. It nevertheless appears that a good part of the initial effect on individuals' disposable income was absorbed by a change in their saving rates.

A third explanation is that fiscal policy as conventionally measured in the national income accounts excludes direct loans of federal agencies and indirect lending via subsidies and guarantees. The figures quoted above follow this practice. Yet it is dubious that direct federal expenditures have an effect on GNP that is sharply different from the effect of federal lending. Federal lending also supports private expenditures which to some extent would not otherwise be made. Of course, some private expenditures financed with federal loans would be made anyway with loans from nongovernmental sources. But, similarly, some direct federal expenditures may also substitute for private expenditures which are then not made. This is apt to be true of certain grants-in-aid to states and localities.

Federal loans are financed by taxes or Treasury borrowing, and their exclusion from the NIA budget makes the reported deficit appear to be smaller. The amounts are substantial. In the second half of 1968, the net acquisition of credit market instruments by federal agencies in the flow of funds accounts—consolidating the federally sponsored agencies that are excluded from the unified budget—was $6.1 billion at an annual rate. That raises the budget deficit in the national income accounts for the second half of 1968 from $1.5 billion at an annual rate to $7.6 billion. The annual rate of deficit in the first half on the same basis was $19.6 billion.

The annual rate of federal lending alone, which declined by $4.5 billion from the first to the second half of 1968, also contributed to fiscal restraint—along with the tax surcharge. It is possible that changes in lending affect the economy with a longer lag than expenditures do, however, because of a lag in the private economy between borrowing and spending. If so, the second half of 1968 was influenced by federal lending activities in previous quarters. Thus the sizable increase in lending in the first half of 1968 over 1967 may have worked to offset the tax surcharge in the second half.

Although all of these complications were known in 1968, they were largely ignored until the surcharge proved wholly inadequate for curbing the runaway inflation. Thus was it possible for fears of "overkill" to freeze monetary policy into disastrous inaction throughout 1968.

Behavior of Interest Rates

Perhaps no other development has confused the conduct of monetary policy more in recent years than the astounding increase in interest rates. From 1965 until mid-1970 Treasury bond yields rose almost three percentage points, municipal bond yields four percentage points, and high-grade corporate bond yields more than five percentage points (figure 4.2). These increases represented about a doubling of 1965 levels. Short-term rates also rose spectacularly, though they peaked at the beginning of 1970. Over half of the increase came after mid-1968. Apart from panics, U.S. interest rates had never climbed so high in so short a period of time. This gave an appearance of intense tightness to financial markets which, in 1965 and again in 1967–68, helped justify faster monetary growth than the inflationary economy warranted.

The increase in interest rates can be attributed in part to monetary restraint in 1966 and 1969, but the restraint, though important while it lasted, had only a temporary effect. Part of the overall increase since 1965 reflected an expanded demand for capital goods. In the second half of the 1960s, the post-World War II "baby boom" began to augment the labor force and, for the first time since the mid-1950s, many industrial plants operated at high levels of capacity.

But these effects seem incapable of fully explaining the behavior of interest rates. Anticipations of inflation also played an important role. Financial assets such as bonds whose principal is fixed in dollars depreciate in real value during inflation. If prices rise 4 percent per year over the life of a bond, a nominal yield of 8 percent returns 4 percent in real terms. Lenders can compensate for this depreciation by obtaining higher nominal rates of return, and they will look for inflation hedges until bonds offer nominal yields which reflect the anticpated rate of inflation. Businesses will try to borrow more funds until higher interest charges take away all the anticipated gains from inflation.

Years ago economist Irving Fisher pointed to this effect of inflation on nominal interest rates. He used it to explain the behavior of bond yields before World War I. Now it helps to account for their rising trend since the mid-1950s. From 1952 to 1955 long-term U.S. bonds fluctuated narrowly around 2.75 percent. Then from mid-1956 to mid-1959, following the 1955–56 inflation, they climbed to 4 percent and stayed close to that level until 1965. Following the reemergence of inflation in that year, they rose much further, as did all other interest rates.

The failure to distinguish nominal and anticipated real rates of interest bedeviled the conduct of monetary policy. The reports of the Federal Reserve Open Market Committee frequently took note of the tightness in financial markets as reflected by the high and rising interest rates, but made no mention of the fact that the anticipated real rate of interest was probably much lower, and often falling rather than rising. The increased difficulty of interpreting interest-rate movements in an inflationary period finally led the committee in 1970 to demote (though, unfortunately, not abolish) the role of interest rates as a major indicator of monetary policy.

Behavior of Prices

Critics of the administration's economic policy during 1969 claimed that monetary restraint was not working. One reason for that claim was that the restraint came, as noted, a half year later than the announced shift in policy. But there was no reason to question the ultimate effect on aggregate demand, which slowed in the fourth quarter; the lag was actually short by historical experience. Yet the critics were right about prices if not about output. Inflation showed little tendency to yield to policy intentions. The unexpected persistence of rising prices made it politically harder to persevere with an orthodox anti-inflation policy (see figure 4.6).

The rate of increase of most prices had declined in the second half of 1966, following the application of monetary restraint. The wholesale price index for industrial commodities, a bellwether indica-

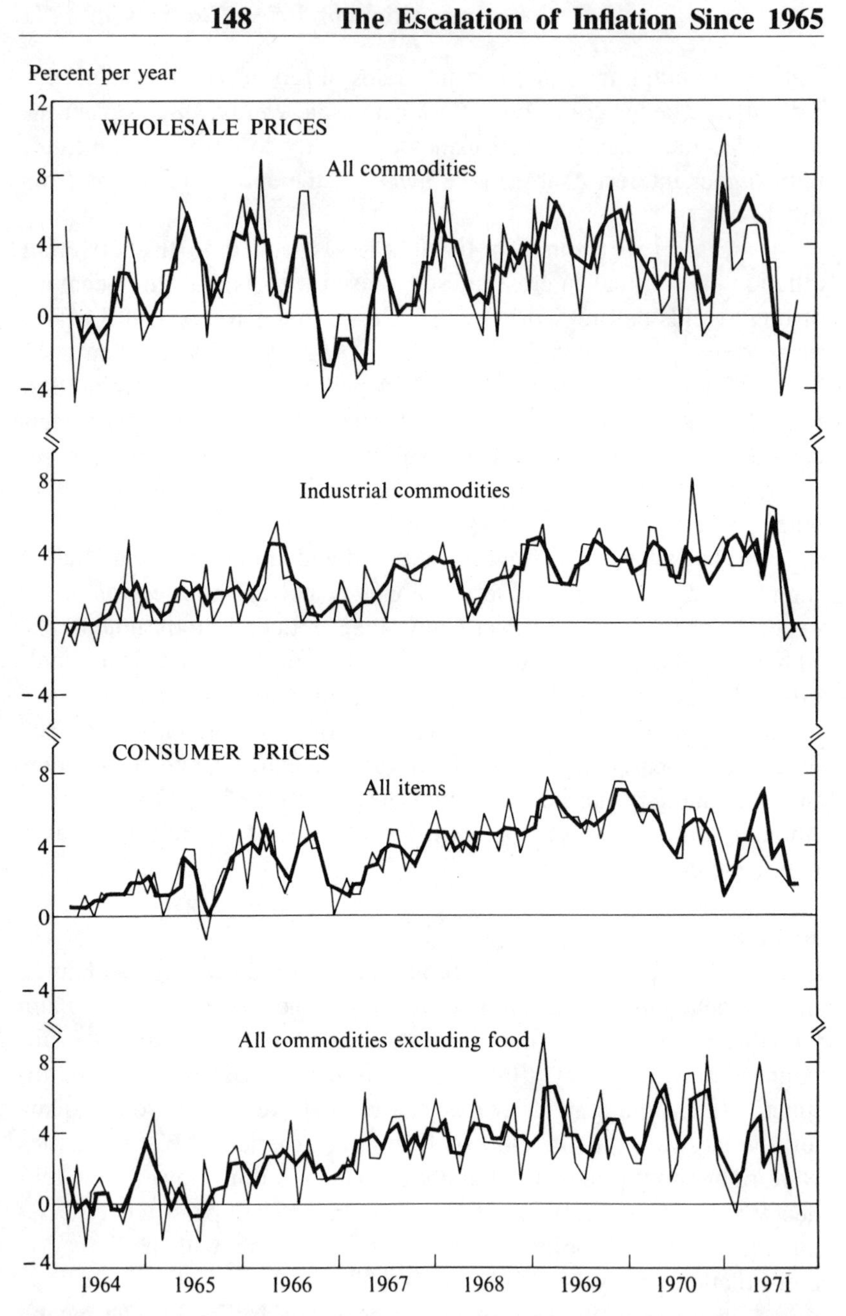

Figure 4.6 Rate of Change of Prices, 1964–71 (monthly change and centered 3-month average at annual rates)

tor of subsequent movements in retail prices, rose at an annual rate of 3.4 percent from January to July 1966 and, over the next six months, at a rate of only 1.2 percent. In the next six months this index was virtually constant. For the consumer price index, the annual rate was 4.2 percent in the first period and 2.5 percent in the second. Excluding foods, the deceleration was only slightly less. By contrast, from the second half of 1969 through the first half of 1970 these indexes showed little deceleration. The index for wholesale industrial commodities rose 4.1 percent per year in the first period and 3.8 percent in the second. The consumer price index rose 5.9 percent per year in the first period and 6.0 percent in the second, and excluding foods accelerated to 6.5 percent in the second period.

It was not that there were no signs of improvement in the year following the 1969 slowdown in activity. Consistent with the usual sequence, wholesale prices of crude industrial materials responded first. They reached a plateau in the second quarter of 1970 and remained roughly at that level for the remainder of the year. Intermediate industrial materials rose at an annual rate of 4.3 percent in the first half of 1970, 2.2 percent in the third quarter, and only 1.1 percent in the fourth. But wholesale prices of all industrial commodities had an annual rate of increase of 3.8 percent in the first half of 1970, and this rate fell only slightly to 3.5 percent in the second half. By and large, the pattern of price response was following the usual sequence, but at a snail's pace.

In the first half of 1971, wholesale price increases speeded up, as was to be expected in the first stage of a business recovery. The industrial component rose at an annual rate of 4.0 percent in the first half of 1971 compared with 3.5 percent in the preceding half year. The consumer price index slowed down, to be sure. For the first half of 1971 it rose at an annual rate of 4.1 percent and, excluding foods, at only 2.8 percent. But much of this improvement reflected the sizable decline in mortgage interest rates which are counted in household services (table 4.2). The private GNP price deflator (chain index), which does not cover mortgage rates, continued rising at 5.6 percent per year in the first half of 1971 (table 4.1).

Why were prices responding so slowly to slack demand? There are really two questions here. First, why did consumer prices rise more than 5 percent during 1970 at a time when unemployment was rising from 3.5 to above 6 percent? Second, why was inflation cooling so much more slowly than in 1966–67?

The common answer to the first question was framed in terms of "cost push." All the old theories of excessive union wage demands and administered pricing discarded in the late 1950s were dusted off and paraded out. No doubt most price increases in 1970 reflected a passing along of higher costs, since demand was too weak to pull prices up. But where did the cost increases originate? "Excessive" increases in administered prices were hard to find. Corporate profit margins were generally declining during 1969 and 1970, which does not indicate a use of administered pricing to maintain profits. In its two "Inflation Alerts" issued during 1970, the Council of Economic Advisers singled out some of the important price increases. Only three were questioned as perhaps not entirely justified by cost or demand pressures—those in petroleum, copper, and cigarettes. Studies of inflation which looked for an influence of concentrated industries generally failed to find that it was disproportionate.

Wages became the scapegoat. One certainly saw plenty of outlandish displays of union power: the construction trades, the teamsters, and the new militancy on the part of state and municipal unions received considerable publicity. Union wage settlements tended to accelerate in 1970 while nonunion wages slowed down slightly. The median increase for 1970 in manufacturing was 7.4 percent per year for union establishments and 5.8 percent for nonunion establishments, compared with 6.9 and 6.0, respectively, for 1969. High union settlements were widely publicized in 1970, giving administration officials cause for hand-wringing despair.

A pattern of union militancy is common to inflation. Unanticipated past increases in the cost of living make workers angry. They feel justified in insisting that their money incomes catch up and provide for future increases over the life of contracts. It is not always clear that even the large gains of over 10 percent put union wages ahead *in real terms*. Such settlements can represent a catching up with past real losses due to cost-of-living increases. The catching up can require 6 to 8 percent for a three-year contract just ended, and the average increase in productivity adds another 2 percent per year. While the data do not indicate that wages in general lagged behind prices in the period since 1965, wages under three-year contracts probably did lag until each contract was renewed. Then, as unions become conscious of inflation, they also bargain to cover anticipated increases in prices over the life of new contracts, which in those years could add another 4 to 5 percent per year. These sizable increases due to anticipations were built into the second and third year of the contracts, as well as the first. The resulting large increases made militant unions heady, and bringing them back to reality was turning out to be difficult.

The increasing power of unions poses a problem here, not in starting inflation, but in keeping it going. Anticipations of inflation are probably no greater for union workers than for the rest of the economy. But their power enables them partly to disregard slack demand and to translate those anticipations into wage increases which are inconsistent with a policy of curbing inflation. The whipsaw process of each handsome settlement giving rise to militant demands by other unions for equal or better treatment created the alarming prospect of a very slow cooling of the rampant inflationary psychology.

While union pressures on wages can greatly delay the response of prices to monetary restraint, the persistence of inflation in 1970–71 cannot be explained solely by unions. Wages and salaries continued to rise on a broad front. Median wage adjustments in nonunion manufacturing establishments were still rising 5.0 percent in 1970 compared with 5.1 percent in 1969, and average hourly earnings of production workers in manufacturing (excluding overtime and interindustry shifts) rose 6.9 percent in 1970 compared with 6.0 percent in 1969. In the first half of 1971 the annual rate of increase was still as high as 6.3 percent. Total compensation per hour for the private economy even accelerated to an annual rate of 8.6 percent in the first half of 1971, compared with 7.0 percent for all of 1970. These increases could not all be attributed to monopoly unions. The wage inflation had much broader origins.

The main reason for the persistence of inflations, even apart from unions, was simply that inflations do not stop immediately no matter how severely activity contracts. Prices and wages are set periodically, each time adjusting to an accumulation of cost influences since the previous setting. A price increase in one sector pushes up costs in others, and each increase then works its way through the price structure. At the stage of final goods and services, price increases add to the cost of living, feeding back on wages and costs in the earlier stages of production, then to work forward again. The process of sequential increases in costs and prices, once set in motion by an excessive aggregate demand, unwinds slowly.

The perplexing question in 1970–71 was why the process was unwinding more slowly than usual. Unions had grown stronger since inflation was curbed in the second half of the 1950s. That seemed to be one reason. Another reason was the greater magnitude and duration of price increases in the preceding years than in any of the previous inflationary periods since World War II. The new outbreak in 1965 added to the upward trend of prices since World War II, making anticipations of future inflation stronger than ever. Despite the 1970 contraction in activity, fears of business recessions had lessened since World War II. Such fears used to contract investment expenditures at the first signs of an economic downturn, but business investment continued at a high level throughout 1970, notwithstanding a slackening in aggregate demand and declining profit margins. (The administration had unintentionally encouraged business optimism during 1969 by predicting a mild slowdown in early 1970 and a resumption of economic expansion thereafter.) Newspapers reported the course of inflation fully, along with a consensus view of economic commentators that no President seeking reelection could any longer safely allow the economy to depart from full employment for very long. The implication was that prices are seldom going to decline, will usually rise, and, even when inflation gathers speed, the counteractions of policy will be mild and not very effective.

The significance of strong anticipations of inflation is that they can reduce the influence of demand on prices, even without strong unions. Cost increases are more readily and fully passed along, despite weakness in demand, if that weakness is viewed as temporary and prices are expected to follow an upward trend. Then the process of costs pushing up prices and vice versa moves along with less friction and is harder to interrupt by curtailing demand. The process only gradually slows down when cost increases are not fully passed along and anticipations eventually respond to a slackening in the actual rate of inflation.

Lessons of the 1965–1971 Experience

The inflation that began in 1965 created an almost made-to-order experiment for testing monetary effects on the economy. Monetary restraint was imposed in 1966 and again in 1969 to curb the inflation under circumstances which left no doubt that the reductions in monetary growth were policy decisions and not an automatic response of the monetary system to changes in the demand for money or credit. The resulting developments provided new evidence on the effects of monetary policy and on the nature and problems of inflation.

Effects of Monetary Policy

Monetary policy had long been downgraded, even by the monetary authorities themselves, as having limited power to influence the course of economic activity. Since changes in the money stock are typically produced via Federal Reserve sales or purchases of financial assets, no immediate effect on business sales or national income need occur. An effect on interest rates and then on investment demand occurs as the public subsequently adjusts to the change in money balances. A common view had been that the ultimate effect on aggregate expenditures is highly uncertain and probably fairly weak.

The experience of 1965–70 made clear, however, that monetary effects are not weak. Inflation began in 1965 when excessive monetary growth pushed the economy into the zone of increasing prices. Economic activity faltered in 1967 and contracted in 1970 after monetary policy became restrictive. There was nothing new here; such effects had been seen in the past. But the causal role of money had been widely doubted on the grounds that monetary growth passively reflects changes in economic activity, not vice versa, or that other influences are responsible for the appearance of a common variation in activity and monetary growth. For these episodes the alternative explanations could be readily dismissed. Monetary policy had finally come center stage.

This experience not only verified that money affects aggregate expenditures but also that it does so with a lag. It is the lag which explains why the effects had often been overlooked. In 1966 and 1969 the length of the lag was about two quarters from the step peak in monetary growth to the peak in the level of economic activity—a lag on the short side compared with previous cycles but not far out of line. (The effects on the *rate of change* of activity occur somewhat earlier.) The lag time is not easy to pin down, largely because it varies from one episode to the next. Predictions of monetary effects are therefore subject to considerable error, and this has often led to confusion in the conduct of monetary policy.

In view of the variable lag in the effects of monetary policy, fiscal policy used to be viewed as the key to stabilizing the economy. The acclaimed success of the 1964 tax cut helped to certify fiscal measures as a practical tool of government policy. But the disappointing failure of the 1968 tax surcharge—first the delay in getting it enacted and then its inability to curb the business boom—raised serious questions about the reliability and practicality of fiscal measures. Neither fiscal nor monetary policy has proven to be an effective stabilizer of the economy in the very short run. It is more accurate to say that both have been major sources of instability.

At the center of these policy shortcomings stands the sorry record of forecasting. Crucial changes in the economy are missed, causing serious policy mistakes. The beginning of inflation in 1965 was generally not recognized until it had gathered momentum. The strength of the business recovery following the slowdown in the first quarter of 1967 was underestimated. The downturn of 1969 was first predicted for early in that year and, when it finally came at the end of the year, its depth and duration were generally underestimated. As a result, the application of monetary restraint in 1966 was late, and its reversal in 1967 was far too strong. The restraint in 1969 also came too late and was overdone.

The financial crunches of 1966 and 1970 resulted from the delay and then overapplication of monetary restraint. The severe restraint unsettled financial markets, raised interest rates sharply, and channeled the limited supply of credit in favor of particular sectors. Housing especially suffered—in large part because savings institutions, which are the main suppliers of residential mortgage credit, could not compete effectively for deposits and were forced to curtail their mortgage lending. The housing problem was partially alleviated by the expansion of federal support of the mortgage market. But to avoid severe contractions of home building, savings institutions needed greater flexibility so that they could offer competitive rates on their deposits and attract funds even in tight markets. Basic reforms were needed to free these institutions from deposit-rate ceilings and other regulations.

The conduct of monetary policy in the 1965–70 period made additional errors by relying too much on movements in bank credit and interest rates as indicators of monetary effects. Both were particularly misleading in those years. Because of deposit-rate ceilings, time deposits experienced wide fluctuations as market rates rose above and then fell below the ceilings. Bank credit reflected these variations in time deposit growth and in nondeposit sources of funds which banks contrived to borrow on the open market until discouraged by the imposition of new regulations in 1969. The variations in growth of bank credit did not indicate parallel changes in the total supply of credit. Interest rates were also a poor indicator, because they reflected more than just monetary policy. In addition to shifts in the demand for credit, anticipations of inflation contributed to the rise in interest rates from 1965 to 1969. On the whole, growth in currency and demand deposits was a better indicator of the effects of monetary policy on aggregate expenditures.

Given the lags in monetary policy and the difficulties of forecasting, a policy of stable growth in the money stock has much appeal. But deposit-rate ceilings and other banking regulations cause problems here too. The large fluctuations in time deposits just described reflect portfolio transfers in and out of other assets, mostly securities but to some extent demand deposits also. Hence, a given growth rate of demand deposits could have varying effects on the economy because of substitutions betwen demand and time deposits. The money stock defined to include demand deposits plus currency is still the best single indicator for monetary policy, given the large fluctuations in time deposits. But, under such circumstances, even this indicator is less than ideal.

The Nature and Problem of Inflation

Inflation proved unexpectedly tenacious during the 1970 recession and subsequent recovery. The earlier inflationary upsurge of 1955–56 did not finally subside until 1958, but many prices had begun to decelerate before or soon after business activity turned down in 1957. This time deceleration came more slowly. Inflation began to slacken in early 1969, but as of mid-1971 gave little indication of a steady decline.

This did not mean that monetary restraint had been ineffective. The restraint had curtailed aggregate expenditures and activity, as noted above. Inflation was a problem because the slowdown in the economy was reflected primarily in output and hardly at all in prices. Price increases developed a built-in momentum which was generated and maintained by the widespread public anticipations of continuing inflation. The anticipation in turn affected prices, indirectly by raising wage settlements and directly by weakening the restraining influence on increasing prices of the slack in aggregate demand.

Until August 1971, policy acted to maintain moderate slack in the economy until inflation came gradually under control. The consequences of inflationary anticipations were that inflation would take longer to curb and, if not curbed, would get worse. Then the administration responded to widespread impatience with the slow signs of progress by abruptly changing course. In August the President announced a 90-day wage-price freeze and other measures to stimulate the economy and to deal with a worsening balance of payments. Since the administration had long expressed opposition to direct controls on the economy in peacetime, the change of mind expanded the range of economic policies that would be considered acceptable in the future.

5

The Economy under Controls, 1971–1973

The Background to Price and Wage Controls

During 1970, as it became clear that prices were responding more slowly to economic slack than they had been expected to, policymakers examined the distasteful choices. To subdue inflation fairly rapidly, unemployment would have to be raised to unacceptably high rates. But if unemployment were reduced to 5 percent or so and held there, which seemed temporarily acceptable even though not permanently desirable, inflation could not be reduced very rapidly—according to some estimates, only one percentage point a year or even less. Even then the reduction of inflation might not go very far, since some economists argued that a permanent unemployment rate of 5 percent or more might be necessary just to keep inflation down to 2 or 3 percent a year. No one could be sure of the final outcome, except that neither permanently high unemployment nor permanently high inflation was generally acceptable. The frustrating lack of a quick solution created a willingness to reconsider direct controls which had previously been stoutly resisted.

The business community was attracted to a wage-price freeze in the belief that this was the only means of stopping runaway wage increases. But a freeze can serve only as the initiating step to other direct controls. Since individual wages and prices cannot be kept absolutely constant for long, increases must very soon be allowed, which requires a sizable agency to decide every allowed increase and

Adapted from an essay originally published in *A New Look at Inflation,* American Enterprise Institute, Domestic Affairs Study 17, September 1973, pp. 1–34.

to try to enforce the decrees. Experience with this apparatus during World War II and the Korean War convinced many of its unattractiveness, especially the government officials who would be responsible for its administration. Also, there was no telling how long such controls might have to be maintained, and few could be sanguine about wrapping the economy up in such a straitjacket for a long time.

Middle-of-the-road opinion outside the government therefore gravitated during 1970 to an "incomes" policy of one kind or another. Proposals covered a wide range: the publication of general "guideposts" for wages and prices, as the Council of Economic Advisers had done in the early 1960s; establishment of a high-level board to review the appropriateness of wage and price increases with authority to publish findings but not enforce them, as Federal Reserve Chairman Burns had proposed; or more elaborate commissions authorized both to review increases and delay them, as Britain had had for several years until it abandoned the effort in January 1970. Earlier the Nixon administration had rejected such schemes as ineffective and philosophically obnoxious. But by the end of 1970 it was prepared to apply selective "jawboning," which relies on publicity to focus public disapproval and other kinds of government pressure on errant unions and firms.

Although the Council of Economic Advisers began in August 1970 to issue periodic reports on inflation which highlighted specific price increases, the administration applied pressure only in a few instances: During 1970, in an effort to counter rising petroleum prices, restrictions were relaxed on the importation of oil from Canada and on the production allowed from federal offshore leases. In January 1971, an announced increase in steel prices was reduced substantially under the threat of a possible relaxation of steel import quotas. In March 1971, the construction unions agreed to help set up a voluntary wage review board for the industry, in exchange for continuing enforcement of "prevailing wages" on federal construction projects under the Davis-Bacon Act. In July 1971, the President called upon management and workers in the steel industry to reach a "constructive settlement" in their new wage contract.

A case could be made for each of these steps on its own. After all, the federal government supports or enforces import quotas in oil and steel, and much of the power of construction unions to raise wages derives from federal legislation. To curb price and wage increases that could not occur without federal support, a reduction of this support was appropriate. Broad sentiment existed for curbing runaway wages in the construction industry, where 1970 contracts awarded a median first-year increase of 18.3 percent while unemployment among construction workers was unusually high.

But such steps, even aside from their limited enforcement, were too selective to have much effect on the general rate of inflation. A general effect required the imposition of wage and price guideposts for all or most of the economy. This step the administration had originally rejected. Aside from objections based on political philosophy, there was little practical evidence of their effectiveness. The Kennedy administration had initiated guideposts in the early 1960s. They were enforced selectively to head off or roll back announced wage increases which deviated, after allowing for certain adjustments, from a projected increase in labor productivity of 3.25 percent per year. Prices, except for special circumstances, were to remain constant. While the pressure appeared to work in some cases, the overall accomplishment was limited.[1]

Experience abroad had been no more favorable.[2] Several European countries had struggled with "incomes" policies having various powers of enforcement. Generally, the policies could not overcome trade union intransigence and gradually crumbled. In the case of every country that tried them, serious difficulties arose when inflation escalated. Governments were in the absurd position of asking workers to refrain from raising wages to match past price increases fully or in anticipation of future increases; in effect, workers' money incomes were not to keep up with inflation. Such a policy has only a slim chance of working when aggregate demand is weak; it had no chance in the runaway inflation of 1965–69.

Those who placed hope in guideposts as a means of curbing inflation in 1970 or 1971, after the demand pull on prices had subsided, had a particular view of why inflation persisted. In this view, the persistence reflected excessive wage settlements due to union power and to anticipation of continuing inflation at the same rate as in previous years. Wage guideposts might counteract union power and reduce anticipations. But, if the rise in wages and prices in 1971 reflected a catching up commensurate with past inflation, guideposts would distort relative wages and prices and would be hard to enforce. For guideposts to be successful, therefore, it was implicitly assumed that the catching up had largely been done before 1971 or that it was possible to enunciate guideposts which allowed for catching up.

Even then, however, advocates of this view faced a practical dilemma in opposing anticipatory increases in wages. To pretend that prices would not increase at all was ridiculous. Yet to select any particular rate of increase put policy in a box: too low a rate invited derision and union opposition, while too high a rate predicted the failure of anti-inflation policy. Unfortunately, these unattractive high and low zones overlapped in 1970–71, providing no middle ground.

One way around this problem was to supplement guideposts for wages with mandatory cost-of-living escalator clauses. Such clauses had been widely used in the 1950s, but had fallen into disfavor because employers often found cost-of-living payments to be larger than expected and unions disliked the limit on such payments which contracts at that time usually specified. Escalators were thought to intensify inflation by speeding up the transmission of wage and price increases through the economy. Yet, it is unfair and futile to rely on a lag in wages to hold back inflation. If the clause has no upper limit, wages remain roughly stable in real terms over the life of the contract. Then, if policy manages to reduce inflation, the increase in nominal wages will be correspondingly low; while if policy fails to slow the inflation, the wage increase will prevent a reduction in workers' real incomes.

Even with escalator clauses, however, guideposts pose serious problems for controlling wages. The expediency of holding increases in all wages equal to the growth in average productivity offers no solution, because there must be allowance for deviations, in particular industries and crafts, from the average. This need makes enforcement of guideposts in specific cases arbitrary and difficult. The problems are vastly more intractable for prices. Yet controls on wages but not prices seemed politically unacceptable; they had to cover both, as well as dividends and perhaps interest.

The administration's step in mid-1971 to impose controls was in many respects restrained. The lid it put on the inflationary steam pot had plenty of holes to let off the pressure. The strategy was to avoid setting up strong political opposition by bending the guidelines upward where necessary, but to achieve a sufficient reduction of increases elsewhere to produce a sense of waning inflation. Then anticipations would weaken and remove their pressure for increases in wages and prices. Confusion over how the new controls would work incidentally served the additional purpose of creating uncertainty, which delayed the business recovery and kept markets slack. But permanent success against inflation depended upon the advance in aggregate demand. The administration knew that, if markets remained slack, a slow unwinding of the inflation could continue. If policy stimulated the economy too rapidly, even a lid with holes could not contain the resulting build-up of inflationary pressures. Such pressures could not be quelled by price controls which merely suppress the immediate symptoms of inflation without changing the underlying demand and supply conditions.

The Economic Stabilization Program

The new program suddenly announced on August 15, 1971, had three basic parts: (1) It set forth steps designed to lead to a devaluation of the dollar through the appreciation of foreign currencies (the dollar was an international reserve currency to which other currencies were pegged and could not be devalued unilaterally), including a temporary surcharge of 10 percent on dutiable imports to use as a bargaining weapon in international negotiations. (2) It reduced selected taxes to stimulate the slow business recovery. (3) It froze prices and wages for ninety days (Phase I) to be followed by controlled increases for an indefinite period thereafter.

The devaluation had far-reaching implications for the international financial system and set off a series of discussions on how to build a system better able to redress payment imbalances. At first the degree of dollar devaluation to occur against each currency was contested. Finally on December 18, in an international meeting at the Smithsonian Institution in Washington, an interim agreement was reached. The various foreign currencies were appreciated by different amounts, producing an average appreciation against the dollar at the end of 1971 calculated at about 8 percent for total U.S. trade. (The gold value of the dollar was also changed from $35 to $38 an ounce, which meant that the appreciation of foreign currencies against gold was less than against the dollar, but this difference was of no significance for international trade.) As part of the agreement, the U.S. import surcharges imposed on August 15 were removed, the permissible band of fluctuation in exchange rates was widened from 1 to 2.25 percent, and plans were laid for further negotiations to modify the mechanism of international financial adjustments. The devaluation was expected to improve the U.S. trade balance, though the full effect would not be felt for several years. (Little effect was in fact discernible during 1972, because the trade balance deteriorated markedly as the business recovery picked up. As a consequence, pressures against the dollar reappeared late in 1972, culminating in a further 10 percent devaluation in January 1973.)

The effects of the fiscal stimulants of the stabilization program mainly came in the final four months of 1971, but they were not of major importance for the economy at large. Except for the import surcharge, they comprised a number of proposed tax reductions designed to encourage spending, including removal of the 7 percent excise tax on automobiles and a tax credit on new investment. The Council of Economic Advisers estimated that these proposals would reduce fiscal year 1972 revenues (excluding the surcharge) by $5.8 billion and expenditures by $4.9 billion. As finally enacted by Congress, the actual revenue reduction was estimated to be $4.6 billion. The net effect on the budget deficit was very small and could not have affected aggregate demand much either way. The main purpose was to encourage early purchases of certain domestic goods that otherwise would not have been made until later.

The wage-price controls were the most dramatic step for the domestic economy and for anti-inflation policy. They were not a substitute for the previous policy of maintaining aggregate demand below potential output, which was not to be abandoned. The purpose of the controls, as implied in the 1972 *Annual Report of the Council of Economic Advisers,* was to hold down price increases made in anticipation of further inflation. Controls were intended to hasten the decline in inflation through their announcement effect on anticipations.

Given the objective of influencing anticipations, an elaborate enforcement agency was not necessary and indeed was economically impractical—in addition to being politically repugnant to the administration. The idea was to do little to disrupt the economy. Controls were to prevent most of the very large union wage settlements and to force firms with "reasonable" profits to absorb some cost increases and so foster public confidence that inflation was gradually coming under control.

Thus, the ninety-day freeze was followed by a Phase II set of regulations administered by a small organization specially set up for the purpose. The key operating centers of the organization were a Price Commission of seven public members to control prices and a Pay Board of fifteen members split equally among business, labor, and public representatives to pass on wages and salaries. The Construction Industry Stabilization Committee for controlling construction wages was incorporated into the organization, and other groups were formed to advise on or deal with dividends and interest, government pay, health services, and rents. Each of these groups had a staff numbered in the hundreds. Public inquiries, complaints, and general enforcement were taken on by the Internal Revenue Service, which assigned 3,000 employees to the task. In fact, very little litigation was instituted. The entire program was run to a considerable extent by voluntary compliance. And it had to be: the full-scale price control apparatus of World War II involved 60,000 paid workers and many thousands more volunteers.

The lack of a large enforcement agency meant that the controls had to be limited in scope. This was done by exempting all but large firms from direct control. The nonexempt firms comprised a Tier I: for prices, the 1,500 firms with annual sales of $100 million or over (45 percent of total sales in the economy) and, for wages, labor contracts affecting 5,000 or more workers (10 percent of all employees). Tiers II and III composed of smaller firms had to follow the guidelines set down for price and wage increases but could act without prior approval (though Tier II firms had to give prior notification). The guidelines were 2.5 percent per year for prices and 5.5 percent for wages (6.2 percent including fringes), with an allowance up to 1.5 percent for catching up. (The 2.5-price and 5.5-wage guidelines were mutually consistent under the assumption that labor productivity would rise on the average 3 percent per year.)

Initially agriculture (including fisheries and forests), exports and imports, pay scales and fees of the federal government, and interest rates were exempt. The exemption was extended, in January 1972, to retail firms with annual sales below $100,000 and to apartments of four or less units or with monthly rents above $500 and, in May, to firms and governmental units of sixty employees or less (with some exceptions).

This confinement of direct controls to large units meant that the sparse enforcement machinery could efficiently narrow its responsibility. But the policy also conformed to the popular view that the inflation originated in the aggressive policies of large corporations and large unions. Only the atomistic markets, such as those for farm and other basic commodities, apartments, and financial assets, were thought to be self-regulating. Contrary to this view, however, the impetus of the inflation was not coming from industries dominated by large corporations; indeed, the general decline in corporate profit margins during the inflation indicated that most corporations were having difficulty simply keeping up with cost increases. Whether big unions were responsible for prolonging the inflation was a more complex question. To a large extent new union contracts simply made up for increases in the cost of living since the last contract and thus were not independent sources of inflation. But many unions also used their power to outdo each other and to cover in new contracts the anticipated future increases in the cost of living. Some of the large settlements seemed to accomplish all this and more, and thus to prolong the inflation. Union leaders were not illogical to conclude that the controls were aimed primarily at union wage contracts. Labor leaders voiced their opposition but failed to dent the public support for restraining union wage demands.

To avoid a knockdown confrontation with labor, the Pay Board wielded its authority cautiously. In the initial weeks it approved large increases negotiated by several powerful unions, explaining that the increases had been previously negotiated or that the wage rates in question had fallen behind so that the increases were allowed under the catching-up or gross inequity provisions of Phase II. But the board gradually tightened its rein: In a well-publicized decision early in 1972 it pared down a settlement of the West Coast longshoremen who threatened a showdown strike but finally backed off. Overall, the increases approved through June 1972 averaged 5.1 percent for union workers and 4.4 percent for nonunion workers.[3] Flexible enforcement of wage controls succeeded in avoiding resentment. Although AFL-CIO President George Meany pulled union representatives off the Pay Board in March 1972 (whereupon the administration reorganized it with seven public members), the board was generally accepted by business, the union rank and file, and the public.

Acceptance and compliance had been uncertain when the controls were first imposed. Other Western countries, notably Great Britain, had instituted various kinds of "incomes" policies during the 1960s, but with little evidence of more than temporary success, as noted. The key differences between the U.S. case and the others appeared to be the slack in the U.S. economy and the fact that controls had not been used since the Korean War, so Americans had been spared a recent opportunity to become disenchanted with them. Of course, 1972 was a year of reduced labor negotiations: major contracts (1,000 employees or more) affected only 2.8 million workers that year, compared with 4.75 million in both 1970 and 1971, and 5 million in 1973.

Prices and Wages under Phases I and II

The ninety-day freeze of 1971 achieved its purpose. Although wholesale industrial prices rose at a 6.6 percent annual rate in June and July compared with a 3.8 percent rate in the preceding six months, suggesting that some firms had a premonition of what was to come, in general the freeze was not expected and a difficult-to-administer rollback of prices did not appear necessary and was not seriously contemplated. During the freeze the recorded prices of covered items did not rise and no evidence of widespread evasion came to light. Many prices rose because of exemptions (which included basic foods, imports, and seasonal variations). But others fell due to market conditions, and the overall wholesale price index was practically unchanged during the period. A special analysis of consumer prices showed little rise in covered prices during the freeze.[4] As to wage increases, with some exceptions, they were stopped.

Of course, this freeze was successful without much enforcement because there was slack in the economy, because adjustments were to be allowed afterward, and because the economy can endure almost anything for only three months. The effect on prices if the freeze and postfreeze quarters are combined was much more modest. Right after the freeze, there were catch-up increases in prices and wages which the Phase II controls attempted to moderate but not prevent altogether. As a result, the rise in the consumer price index (annual rate) jumped from 1.9 percent during the freeze to 4.8 percent during the three months following the freeze. For the six months combined the annual rate of increase was 3.4 percent, compared with

4.0 percent for the preceding six months. Allowing for the fact that the inflation had been declining due to reduced aggregate demand, the additional decline that could be attributed to the freeze was slight.

The postfreeze offset was not unexpected or thought undesirable by policymakers, because the controls had not been intended to cut too radically into inflation for fear of disrupting business activity. The freeze satisfied the public's clamor in mid-1971 for some dramatic new initiative against inflation and, at the same time, constituted a needed holding action while the Phase II controls were planned and set up. The planning operation could not have been kept secret and, without the freeze, would have touched off a spate of anticipatory price increases.

Under Phase II inflation fell appreciably. This was not widely recognized at first because of the attention paid to price increases for exempt foods and other basic commodities. But by late summer consumer prices showed substantial deceleration (figure 4.4). The private GNP deflator (chain index) rose 5 percent at an annual rate in the first half of 1971, whereas its annual rate averaged 2.6 percent in the second and third quarters of 1972 after the catch-up increases in the first quarter (table 4.1).

The coincidence of controls and deceleration convinced the public that controls were effective. Yet the deceleration could not have been caused solely by controls, since it had started earlier in many sectors in response to slack demand.

How much of the deceleration from mid-1971 to the end of 1972 can be attributed to controls? The initial acquiescence of the business community to the burden of operating under controls reflected a belief that only controls could stop the wage explosion. The large increases in union settlements apparently did moderate faster with the help of controls. The Construction Industry Stabilization Committee, which began operations in March 1971 before the freeze went into effect, helped to restore order to a chaotic wage structure. First-year wage increases in construction contracts, which had averaged 9 percent in 1968, started rising again in 1969, and reached 21 percent in the second half of 1970. They came down to 11 percent by the end of 1971 and to 6 percent by the end of 1972. For other workers as well, the frequency of large settlements was reduced. First-year wage increases were above 9 percent for 56 percent of the workers under new union contracts of 1,000 workers or more in the first half of 1971 but for only 27 percent in the first half of 1972 and 20 percent for all of 1972.[5] In manufacturing, first-year increases in union wage settlements averaged 8.3 percent in the first half of 1971, slightly above their 7.8 percent average rate for 1970, and declined substantially to 6.3 percent in the first half of 1972—although the corresponding decline for nonunion settlements was smaller, from 5.2 to 4.6 percent.

While controls had a substantial effect on union settlements, their overall impact on wages was less dramatic. Total compensation per hour for the private nonfarm sector rose 7.2 percent in the year ending June 1970 and 7.5 percent in the year ending June 1971; in the freeze and postfreeze catch-up periods combined (third-quarter 1971 through first-quarter 1972), it rose 6.2 percent at an annual rate, and then in the next two quarters decelerated to 5.2 percent. But in the fourth quarter of 1972 it shot up to an annual rate of 7.6 percent, and averaged 6.1 percent for the last three quarters of 1972. So the average deceleration was about 1.5 percentage points. But this statistic is affected by cyclical changes in overtime pay. A better indicator is average hourly earnings for the private nonfarm sector adjusted for overtime in manufacturing and interindustry shifts, which exhibited a similar pattern but less deceleration. Its annual rate of increase was around 7 percent during 1970 and the first half of 1971. In the freeze and postfreeze catch-up (August 1971 through March 1972) it averaged 6.0 percent and, for the remainder of 1972, 6.3 percent. For this index the total deceleration from 1970 to the last three quarters of 1972 was less than 1 percentage point. Moreover, not all of this deceleration could be attributed solely to controls in view of the fact that a 6 percent unemployment rate persisted until June 1972 and a 5.5 percent rate until November.

Unit labor costs decelerated considerably, chiefly because of the stepped-up growth in output per hour of labor beginning in early 1970. This allowed prices also to decelerate and, at the same time, some improvement in depressed profit margins. To the extent that the reduction of inflation reflected a deceleration of unit labor costs, it was due primarily to business cost cutting and the economic recovery.

If controls had a direct effect on prices in addition to the small indirect effect via wages, profit margins had to be squeezed. This indeed seems to be the explanation for the greater deceleration of prices under Phase II than during the year and a half preceding controls, a deceleration that was too sharp to be dismissed as accidental. Controls held back those price increases that would otherwise have occurred to improve profit margins. The margins generally advanced in 1971–72, to be sure, but presumably not as much as would otherwise have resulted from the business recovery.[6]

The effect of price controls on profit margins works against market forces and distorts business incentives. Controls do not change the long-run relation between prices and unit labor costs determined by market forces. The margins tend to gravitate toward their market-determined levels, either through evasion of the controls or eventually when the controls are removed. There is then no lasting effect.

Any lasting effect of controls had to reduce the anticipated rate of inflation incorporated in union as well as nonunion wage increases. The impact on adjusted average hourly earnings was, as noted, about 1 percentage point—a third of the deceleration in the consumer price index from 6 to about 3 percent per year by the end of 1972. That is indicative of the lasting effect of the controls via anticipations, and it is a maximum estimate because it includes the independent contribution of slack demand. The other two-thirds of the deceleration in consumer prices reflected improvements in productivity and a squeeze of profit margins due partly to slack demand and partly to the controls.

After the initial deceleration in wage increases from above 7 percent to 6 percent per year by the end of 1971, there was no further decline during 1972. With a projected growth in labor productivity of 3 percent per year, a wage increase of 6 percent was consistent with 3 percent inflation, to which any recovery in profit margins would be added. Notwithstanding the optimism with which the public first greeted the imposition of controls and the belief that inflation would somehow be eradicated quickly, it was winding down slowly. During most of 1972, slack in the economy created the conditions for a reduction of inflation, and controls did not have to fight against the tide. This favorable situation lasted until nearly the end of the year and was deceptively conducive to an expansive monetary policy.

Monetary Policy and Business Activity under Controls

Notwithstanding the squeeze of profit margins, the Phase II controls did not produce the obvious restrictions on supplies that would be indicated by shortages and black markets. There is little evidence, therefore, that controls impeded the business recovery directly in the 1971–72 period.[7] They may have done so indirectly by creating uncertainty. The sluggish recovery of the first half of 1971 was no doubt prolonged to some extent into the third quarter by the uncertainties of international finance and of the price freeze. But the dark clouds soon cleared, and the expansion began to pick up by the fourth quarter. Then, in early 1972, as confidence grew that the economy would not be hamstrung by controls and that controls would somehow hold inflation in check, consumer expenditures rose and the laggard business recovery took off. Industrial production spurted. Real GNP rose 7.6 percent from the fourth quarter of 1971 to the fourth quarter of 1972. The increase in real GNP for the two years 1970–72 was stronger than in the two years following each of the cyclical recoveries beginning in 1954, 1958, and 1961, whereas comparison of real growth in just the first year of these recoveries shows 1971 to be the weakest.

The unemployment rate stubbornly did not begin to decline until 1972, and then slowly at first because of increased growth in the labor force. This growth was finally absorbed, however, and by year-end the unemployment rate fell to 5.1 percent. The decline in unemployment occurred despite continuing large gains in labor productivity. In the first three quarters of 1972 unit labor costs advanced at the the lowest rates in many years, which made possible slower price increases.

Unfortunately, satisfaction with the cooling of inflation in the first half of 1972 led monetary policy to err on the expansive side, with disastrous results that did not become apparent until the year was over. The attitude that fostered this error was prophetically expressed at the beginning of the year in the 1972 *Annual Report of the Council of Economic Advisers:*

The establishment of the direct wage-price controls created room for some more expansive measures, because it provided a certain degree of protection against both the fact and the expectation of inflation. This situation had to be approached with caution, because excessive expansion could make the price-wage control system unworkable. Still there could be no doubt that the tolerable rate of expansion had been increased.[8]

The halfhearted plea for caution in this statement went unheeded.

In early 1972, anxious to speed the recovery of production, the Federal Reserve Open Market Committee called for "moderate" growth in the money stock (excluding time deposits), which apparently meant the same 6 percent average rate achieved during 1970 and 1971. But during the year the growth rate exceeded 6 percent in most months; it also experienced a sharp increase in July, which was not offset in subsequent months, and again in December due in part to the Treasury's year-end disbursement of revenue-sharing checks to state and local governments. The overall result for 1972 was monetary growth of 8.3 percent, and the increase for the year from January to January (which downplays the unintended December spurt) was still 8.2 percent (figure 6.4 below).

The business recovery, which had proceeded sluggishly during 1971 and gathered speed during the first part of 1972, now reached boom dimensions. Real GNP rose at an 8 percent annual rate in the final quarter of 1972 and first quarter of 1973. Production rose to near-capacity levels, triggering an expansion in business plans for investing in new capacity. Although wholesale prices of crude materials, foods in particular, had started rising rapidly in the latter part of 1972, they literally exploded in early 1973. Wholesale food prices rose at an annual rate of 47.5 percent seasonally adjusted in the first half of that year. Special supply conditions were offered to explain the inflationary significance of skyrocketing food prices. The chief explanation was the devaluation of the dollar, first in 1971 and again in January 1973, which had brought about higher domestic dollar prices for basic commodities traded on world markets. Also, the special sale of U.S. grains to Russia had reduced stocks, the beef-production cycle reached one of its periodic low points, and weather conditions were adverse for many farm products.

All these events contributed. They are discussed in chapter 6. Nevertheless, rising aggregate demand was a major factor. While the first markets to reflect the business boom were as usual those for basic commodities, pressures on a broader range of prices came in due course. Wholesale prices of industrial commodities rose 12.5 percent at an annual rate seasonally adjusted in the first half of 1973 compared with 2.9 percent in the preceding half year. Even the less volatile prices of finished manufactured goods took off. The wholesale prices of consumer finished goods excluding foods experienced a rate of increase of 12.2 percent seasonally adjusted in the first half of 1973 compared with 2.1 percent in the preceding half year and the rates for producer finished goods were 5.2 percent in the later period and 1.2 percent in the earlier period. These price increases reflected not only temporary supply scarcities but also the raging inflation of a business boom.

How can the failure of monetary policy to become moderately restrictive during 1972 be explained? Understandably, the monetary authorities had not wished to thwart a business recovery, and it is difficult to achieve restraint in monetary growth when a business expansion is gaining strength. Reports of the Federal Reserve Open Market Committee indicated a desire early in 1972 for slower monetary growth than was being achieved. In February the committee began to state its monetary objectives in terms of reserves against deposits held by the public, a technical refinement which seemed to promise closer control over monetary growth. Rising short-term rates cautioned against pushing restraint too rapidly—though some members of the committee voted for a less expansionary policy. As was to be expected in a strong business recovery, short-term interest rates rose. From a low of almost 3 percent in February 1972, Treasury bill yields rose to 4 percent by July and to 5.5 percent in early 1973. A majority of the Open Market Committee still harbored a traditional reluctance to abandon interest rates to the pull of market forces.

These reasons, however, could only partly account for the failure to achieve restraint after mid-1972 when it had become clearly appropriate. Instead, policy pursued a goal of driving the economy toward full employment without regard for the lag in monetary effects and for the need to slow the pace of economic expansion as the goal was approached. Given the well-recognized imprecision of forecasts and of monetary control over the economy, such a policy invited a resurgence of inflation. When it burst out, it was stronger than expected, but serious consequences should have been foreseen. During the painfully slow progress against inflation in 1969, 1970, and 1971, Federal Reserve and government authorities pledged not to fritter away the hard-won gains and repeat the mistake made in 1967 of overstimulating the economy as it recovered. But, in fact, the inflationary pressures which erupted in early 1973 were much stronger than those which followed the monetary slowdown of 1966–67. Although they were exacerbated by foreign influences and supply conditions, the failure of policy in 1972 to restrain monetary growth was a monumental blunder.

Phase III as the "Culprit"

In January 1973 the administration relaxed the mandatory compliance of Phase II for all price and wage increases, except in food processing and distribution, construction wages, and health services, and substituted guidelines for the rest of the economy. The Price Commission and Pay Board were abolished, and the Cost of Living Council was authorized to see that the guidelines were followed. There was no intention of policing the guidelines, but mandatory controls could be reinstated on particular sectors if the guidelines were seriously breached. Pressure was to be applied primarily to the largest corporations and unions, but it was not used widely. Phase III guidelines were not rigid and offered more play to market forces. They started as a cross between the voluntary guideposts on wages and prices of the early 1960s, which had modest effects, and the mandatory but loosely enforced limits of Phase II.

The timing of the shift to Phase III led the public to believe that prices spurted because of the removal of Phase II controls. The amount of truth in this belief is miniscule. Although the ending of Phase II allowed firms to post catching-up price increases, most of the largest increases of early 1973 came in basic commodities which were uncontrolled under Phase II. Moreover, the pressures under prices that surfaced in 1973 had a force that would eventually have buckled the Phase II controls.

The administration ended Phase II in January 1973 under the impression that inflation was subsiding (showing once again that crucial economic turning points are seldom recognized at the time they occur) and that the economy seemed ready for uncontrolled prices, which the administration preferred. By chance, therefore, Phase II ended before its inability to contain a strong inflation was revealed. In a few months the public was clamoring for a tightening of price controls. The skyrocketing prices of foods brought housewives out in angry protest. The public outcry over soaring meat prices forced the administration to freeze them in March, and the broadening inflationary pressures led to a second step back to controls in May (corporations with annual sales over $250 million were required to gain prior approval of price increases above 1.5 percent of the January 10 level).

During the first half of 1973 the administration resisted further increases in the federal budget and talked of applying monetary restraint to moderate the boom. These policies, together with larger agricultural supplies expected in the fall and continued moderation in wage increases, were thought to promise a desired cooling of inflation by the end of the year. It is true that some signs still pointed to that possibility. Output per hour of labor for the private nonfarm sector rose 4.3 percent at an annual rate in the first quarter of 1973, up from 3.6 percent in the previous quarter, and this helped moderate the increase in unit labor costs (table 4.1). While the comparable rate for compensation per hour jumped from 7.6 percent in the preceding quarter to 10.4 percent, much of this acceleration reflected increases in social security taxes and overtime pay. For negotiated wages and benefits in the first year of contracts covering 5,000 workers or more in all industries, decisions in the first quarter had an annual rate of increase of 7.3 percent, the same as in the preceding quarter and well below the rates of recent years. Wage increases for nonunion workers in manufacturing also continued to moderate. But, with the economy near full capacity, substantial gains in productivity and continued moderation in wage demands became less likely. Although settlements during the first half of 1973 generally stayed within the guidelines, fears of stepped-up demands figured prominently in the administration's willingness to tighten controls. As the resurgence of inflation broadened (with some increases no doubt occurring partly in anticipation of a change in Phase III rules), talk of the need and possibility of a new set of controls spread.

On June 13, 1973, Phase III ended with the imposition of a new freeze on all prices and wages except farm products (which were in effect controlled by the inability of processors and distributors to pass along any increases). This was followed in August by a Phase IV program similar to Phase II. The change in policy was intended to signal the failure of Phase III and its replacement with a "certified" program of controls. But Phase III mainly confirmed both the failure of monetary policy to moderate aggregate demand and the widespread appeal of rigid price controls despite the evidence of meager previous accomplishments. While the first freeze and Phase II did not disrupt the economy because demand was generally slack, the second freeze and Phase IV came when most markets were tight. For this reason, they were not able to avoid some disruptions. But, in general, these were minor because Phase IV had little effect in moderating price increases.

The Phase IV controls ended with little notice on April 30, 1974, when the Economic Stabilization Act expired.

Summary and Evaluation

Progress against Inflation

When the Nixon administration took office in 1969 and announced that curbing the inflation was its number one domestic priority, it thought the job would take two years at most. The 1955–59 inflation, which stood as a warning to this optimism, was generally forgotten. Yet, the inflation was even harder to subdue than previous ones, in part perhaps because it had lasted longer. First the excessive growth in aggregate demand had to be slowed by a cut in monetary expansion. The monetary restraint initially tightened financial markets and after a delay slowed economic activity, which produced the 1970 recession. From the decision to restrain the economy to the beginning of the recession took a year by itself. Then, to general dismay, prices rose just as rapidly during the recession as they had before, carried along by the momentum of rising wages, costs, and anticipations of continuing inflation. The inflation rate reached a peak during 1970, but signs of a change in direction were unclear at the time, and no one could be sure that it had actually occurred. Many people concluded instead that the orthodox method of fighting inflation by restraining aggregate demand was a failure.

A process of unwinding the inflation was nevertheless at work beneath the surface. Excess productive capacity brought about by the business recession induced cost cutting. During the middle and later stages of the inflation, profit margins had fallen to low levels, and the recession-slack in demand and associated layoffs of workers created the conditions for intensified efforts to hold down costs. Output per hour of labor, which had not advanced during 1969, began to improve markedly. Such improvement is typical of business contractions and recoveries, and in this instance it started in the second quarter of the recession, sooner than usual, and speeded up when business recovered. Many of the benefits of cost cutting completed earlier did not appear until later when production rose in the business recovery without the need for a commensurate addition to the work force. As productivity improved, unit labor costs decelerated appreciably despite the continuation of large wage increases. Initially this led to an improvement in profit margins rather than to smaller price increases. Historically, prices have reflected changes in unit costs after a lag of several quarters, and here too the growth of productivity exerted little restraint on price increases until the end of 1970, and then not as much at first as in past cycles.

By 1972, three years after the application of monetary restraint in 1969, the economy was finally recovering from the effects on output, and the inflation was half cured. The restraint had not been extraordinarily severe, and the execution of policy in 1969–70 was probably as competent as could reasonably be expected under practical circumstances. The problem had been the exasperating delay in getting results, a problem which indicates how long it takes to formulate and execute a change in direction for the economy. It was a sobering lesson on the difficulties of recovering from an inflationary binge.

Price Controls

Phases I and II came in the midst of this process. Their effect is not easily determined because inflation was subsiding and would have continued to do so, at least for a while, even without controls and also because the strengthening business recovery during 1972 was bound to exert upward pressures on some prices that controls could not hold back. Adding to the difficulties of assessment, the key price indexes differed in their measurement of the timing and extent of the initial deceleration. The consumer price index (excluding foods and mortgage interest) decelerated from a 6 percent annual rate of increase in 1970 to 4.5 percent by mid-1971, *before* the imposition of controls, and to about 3 percent thereafter (table 4.2). The private

GNP deflator, on the other hand, decelerated from 5 to 3 percent per year, and most of the reduction came after mid-1971, *during* controls (table 4.1).

To be effective, controls had to hold down the advance of wage costs, and the Pay Board's success in chopping down some of the eye-catching union wage demands has been cited in support of Phase II. But the deceleration of wage increases in the economy at large was not great, and even part of that reflected the slack in the economy. The increase in adjusted average hourly earnings fell from 7 percent in 1970 to 6 percent or so in 1972. It took time to slow the momentum of these increases, and, for some wages, the controls did well at first just to impede further acceleration.

Although much of the initial business support for controls presumed that they would curtail wage increases, their main contribution was to hold back the improvement in profit margins (controls had little to do with gains in output per hour of labor). This effect could not be permanent, since the widely imagined profiteering[9]—an obvious target for controls—did not exist. Profit margins had declined sharply in 1969 and 1970 and remained low in 1971. They rose moderately with the business expansion in 1972 and finally spurted only with the surge of aggregate demand in the first quarter of 1973. Sooner or later profit margins gravitate to their market-determined levels. Controls can delay but not prevent those adjustments.

However, a temporary reduction in the inflation rate achieved by holding down profit margins might have lasting benefits if it contributed to lower anticipated rates of inflation. This, in turn, would reduce the upward pressure on wages and thence prices. Such a contribution is the main rationale for controls. But the maximum effect of Phase II on anticipations could not have exceeded the total deceleration of wages of one percentage point—and probably was much less. Apparently the anticipated rate of inflation had not previously risen much above the rate that the controls were expected to allow. Perhaps, too, anticipations of inflation played a much smaller role in price and wage setting compared with catching-up adjustments than this rationale for controls presumed.

The public attributed the earlier cooling of inflation to the Phase I and Phase II controls and its resurgence to relaxation of controls under Phase III. The administration, which had sought to disengage from the labyrinth of controls by abandoning mandatory guidelines under Phase III, bowed to political expediency in mid-1973 and announced another cycle of a freeze and a follow-up program of controls. Problems of scarcity and cost-price disparities immediately arose, indicating that the slack markets which made Phase I and Phase II relatively innocuous had become tight. Controls presuppose that the demand and supply costs of different products maintain uniform relationships over time, so that all prices can be allowed the same increase, whereas inflationary conditions disrupt such uniformities.

Whatever limited effect controls had under the conditions of slack demand in 1971–72, a return to a freeze and rigid controls in the tight markets of 1973 made no economic sense. Yet, despite the near-unanimity of professional economists that controls are not effective against demand-pull inflation, they have enormous appeal to the general public. The public believed that the relaxed Phase III controls were responsible for the surge of prices in 1973. In addition to the inequities and inefficiencies of controls, the danger in that belief is that controls divert attention from monetary policy and encourage a postponement of the restraint which is necessary to curb inflation. This was the tragic outcome of the overly expansive monetary policy under Phase II.

Monetary Policy

After mid-1972, as the economy approached full capacity, storm clouds appeared in tightening commodity markets. Yet monetary policy continued to support a strong business expansion, which by then had attained boom dimensions. In early 1973 the economy plunged headlong into demand-pull inflation. Even had Phase II controls still been in effect during the first quarter of 1973, they could not have contained the spectacular increases in the prices of basic commodities, for these commodities were exempt under those controls.

Phase II controls led the authorities to believe that little of the monetary stimulation of aggregate demand would affect prices and nearly all of it would go to raise output. Monetary growth had averaged 6 percent per year in 1970 and 1971, which was reasonable for those years of slack demand. But it speeded up to 8 percent in 1972 and continued at 7 percent in the first half of 1973. To avoid overstimulation of the economy, policy should have slowly *reduced* monetary growth during 1972.

The failure to do so appears to be yet another case of the lag in monetary effects tripping up policy objectives. The previous case occurred during the mini-recession of 1967 when policy turned sharply expansive to stimulate economic recovery, only to find a year later that it had fueled another round of inflation. Policymakers vowed not to make that mistake again. The resurgence of inflation in 1973 showed that they had been no more successful the next time. A flexible policy is supposed to avoid the cycle of bust to curb inflation followed by boom-producing expansions to speed the ensuing recovery. But a flexible policy is subject to the hazards and pressures of dealing with economic developments as they unfold. The nation returned in 1973 to square one in the battle against inflation, and the cumbersome reliance on government fiat to control prices under Phase IV only added to the tragic consequences.

6

Foreign Influences in the Inflationary Outburst of 1973–1974

The New Environment

In 1973 and 1974 policies to subdue inflation not only suffered another setback because of the resurgence of domestic inflation but also appeared to have entered a hostile new environment subject to inflationary disturbances from outside the country. In addition to braking the momentum of the ongoing inflation, policy somehow had to combat the effects of new outside pressures as well.

Before 1973, inflation had with few exceptions reflected an overexpansion of aggregate demand from too rapid monetary growth, for which the policy prescription is first to persevere in mild restraint until inflation simmers down and thereafter to avoid overexpansion. In that case inflation is the vehicle by which excessive money balances are reduced to the desired level in real terms. But part of the inflation in 1973 appeared to be different. Special conditions conspired to raise the prices of many basic commodities well beyond a level attributable to prior monetary growth. When these increases passed through to prices of finished goods and services, real money balances were reduced *below* the desired level. Faced with deficient balances, the public attempted to restore them to the desired level by selling other assets and reducing expenditures. Monetary policy was then faced with a range of choices from (1) accommodating the

Adapted from an essay originally published in William Fellner, ed., *Contemporary Economic Problems*, pp. 17–53. Washington, D.C.: American Enterprise Institute, 1976.

increases in the price level by expanding the money supply faster until real balances reached the desired level to (2) holding back and enduring a period of economic retrenchment during which desired real balances would be reduced to the lower actual level. In view of the severity of the 1973–75 recession, monetary policy can be described as having pursued a course closer to the second than to the first of these two extremes.

Foreign Influences on U.S. Prices

The fury of the inflationary storm that burst upon the Western economies in 1973 reflected a variety of international developments. World prices of basic commodities rose sharply, beginning late in 1972 with food grains reduced in supply by crop failures, spreading to nonfood materials under the demand pressure of cyclical upswings in most of the industrialized countries, and capped by the quadrupling of the price of petroleum by the OPEC cartel in late 1973. There was in addition to these worldwide developments the devaluation and floating of the dollar exchange rate beginning in 1971, which raised the prices of U.S. imports.

None of these foreign influences was the result of a concurrent rise in U.S. aggregate demand. The devaluation reflected past U.S. inflation, and in the floating of the exchange rate, dollar prices of imports previously held in place by a fixed exchange rate were set free to adjust upward. The explosion in world commodity prices was fueled by expanded monetary growth in the major industrial countries in 1971–72, which was in turn supported in no small measure by a growth in world monetary reserves from an outflow of U.S. dollars.[1] Although not independent of prior U.S. developments, the price increases of basic commodities nevertheless came mostly in response to world demand and supply conditions and were much greater (as shown below) than demand conditions within the U.S. economy alone could explain. Once under way, the price increases generated their own effects on U.S. incomes. The main effects occurred through the balance of foreign payments and the terms of trade. The sharp rise in the price of petroleum reduced U.S. incomes in real and nominal terms in early 1974, though from the third quarter of 1973 to the first quarter of 1974 U.S. incomes rose because increased grain exports at increased prices expanded farm receipts from abroad. But the resulting effects on net aggregate U.S. expenditures, relatively minor from an overall view, were temporary. Given that monetary growth did not rise to sustain them, and other things the same, the rising prices of the scarce commodities reduced the demand for all other goods and services, and aggregate demand did not change, except perhaps temporarily.

Yet, while aggregate demand is the main determinant of the general price level in the long run, the price increases of imports were passed through the economy as cost increases and thereby raised the general price level before offsetting demand pressures on other prices took effect. Demand pressures work very slowly; their impact is initially on output and only much later on prices. Consequently, the run-up in the price level resulting from the cost increases can be reversed, given unchanged monetary growth, only after a long period of reduced output. In the meantime, wages advance in response to the higher cost of living, making the period of reversal very long indeed.

The importance of foreign influences in 1973 and 1974 is indicated by the rise in U.S. import and export prices relative to general prices. From the fourth quarter of 1972 to the second quarter of 1974, while the consumer price index rose 15 percent, the unit value of total imports rose 68 percent, and even with fuels excluded it rose 39 percent—which was also the rise in the unit value of total exports (see table 6.1). The effective dollar exchange rate depreciated 7 percent. Even with fuels excluded, therefore, import and export prices rose about six times more than the depreciation in the exchange rate and two and a half times more than the consumer price index.

To what extent did these increases raise costs and push up other prices? The direct effect of a rise in input prices on output prices in the various sectors of the economy can be estimated with the use of input-output weights for U.S. industries. To be complete, the estimates must make some allowance for the effects on substitutes, because a rise in import prices will pull up the prices of substitute domestic inputs. A study for the Joint Economic Committee, which made such estimates,[2] found that the effect on general prices was moderate from the third quarter of 1971, when the dollar was first devalued, to the second quarter of 1974. In that period the price deflator for personal consumption expenditures rose 18.6 percent. The study attributed a rise of less than 1 percent to the depreciation of

Table 6.1 Indexes of U.S. Domestic and World Prices, 1972-IV to 1974-II

Year and Quarter	*U.S. Dollar Price of Weighted Foreign Currencies*	*Import Prices (unit values)*		*Export Prices (unit values)*	*Consumer Prices*
		Total	*Nonfuel*		
1972 IV	100.0	100.0	100.0	100.0	100.0
1973 I	104.1	103.8	103.6	103.9	101.5
II	106.9	112.5	112.6	108.7	103.7
III	108.8	116.8	116.1	116.1	106.0
IV	106.9	127.0	123.3	124.2	108.5
1974 I	104.0	147.8	126.6	134.3	111.5
II	107.2	168.3	138.9	139.2	114.8

SOURCE: Berner et al. (1975), p. 5.

the dollar and a rise of 4.5 percent to the effect over and above exchange depreciation of higher import prices including sympathetic rises in domestic substitutes. The combined effect of depreciation and additional increases in import prices accounted for three-tenths of the total inflation over the period. We must also add the pressure of foreign demands on U.S. commodities traded in world markets, which raised the input costs of these commodities to the U.S. economy. Even with this addition, it still appears that a substantial part of the 1973 inflationary outburst in the United States reflected excessive domestic demand.[3]

It took about two years for all the foreign-induced cost increases to pass completely through the price structure. This can be seen in figure 6.1 from the timing of quarterly price movements in wholesale prices of three stages of production. Wholesale crude materials rose 15 percent in 1972 and 39.5 percent in 1973. These prices then stopped rising and fell in the first half of 1974. According to the monthly data, the index fell at a 16.5 percent annual rate over the first half of 1974, but the decline erased only a fraction of the 1973 increase. Although the index fell 14 percent from its peak in August 1973 to a trough in June 1974, by the end of 1974 it had recovered and was below the earlier peak by only 5 percent. For all of 1974 the index actually rose 7 percent (in quarterly averages), bringing the total increase for 1973 and 1974 to 49 percent. The contribution of this increase in materials prices to manufacturing costs took a year to pass through the entire economy: wholesale prices of intermediate materials and finished goods did not begin a comparable rise until

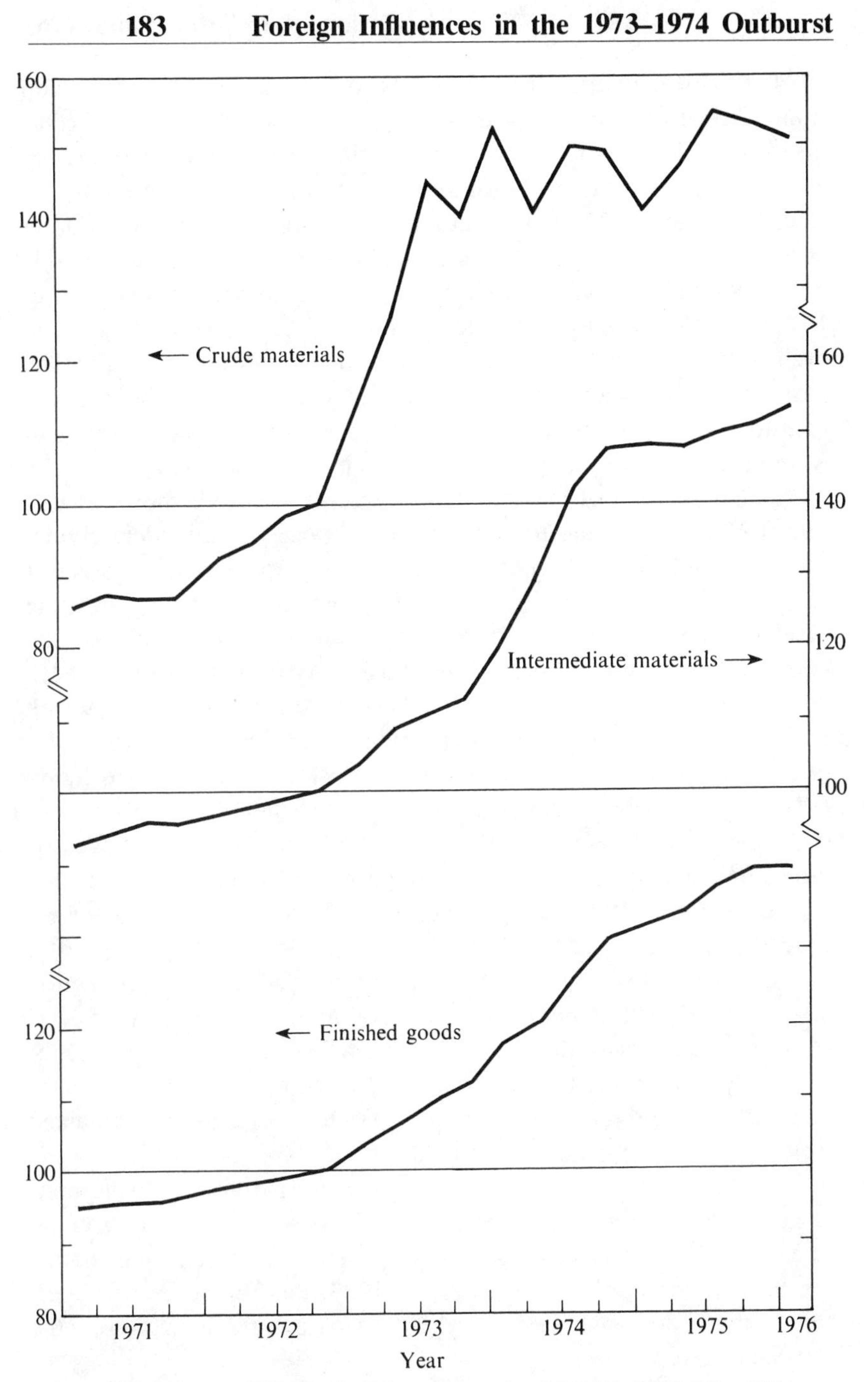

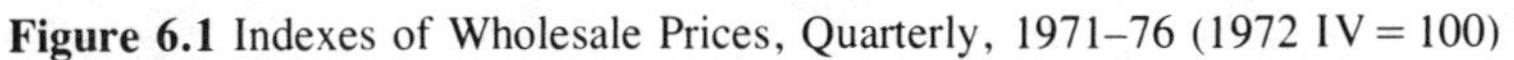
Figure 6.1 Indexes of Wholesale Prices, Quarterly, 1971–76 (1972 IV = 100)

1974. Prices of intermediate materials rose 30.5 percent in 1974, up from 12.5 percent in 1973, and prices of finished goods 18.5 percent, up from 11.5 percent. These high inflation rates came down sharply during the first half of 1975 (in the case of intermediate materials to a level below the 1972 rates), and then partly recovered in the ensuing business recovery during the second half of 1975. Finished goods prices continued rising more rapidly than the other two indexes in 1975. (The lag in the price index of finished goods would have been even longer if it were not for the inclusion of consumer foods.) The passing of price increases from crude to intermediate materials and then to finished goods with a year's lag meant that the total index of wholesale prices rose substantially in both 1973 and 1974.

The pattern of these price movements therefore shows a large blip from materials and food costs superimposed on a moderately accelerating inflationary trend: the blip was a sharp rise in the level of prices which temporarily raised the rate of increase, and the accelerating trend reflected the accumulation of past pressures and the emergence of new pressures as the business expansion gained speed during 1972. The price deflator for the private nonfarm sector, which in the first quarter of 1973 had an annual rate of increase of only 4.2 percent, then had a 9.3 percent rate in the fourth quarter (see figure 6.2). Not all of that acceleration yet reflected the 1973 blip in materials costs, which subsequently passed through successive stages of production and by the end of 1974 raised the inflation rate for the private nonfarm sector to 13.4 percent. The rate for this sector receded in early 1975 at the trough of the recession, but the blip left a trail of cost increases that continued coming through the production pipeline for a time thereafter, not to mention an accumulation of cost-of-living increases in the wage "catch-up" of negotiated labor contracts later on. While the inflation rate for the private nonfarm sector had declined by the fourth quarter of 1975 to 7.3 percent, it remained well above the 2.8 percent of 1972.

On the assumption that the 21 percent rise in the private nonfarm deflator from mid-1973 to mid-1975 would, if there had been no price blip, have instead roughly equaled the 5.1 percent annual rate reached in the middle two quarters of 1973, the blip added 10.5 percent to that index—which doubled the increase in the index—over the two-year period.[4]

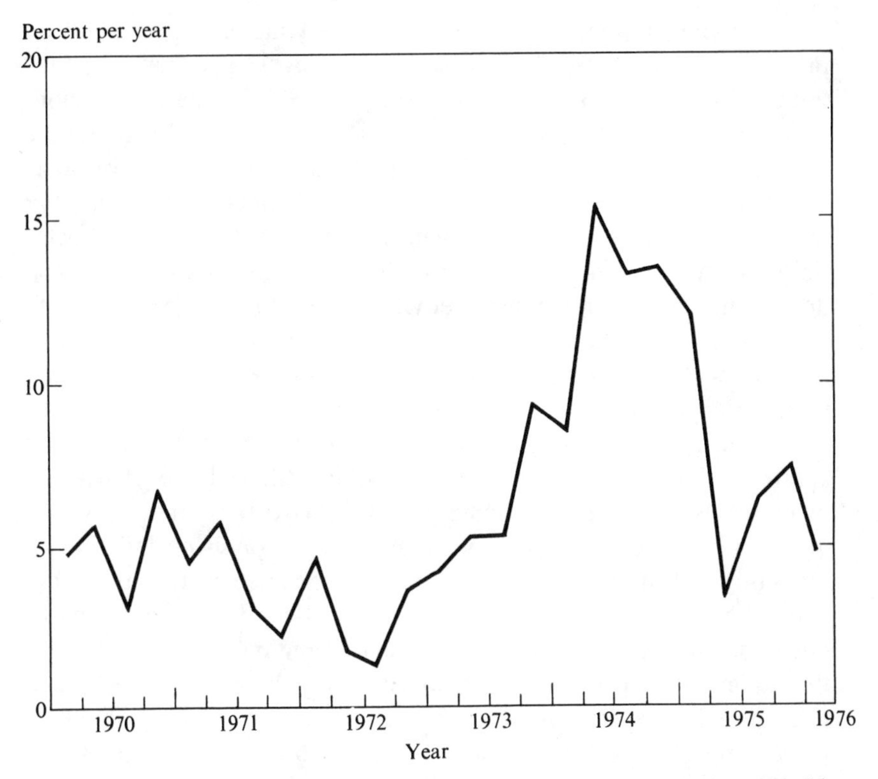

Figure 6.2 Rate of Change of Prices, Private Nonfarm Sector, Quarterly, 1970–76

Overexpansion in 1972

The foreign influences would very likely have had much less effect on prices than they did if the domestic business expansion had not accelerated price increases at the end of 1972 by pushing the economy into the zone of demand-pull inflationary pressures. Recovery from the 1970 recession had begun slowly but progressively picked up speed. By 1973 capacity utilization in manufacturing had returned to the neighborhood of the peak rates reached in the booming second and third quarters of 1969.[5] Supply bottlenecks developed in various industries. Unemployment fell below 5 percent, a level which because of changes in the composition of the labor force was no longer consistent with a stable or falling inflation rate.

Nominal wages were not a source of increasing pressure on prices. As is usual for the late stages of a cyclical expansion, they trailed price increases. Average hourly earnings for the private nonfarm sector rose by 6.5 to 7 percent during 1972 and 1973, about the same rate of increase as in 1971. But unit labor costs rose considerably faster in 1973 and 1974 than in 1972, as output per hour of labor fell sharply. It does not seem implausible to attribute the serious deterioration in productivity growth to the spreading inefficiencies and distortions of an inflationary environment. In any event, profit margins generally fell, so that the decline in productivity growth, together with the rise in materials costs, accounted for the increasing pressure on prices.

Instead of slowing monetary growth during 1972 as activity approached full capacity, monetary policy allowed the growth to increase, as recounted in chapter 5. The Phase II controls in effect during 1972 held back some of the early signs of rising inflationary pressures and lulled policymakers into the belief that unemployment could be pushed to around 5 percent without inflationary consequences. The rate was above 5.5 percent during most of 1972, but, as the expansion gained speed, it dropped during the closing months and fell below 5 percent at the beginning of 1973. Complacency about renewed inflationary dangers turned out to be a disadvantage of the controls more serious than their allocative distortions.

Such complacency was widely shared, to be sure, as late as the first quarter of 1973. The sixty-odd professional forecasters in the ASA survey[6] of December 1972 expected on average that the GNP deflator in 1973 would rise 3.5 percent, up only slightly over 1972. In the February 1973 survey they expected a small bulge in the inflation rate for the first quarter of 1973 then under way, but no lasting escalation, and the expected rate for the year remained at 3.5 percent. The actual rate for 1973 was 7.6 percent, and it was climbing further as the year ended.

The Recession of 1973–1975

As a result of the price explosion, real money balances fell 9.75 percent from mid-1973 to mid-1975 (see figure 6.3), which happens to correspond in timing and magnitude to the price blip of 10.5 percent noted above.[7] Without the blip, in other words, monetary growth would have kept real balances constant. Insofar as the price blip originated from crop failures and demand conditions outside the U.S. economy (as it did for the most part) and monetary growth was not at the same time expanded commensurately, the blip reduced real money balances *below* their desired level. Such a reduction had consequences altogether different from those of a reduction following monetary overexpansion, in which the resulting spurt of prices reduces real money balances *toward* their desired level. The economic effect of reducing real balances below their desired level is contractionary, just as though nominal monetary growth had been curtailed, and the immediate effect was a rise in short-term interest rates. Prime commercial paper rates rose above 10 percent in the second quarter of 1973, receded somewhat during the next two quarters, and then rose steeply to almost 12 percent by mid-1974. Part of this rise in interest rates may have resulted, to be sure, from the increase in inflation

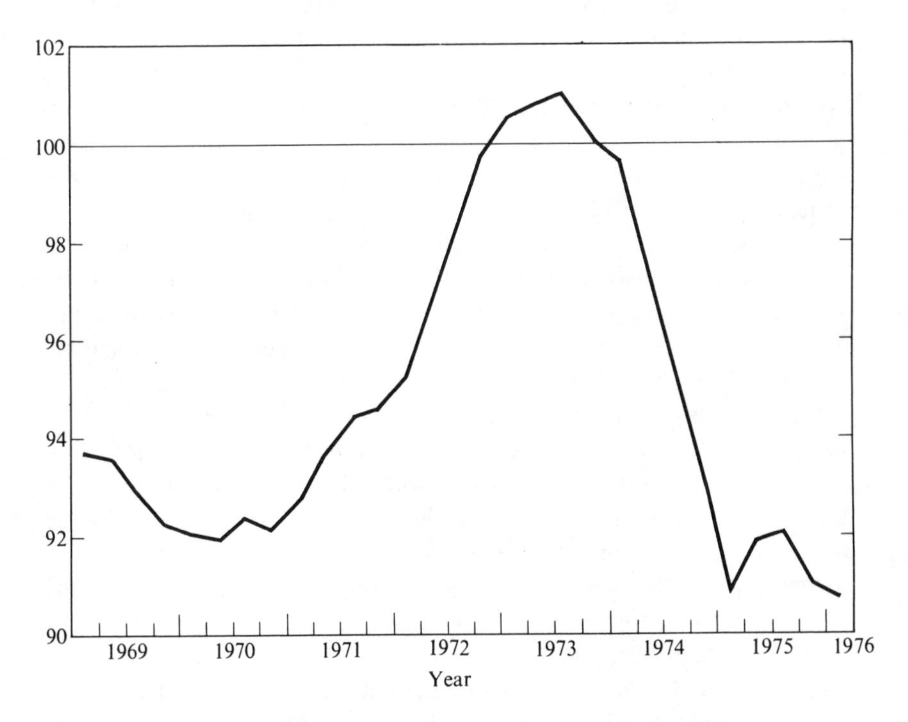

Figure 6.3 Real Money Balances, Quarterly, 1969–76 (1973 IV = 100)
NOTE: Ratio of money stock excluding time deposits to private nonfarm GNP deflator.

rates, as compensation to lenders for the depreciation in the purchasing power of dollar securities. To that extent the rise in nominal interest rates reduced the demand for money balances and offset the tightening effect of the actual reduction in real balances on the economy. But it seems unlikely that a full adjustment of interest rates to the change in the inflation rate occurred so quickly. The subsequent fall in aggregate demand points to a decline in real balances *below* their desired level. This decline contributed to the tightening of financial markets, to the rise in interest rates, and thus to the deepening contraction in economic activity in the fourth quarter of 1974 and the first quarter of 1975.

What could policymakers do about the decline in real money balances? Monetary growth cannot affect real balances in the long run, since economic behavior adjusts them to the desired level as determined by public preferences, GNP, interest rates, and other variables. But when actual real balances deviate from the desired level in the short run, monetary growth can have an effect on real balances by bringing them closer to the desired level or by influencing the desired level itself through effects on GNP and interest rates. In 1973–74 a speedup in nominal monetary growth could have counteracted the effect of the rise in prices in reducing real balances. That would have kept the balances at the desired level and have prevented the subsequent contractionary adjustments in aggregate demand.

To have expanded monetary growth, however, would have precluded any resistance to the outburst of inflation. The Federal Reserve authorities favored the standard response of monetary restraint. Monetary growth excluding time deposits remained around 6 percent per year through most of 1973 and early 1974, down from around 7 percent for most of the second half of 1972 (see figure 6.4). It is likely that the authorities desired even slower monetary growth in early 1974 but compromised in an effort to hold back the sharp rise in interest rates. The authorities revealed their preferences by reducing monetary growth after midyear when interest rates finally fell. In the second half of 1974 monetary growth dropped to 4 percent per year, resulting in a further reduction in real balances. The mild business recession which began at the end of 1973 became severe in the fourth quarter of 1974 with a precipitous decline of industrial production—12 percent in six months. The decline in growth of the money stock does not itself appear sufficient to have precipitated such a severe downturn in activity, and the large reduction in the real value of money balances also apparently contributed.

In 1974 one problem for policymakers was the unusually confusing business picture in the first three quarters. At first the mild decline in output seemed to result from production cutbacks necessitated by the oil embargo from October 1973 to March 1974. Despite declining real final sales for the national economy after a peak in the third quarter of 1973, inventory accumulation was extremely large. The rapid increases in crude materials prices engendered fears of shortages, and users of crude materials sought large inventories as insurance against supply shortages and as a speculation on further price

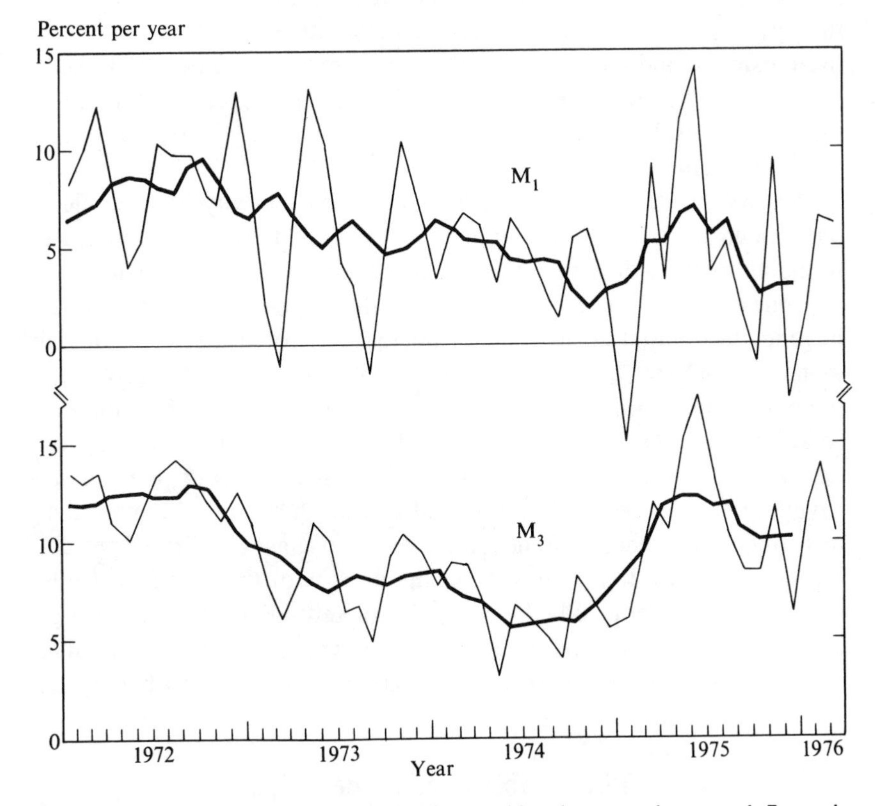

Figure 6.4 Monetary Growth, 1972–76 (monthly change and centered 7-month average at annual rates)

NOTE: M_1 is currency outside banks plus demand deposits at commercial banks. M_3 is M_1 plus time deposits at commercial banks other than large negotiable CDs plus deposits at thrift institutions and credit unions.

increases. In the three quarters from the fourth quarter of 1973 to the second quarter of 1974, inventory investment was two-thirds larger in real terms than in the preceding three quarters when sales were still expanding. The inventory accumulation could not have been primarily an unintended result of a shortfall in sales. The accumulation was much larger than could conceivably be attributed to estimates of higher sales. It turned out to be excessive, and suddenly in the fourth quarter of 1974 the inventory overhang seemed to be recognized as unnecessary, unprofitable, and oppressive, so that purchases for stock, new orders, and production all plummeted. As these events were unfolding, President Ford held his conference of experts and public opinion leaders to discuss policies to curb inflation. For ill-timing, this matches President Truman's strictures against inflation in the closing months of 1948 as the economy, it became clear later, was sliding into recession. A big difference, however, was that, although wholesale prices declined sharply in the 1948–49 recession, they kept rising rapidly in the recession of 1973–75.

As the depth of the decline in business activity became clear by the end of 1974, some commentators[8] called for a large increase in monetary growth to make up the reduction in real money balances. But the Federal Reserve was afraid that open market purchases beyond the normal scale of such operations would disrupt financial markets[9] and (by heightening expectations of inflation) worsen the tradeoff between inflation and output. In retrospect the Federal Reserve could have cushioned the decline in real balances and moderated the fall in economic activity, which turned out to be more severe than was desirable. Yet it is also clear that raging inflation distorts and clouds economic developments and makes it difficult to determine a policy that will subdue inflation with the lowest feasible unemployment path. Whether an error in setting policy once recognized can be quickly rectified is not known, but certainly massive shifts in policy are not part of the traditional art of central banking.

The Problem of Price Blips

Blips in the rate of inflation such as the one produced by foreign influences in 1973–74 present a perplexing problem. Should monetary policy ignore or accommodate them? The problem is similar for any exogenous source of inflation—a category which in some views includes union wage demands, administered pricing in concentrated industries, and purchases of scarce commodities in wartime. Only wage pressures have been a serious recurring problem, and then only in a period of excess demand and subsequently when wages catch up with past inflation. The events of 1973–74 introduced foreign influences as a potential source of sudden large price increases which policy has little chance of preventing and which can only be reversed through prolonged restraint on aggregate demand. Foreign trade previously played a small role in the U.S. economy, and such disturbances had not seemed important. World agricultural prices had risen sharply in previous episodes (such as 1920–21 and 1950–51), but the repercussions on the aggregate price level were short-lived and reversible. Although it is not clear when the situation changed, the United States was no longer an isolated economic island. Many countries had long experienced the vicissitudes of foreign trade effects, but, with expanded international trade and with inflation rampant throughout the world, outside influences had become stronger than ever for all countries.

Floating foreign exchange rates, instituted in 1971, in theory insulate the domestic economy from some foreign influences, but they do not solve this problem. The exchange rate accommodates changes in the general price level between countries, but changes in prices of selected traded materials affect relative prices and cannot be offset by movements in exchange rates. If a rise in world prices of crude materials were to increase the value of imports and exports equally, the exchange rate would not change. If imports rose more, the exchange rate, if not held constant by the intervention of governments, would depreciate, reinforcing the effect of world price increases on domestic costs. Only if our exports increased more than our imports would the exchange rate appreciate and offset part of the rise in world prices.

Changes in world prices of crude materials and foods will therefore occasionally initiate cost increases in the economic pipeline and thereby begin to raise domestic prices. If aggregate demand is not raised to allow for a higher price level, the economy will adjust through a long period of slack demand in which other prices rise less rapidly than they otherwise would have until the price level as a whole falls in line with the unchanged path of aggregate demand. If the trend of prices is otherwise upward, the level need never actually decline, but its rate of increase would have to slow for a while after the initial spurt.

To avoid the effects of such an adjustment on output and employment, monetary policy could accommodate the growth path of aggregate demand to price blips. An accommodative policy raises aggregate demand to absorb the price blip, allowing a higher rate of price increase temporarily to attain a higher level of prices, after which the special influence ends and the inflation rate is again determined by domestic conditions. In 1973 and 1974 this appeared to mean an extra 10.5 percent growth in the money stock, since the foreign influences raised prices by approximately that amount. The argument for such an accommodation is that policy is confronted with a *fait accompli*. The fundamental problem is that cost increases pass through the price system rapidly while the offsetting effect of deficient demand works slowly. Policy cannot stop the cost increases from passing through to prices and can subsequently reverse the effect on prices, therefore, only by a prolonged period of restraint.

While avoiding the loss of output from slack demand, a policy of accommodation subjects prices to higher and higher levels with every upward blip, unless downward blips occur with the same frequency and can be accommodated with equal ease. Most materials prices fluctuate up and down with considerable volatility but are partly offsetting and do not ordinarily affect the general level of prices. But 1973 showed that coordinated movements can occur on a scale that provides strong upward pressure on the general price level. Perhaps if prices and wages were more flexible these increases would not become embedded in the price structure and would be easily reversed. But we do not expect them to be reversed or to be offset by downward blips, in part because policy steps in to prevent deflationary episodes and in part because market participants do not expect deflation and behave in such a way as to reduce its likelihood. In this way the price system has become increasingly prone to inflation.

We cannot simply adopt the rule of accommodating every blip that comes along, however. Some price increases, though interpreted as an exogenous development, could result in part from prior monetary growth and, if accommodated, would lead to a self-reinforcing inflationary process. Since the origin of price increases is not always an easy matter to determine, such an outcome is a distinct possibility. There is also the matter of implementation. Which price increases are to be accommodated? Some would soon reverse themselves if not accommodated, since not all commodity prices are equally passed through to manufacturing prices. Policy cannot wait to see the effects on the price level, for to do so would entail the decline in output which an accommodative policy is intended to avert. The main problem of accommodating blips, however, is that such a policy would almost certainly result in a higher rate of inflation in the long run. It would mean that every rise in the relative price of certain commodities would require a rise in the entire price level. The rise in the price level would perhaps even induce a further rise in the initiating commodity price (as by an oil cartel) in order for that price to maintain its higher level relative to all other prices, subjecting the initial rise to a multiplier effect. The resulting higher trend of prices over the long run could not fail to affect expectations of the average inflation rate and so make basic commodity prices influenced by speculation quicker to rise when any disturbance occurred.

Yet a hard line according to which disturbances are not allowed to raise the long-run price trend will prove equally difficult to follow. The foreign price increases in 1973–74 reduced real money balances and contributed to the severity of the recession. Because of the difficulty of reducing the underlying inflation rate, it does not seem likely that policy can be sufficiently restrictive to reverse the foreign influences, inasmuch as reversal would require that the price level end up no higher than it would have been had these influences never occurred. Monetary policy had been seeking a reduction of the inflation rate, yet there was no intention and little likelihood of *reversing* the effects of the 1973–74 foreign price increases on the domestic price level.

To avoid the long-run inflationary consequences of accommodation, a middle course would be to accommodate unusual price blips, but no more frequently than the occurrence of past wartime inflations, and force the economy to adjust to all others through changes in relative prices and not in the general level. This would require that outbursts of world inflation as in 1973 be rare occurrences. Given the U.S. contribution to world monetary developments, control of domestic demand pressures could help dampen the future development of world inflationary pressures. But if the pressures continue, it is doubtful that any country can cut itself off from their domestic influence. A middle course of not accommodating most world inflationary disturbances will not, therefore, be easy to pursue.

7

Recovery from the Recession of 1973–1975

The steep decline in economic activity hit bottom in the first quarter of 1975. With the aid of expanded monetary growth and a tax reduction and rebates, most of the inventory paring ended and the economy turned around. The rebound was vigorous. Real GNP rose at an annual rate of 8.5 percent in the second half of the year. Excess capacity, however, remained large (about 30 percent), and unemployment was still above 8 percent at year-end.

With the recovery well under way in the second half of 1975, attention turned to the appropriate policies for a strong expansion that would reduce the large unemployment without at the same time interfering with a further decline in inflation. In the prevailing view, the unemployment and inflation goals were not considered in conflict, because the business trough had been so low that two years of strong expansion would not remove all the excess capacity in the economy. So long as a return to excess demand was avoided, inflation would decline as cost increases from past excess demand worked their way through the price system and eventually petered out. Strong fiscal and monetary stimulants were widely proposed, since without them most forecasters saw a sluggish recovery. Despite the strong rebound in the third and fourth quarters of 1975, forecasts at the end of that year predicted a relatively slow recovery of 6 percent growth in real GNP for 1976 and less in subsequent years, a forecast with which the administration concurred. For such a path, unemployment would remain above 7.5 percent through 1976 and 1977.[1]

Adapted from an essay originally published in William Fellner, ed., *Contemporary Economic Problems*, pp. 17–53. Washington, D.C.: American Enterprise Institute, 1976.

The arguments for expanding monetary growth given in early 1975 could be applied equally to the 1976 recovery. If the momentum of rising prices at 6 to 7 percent per year had been built into the economy for the year ahead, as was generally believed, outstanding money balances would depreciate at that rate without having much immediate effect on the rate of inflation. On this line of reasoning, the best policy was for the money stock to grow at a rate sufficient to provide for short-run growth in real balances and output. Then, as the inflation rate gradually moderated, growth in the money stock could be reduced commensurately. Without growth in real balances in the short run, however, the drag on aggregate demand would for some time depress output rather than the inflation rate. Alarm was sounded in the press that without adequate stimulus the recovery could be aborted.

Proponents of this view were ready to admit that, in past cyclical recoveries, output expanded faster than real balances. The typical increase in velocity (ratio of GNP to the money stock excluding time deposits) had been 6 percent in the first year of recoveries since 1954, though less in the second year. The forecast of 6 percent growth in real GNP implicitly assumed such a rise in velocity in 1976. But many critics found this outcome unsatisfactory and wanted faster growth in output to remove the excess unemployment within two years. Some called for 10 percent or more output growth in the first year.[2] With built-in inflation of 6 to 7 percent, that meant 16 to 17 percent growth in dollar GNP. This implied monetary growth of 10 percent if velocity rose the typical 6 percent, and it was thought that velocity might rise much less (its first-year recovery from the 1970 recession had been 2.5 percent). Velocity did rise at a surprising 10 percent annual rate in the second half of 1975. But the rapid rise reflected an initial spurt from a deep recession and was thought unlikely to continue. Moreover, some argued that a further rapid rise in velocity was not all to the good, because such a rise usually came about through a rise in interest rates. With the large projected Treasury deficit, a sharp rise in interest rates would crowd out private investment and partially offset the fiscal stimulus—and many thought the administration budget provided insufficient stimulus to begin with. To avoid this crowding-out, some proposed that stable interest rates be made the target and high monetary growth (10 percent or more) be made the means to achieve vigorous business recovery.[3]

The Federal Reserve was sympathetic to those who wanted stable interest rates but was not prepared to pursue such high monetary growth. In May 1975 and subsequently during the year, it announced a target growth path for monetary growth between 5 and 7.5 percent for the year ahead[4] in line with monetary growth in 1973 and the first half of 1974. This target allowed for virtually no rise in real money balances until inflation slowed considerably.

Economic events have a way of giving an ironic twist to the best-laid proposals of economists. During the second half of 1975, financial markets were unexpectedly easy despite the spurt in output and the large Treasury deficit, and interest rates generally declined. The Federal Reserve refrained from pursuing monetary expansion aggressively, and monetary growth actually fell below the announced target. Monetary growth slowed in the second half and rose only 4.5 percent for the year.

Usually interest rates rise in a business recovery, and proponents of a stable interest-rate target then call for faster monetary growth to hold down the rising rates. On the other hand, those who believe that monetary growth should be kept stable argue for the contrary policy—not to accommodate the expanding demand for credit but to allow interest rates to be pulled up by market forces. Events in the second half of 1975 upset both views. Proponents of stable interest rates, who wanted a vigorous recovery, could not by the logic of their position criticize the low monetary growth so long as interest rates did not rise. Proponents of stable monetary growth, who were leery of overstimulating the economy through overfast monetary growth, had in consistency to urge that interest rates be reduced further in keeping monetary growth from falling below the target. The Federal Reserve could relish the confusion visited upon its critics on both flanks.

Under the circumstances in 1975, it appeared that the decline in rates reflected a weak demand for inventory and capital financing, more than offsetting the effects of the large Treasury borrowing. (Treasury securities may also have gained new takers who had become wary of municipal offerings as a result of New York City's well-publicized difficulties.) To counter a decline in business borrowing, the appropriate policy was to reduce interest rates even further by maintaining or even raising the original monetary growth path. In that event stable monetary growth was closer to a stimulative policy than was the actual growth or the growth which a stabilization of interest rates would have produced.

The 4.2 percent growth of money excluding time deposits (M_1) in 1975 was not viewed by the Federal Reserve as a departure from its announced policy. Although the M_1 growth was low, the growth rates of the other monetary aggregates stayed on target. M_3, for example, grew 12 percent to meet its targeted range of 10 to 12 percent (see figure 6.4). The divergence of M_1 from target was attributed to a shift in public preference from checking accounts to savings deposits, to which the slowing of M_1 growth was an appropriate accommodation. Partial support for this interpretation came from a November 1975 change in Federal Reserve regulations—a change that allowed businesses to acquire and hold savings deposits with commercial banks. A survey estimated that $2 billion in savings deposits had been subsequently acquired. In line with this interpretation, the Federal Reserve widened its M_1 target in February 1976 for the year ahead to 4.5 to 7.5 percent and kept its targets for the other aggregates unchanged.[5]

After the initial rebound, the recovery in business activity became sluggish. In 1976 real GNP rose 4.7 percent, and M_1 growth of 6.0 percent stayed within the Federal Reserve's target. Unemployment remained high. As is typical of slow recoveries, however, the pace gradually quickened. In 1977 real GNP rose 5.9 percent, and monetary growth advanced to 7.7 percent. Unemployment began to decline after midyear and fell to 6.5 percent by year-end and then to 6 percent in early 1978. It was clear after mid-1977 that the economy was advancing smartly, and it was not too early for policy to tighten the reins. But the administration was mainly concerned during 1977 over continued slack in the economy and proposed a tax reduction in the 1978 budget as a fiscal stimulus to aggregate demand. The administration's concern switched to inflation during the first half of 1978, however, as the acceleration of price increases during the winter months gave indication that the underlying rate of inflation was again on the rise.

During 1975 and 1976 inflation had declined sharply from the high rates of 1974. The rise in the consumer price index (December to December) had been 12.7 percent in 1974 but only 7 percent in 1976 and 1977. The underlying rate in 1977 was thought to have been 6 percent and to have been temporarily raised to 7 because of the bulge during the severe winter months. A 6 percent rate was still almost double that reached in 1972 before the 1973–74 outburst. Forecasts made at the beginning of 1978 saw no decline in the underlying rate of 6 percent during that year and were scaled upward as the year unfolded. It appeared that all the reduction in inflation that was to be achieved from the 1973–75 recession and the ensuing mild recovery had already occurred by the end of 1975.

Judging by the 1969–70 and 1973–75 recessions, a contraction in economic activity cuts the inflation rate reached at the preceding business peak roughly in half before the next cyclical expansion raises it again. Whether the inflation rate rises or declines on average from one business cycle to the next depends upon how high it is carried by each business expansion. So far since 1965 the effect on the inflation rate of the succession of overheated cyclical expansions had outweighed the effect of the intervening cyclical contractions. Until that pattern was broken, inflation would persist and probably intensify.

Part III

Policy Issues

8

The Reduction of Inflation and the Magnitude of Unemployment

This chapter discusses three long-standing propositions that weaken the case for the maintenance of a firm anti-inflationary policy in the management of aggregate demand. The first proposition is that unemployment rates of recent years are excessivly high according to the full-employment standard. The second is that inflation is the cost we incur to keep unemployment lower than it would otherwise be. And the third is that the total amount of unemployment produced by a reduction in the inflation rate is less if inflation is reduced slowly. The first proposition requires revision in the light of new estimates of the full-employment rate. The second two propositions are based on the assumed shape of the Phillips curve, but it can support only one or the other of them, not both.

Why Is the Unemployment Rate So High?

The overall unemployment rate declined from a high of 8.9 percent in May 1975, remained at about 7.9 percent during the second half of 1976, and fell by the end of 1977 to 6 percent. From an historical perspective these rates are high (see figure 8.1). In 1948 the overall unemployment rate was between 3.5 and 4 percent, and during the Korean War period it fell as low as 2.5 percent. Since then its trend

Adapted from an essay originally published in William Fellner, ed., *Contemporary Economic Problems 1977,* pp. 15–52. Washington, D.C.: American Enterprise Institute, 1977.

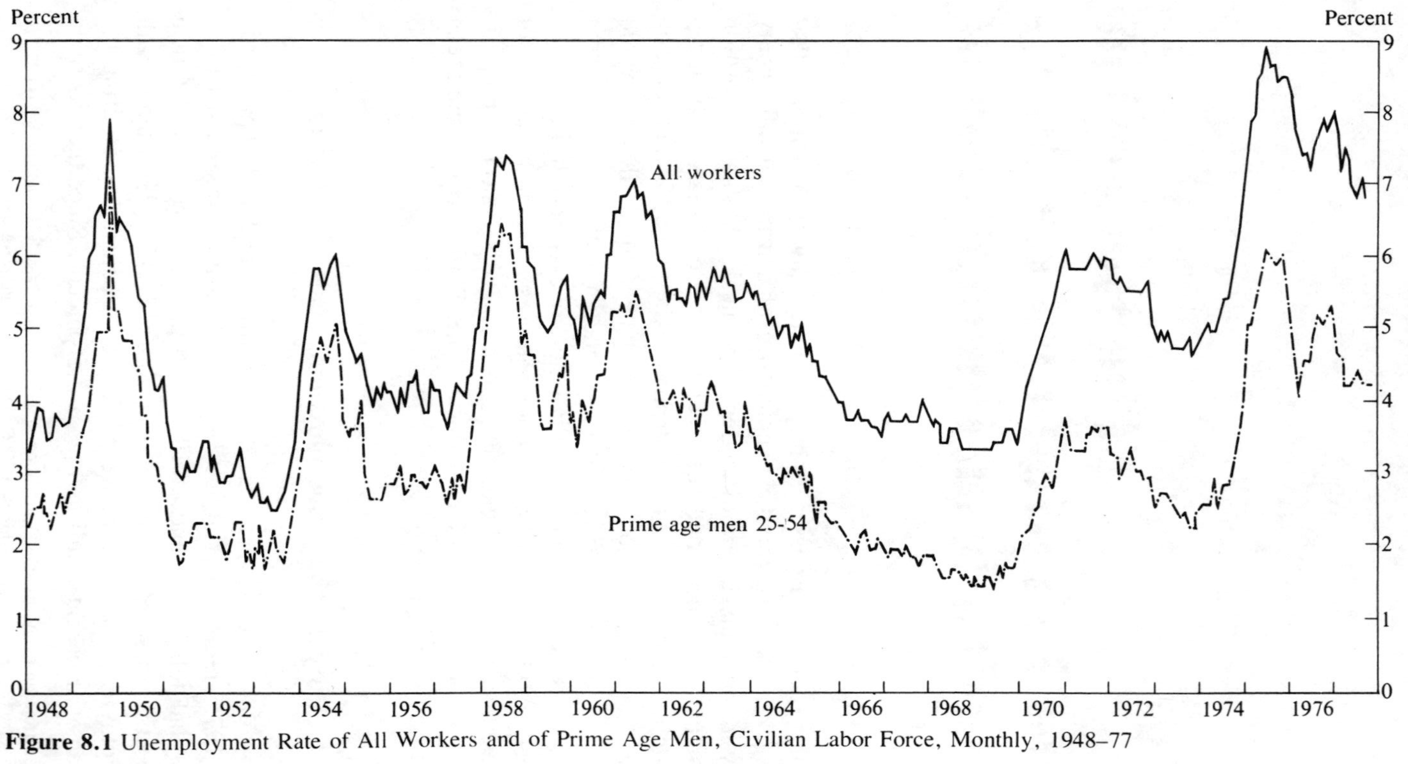

Figure 8.1 Unemployment Rate of All Workers and of Prime Age Men, Civilian Labor Force, Monthly, 1948–77

has been upward. In the early 1960s, when the rate varied between 5 and 6 percent except during the 1960–61 recession, the Kennedy administration chose a 4 percent rate as its interim target.[1] This level of unemployment was thought at that time to reflect a conservative definition of prosperity, since a 3.5 percent rate had been surpassed in the early 1950s and had almost been achieved at the cyclical peak of 1957. In fact, the 3.5 percent rate was often spoken of as the full-employment rate to be achieved after reaching the interim target. The economy finally achieved a 4 percent rate in December 1965 (along with the first signs of inflation) and then a 3.5 percent rate in the second half of 1968, though by then inflation had become rampant.

The 4 percent rate was enshrined as a goal of public policy despite an inability to attain it without inflation or since January 1970 even with inflation. Federal budget projections made at the beginning of 1975 targeted a decline in unemployment to 4 percent over the ensuing four-year period. The government based projections of potential output and of revenues on the 4 percent rate. In fact, as late as 1977, the Humphrey-Hawkins bill before Congress reaffirmed the government's commitment to 4 percent unemployment. In the same year, however, the Council of Economic Advisers acknowledged that the full-employment rate had changed. In its annual report for 1977, the Council reviewed the evidence and said that the full-employment rate was then at least 4.9 percent and perhaps as high as 5.5 percent. Previously professional economists outside the government had also been reluctant to become bearers of the unpopular tidings that the full-employment rate was higher than had been thought.

Unemployment is a focus of public concern and the most widely publicized indicator of economic conditions. It is important to set and pursue policies which keep the social waste of undesired unemployment at a minimum. But unemployment is also central to the control of inflation through the management of aggregate demand, because the unemployment rate cannot be pushed below a critical level without creating additional inflationary pressures. The level at which the inflation rate begins to rise may be considered a practical definition of full employment. The critical level changes over time because of demographic trends and government manpower programs. It might be reduced through programs to help those seeking work qualify for the jobs available or find new jobs more quickly, but it cannot be reduced permanently by stimulating aggregate demand.

Unfortunately, manpower programs have been largely unsuccessful in reducing unemployment, and efforts to achieve the elusive 4 percent goal have fallen by default upon demand management without much consideration of feasibility.

The Noninflationary Rate of Unemployment in 1956

An unemployment goal of 4 percent was chosen because that was the rate attained in the 1950s when inflationary pressures were purportedly absent. However, the rate of unemployment at which inflation tends to be unchanging has been consistently higher than 4 percent. Estimates are presented in chapter 9 of the unemployment rate for prime-age men that corresponds to an unchanging rate of inflation. These estimates are on the order of 3.5 percent. This can be translated into a 1950s rate for overall unemployment: in the period May 1955 to August 1957, when both rates were roughly constant, the overall rate averaged 1.1 percentage points higher than the rate for prime-age men. Therefore, a noninflationary unemployment rate of 3.5 percent for the latter group corresponds to an overall unemployment rate of 4.6. A similar estimate was obtained by Modigliani and Papademos using a conventional Phillips curve with the inflation rate as the left-side variable.[2] They estimated the overall unemployment rate which is noninflationary to be 4.8 percent in 1956. Consequently, the 4 percent target rate turns out to be too low even for 1956 if full employment is to be noninflationary. It should be emphasized that, at this noninflationary rate of unemployment, the inflation rate, while neither increasing nor decreasing, may be at any level.

Based on a 4 percent or even a 4.8 percent rate, the 1976 unemployment rates close to 8 percent appeared to be unusually excessive. Yet evidence indicates that the full-employment rate of unemployment is now much higher than the rate applicable to 1956. The explanation is twofold: first, the proportion of people who frequently move in and out of the labor force has grown; second, the government has expanded programs which encourage workers to remain unemployed longer or discourage employers from hiring inexperienced workers.

Changes in the Composition of the Labor Force

Women and young workers have altered the composition of the labor force. The proportion of women in the labor force has increased from 31 percent in 1956 to 40 percent in 1976. This increase reflects a rise in their participation rate from 37 to 48 percent and a decline in this rate for older men. The proportion of young workers aged sixteen to twenty-four in the labor force has increased from 17 percent in 1956 to 24 percent in 1976 because of demographic trends. Both women and young workers tend to experience frequent periods of unemployment as they enter, leave, and reenter the labor force and shift between jobs in search of better opportunities. In the high-employment year of 1973, men between the ages of twenty-five and fifty-four had an unemployment rate of 2.5 percent, whereas women had a 6.0 percent rate and young workers had a 10.5 percent rate. The overall unemployment rate has therefore been rising with the relative growth of those groups in the labor force subject to higher unemployment. As shown in figure 8.1, the unemployment rate for prime-age men has a more or less flat trend.

If we compare the data for 1956 and 1973, both years of strong demand and vigorous business activity, the unemployment rate was higher in 1973 by 0.7 percentage points, not only because the groups with high unemployment rates had grown in relative size, but also because their respective unemployment rates had increased relative to those for prime-age men. To focus solely on the change in composition of the labor force, we may calculate the 1973 rate supposing that subgroups classified by sex and age had the same unemployment rates as in 1956. This hypothetical 1973 rate is higher than the 1956 rate by 0.46 percentage points, attributable to the change in the composition of the labor force.[3]

Women and young workers also account for a greater fluctuation in the size of the labor force.[4] As job prospects decline during a period of business contraction, many of these workers leave the labor force, to return en masse when conditions improve. This phenomenon results in the "hidden" unemployment which is not included in the regular unemployment rate, though many workers may intend to make such periodic withdrawals from employment and synchronize them with fluctuations in labor demand. In any event, this makes the labor-force participation rate fluctuate more over the course of the business cycle. One reason for the high unemployment rates in 1974–75 is that women did not withdraw from the labor force to the same degree that they had during previous business contractions. It is an open question whether these greater fluctuations in the size of the labor force have affected the average rate of measured unemployment over the length of the business cycle. They nonetheless seem unimportant so far as changes in the full-employment rate are concerned.

In addition to compositional changes in the labor force, long-run increases in the unemployment rates of the various subgroups have also affected the overall rate. Most of these long-run increases appear not to be related to aggregate demand but instead to be related to changes in the behavior of workers. In part they reflect changes in life styles which are difficult to quantify, and in part they reflect the introduction and expansion of government programs which have quantifiable effects on unemployment.

Unemployment Insurance

This is one of the largest programs affecting unemployment. Expansions of the insurance program to cover more workers or to add benefits or to allow more lenient acceptance of claims has tended to raise unemployment in various ways: First, such expansions make it easier for more workers to search longer for attractive jobs. Second, covered industries that meet cyclical or seasonal demands tend to hire more workers at the same pay (the industries do not bear the full cost of the insurance), then to lay them off more frequently for temporary periods.[5] Third, sporadic workers such as students and seasonally employed workers can claim unemployment benefits during nonworking periods and be counted as unemployed, whereas previously they either took jobs or dropped out of the labor force at such times. Fourth, the earned-income limitation of social security increases the number of retired people who work part of the year and claim unemployment benefits for the remainder (social security payments are not affected by unemployment benefits, and only thirteen states reduce or deny unemployment benefits to retired persons on social security).

These effects of unemployment insurance will be greatest when take-home earnings forgone are lowest relative to unemployment compensation (which is not taxed), that is, in the case of low-paid workers and of those in high marginal tax brackets, such as married workers with well-paid spouses. Thus the greater number of women in the labor force increases unemployment as they take advantage of unemployment insurance to accept and leave jobs and be unemployed more often, and as their husbands remain longer between jobs.

Lacking comprehensive studies of these effects on unemployment rates, we may make rough estimates of the changes from 1956 to 1973. The effects of increases in coverage and benefits alone have been fairly small. The proportion of the labor force covered by unemployment insurance was 64.2 percent in 1956 and 78.8 percent in 1973, an increase of 14.6 percentage points.[6] Estimates of the effect on unemployment of this increase in coverage can be derived from the effect on the duration of unemployment, which can then be translated into unemployment rates. One estimate of this effect is that the duration of unemployment in 1968 increased 1.1 weeks for each $10.00 of additional benefits.[7] The $10.00 was 7.9 percent of gross weekly earnings in covered employment in 1968. The same 7.9 percent of weekly earnings of covered workers in 1973 was $12.95, when average weekly benefits were $59.00 or 4.6 times greater. According to the cited effect for the group surveyed in 1968, therefore, average benefits in 1973 would increase the duration of unemployment for the newly covered unemployed by (1.1 × 4.6) five weeks. In 1973 an average of 101,000 workers began receiving unemployment payments each week under state programs. Hence, the estimated increase in the 1973 unemployment rate due to the expansion of coverage since 1956 is:

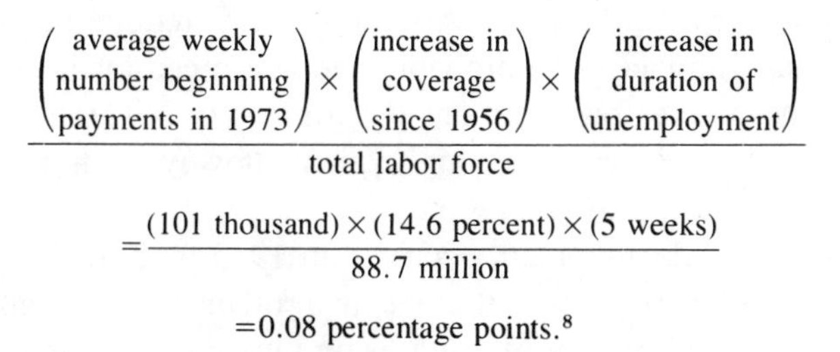

$$\frac{\begin{pmatrix}\text{average weekly}\\ \text{number beginning}\\ \text{payments in 1973}\end{pmatrix} \times \begin{pmatrix}\text{increase in}\\ \text{coverage}\\ \text{since 1956}\end{pmatrix} \times \begin{pmatrix}\text{increase in}\\ \text{duration of}\\ \text{unemployment}\end{pmatrix}}{\text{total labor force}}$$

$$= \frac{(101 \text{ thousand}) \times (14.6 \text{ percent}) \times (5 \text{ weeks})}{88.7 \text{ million}}$$

$$= 0.08 \text{ percentage points.}$$ [8]

This small effect would be reduced to insignificance if we took the increase in duration to be less than five weeks (as suggested by some other studies cited in note 7).

Increases in benefits had an even smaller effect on the unemployment rate. The ratio of benefits to average earnings increased only 2.7 percentage points from 1956 to 1973, and had a negligible effect. The duration of unemployment benefits, however, has at times increased appreciably. The time limit for receiving benefits for each episode of unemployment has generally been twenty-six weeks except in the case of special thirteen week extensions during recessions.

Legislation passed in December 1974 and March 1975 increased the time limit temporarily to sixty-five weeks. This allowed workers who would otherwise have exhausted their benefits after the initial thirty-nine weeks to continue receiving them longer. Such an incentive to remain unemployed increases the overall unemployment rate, but since the extensions generally occur during periods of high unemployment, their effect on the full-employment rate when the actual rate is low will be minor.

In December 1974 federal legislation also extended coverage to 12 million more workers, and by further legislation in 1976 about three-quarters of these workers received permanent coverage under regular state programs.[9] According to the preceding formula and to 1973 figures, this additional coverage increased the unemployment rate at full employment by 0.06 percentage points. This may be an overestimate because these newly covered workers are subject to fewer episodes of unemployment than are the previously covered workers.

These estimates do not take into account the incentive that unemployment insurance gives to workers to incur temporary or seasonal layoffs. The estimates take the incidence of unemployment as given and show only the additions to the overall rate induced by extended coverage and duration. Also, eligibility requirements for unemployment insurance have probably been enforced more leniently in recent years than before, particularly for newly covered workers.[10] These two effects increase unemployment; however, there exists no accurate estimate of how much they increase it.

A special development occurred in 1975 with the extension of coverage to educational institutions and other seasonal industries. Employees took advantage of a provision that allowed unemployment benefits in off months (except for teachers and administrators who had a work contract for the next season). It has been estimated that this development added 0.2 percentage points to the unemployment rate.[11]

The Minimum Wage

This law discourages employers from hiring low-skilled or inexperienced workers, particularly new entrants into the labor force. In 1956 the federal minimum wage was increased to $1.00 per hour or 55.6 percent of average hourly earnings in the private nonfarm sector. By

1973 it had risen to $1.60 and by 1975 to $2.00 per hour, but had declined as a percentage of average hourly earnings in the private nonfarm sector. If we take an average of hourly earnings in major sectors of the economy (excluding the low-wage farm sector), weighted according to the proportion of workers in each sector covered by the minimum wage, we find that the minimum wage as a percentage of this average rose from 30.7 percent in 1956 to 42.6 percent in 1968.[12] This percentage tends to fall from year to year, as nominal and real wage advances whittle away its importance, and to increase in particular years when the minimum wage is raised. The increase in this percentage over the past two decades is probably understated because it does not allow for the rising proportion of young workers in the labor force, a shift in relative supplies of labor which has tended to reduce the average wage of this group relative to that of older workers and to the minimum wage.

For various reasons the effect of the minimum wage is not easy to estimate. First, it affects labor-force participation as well as employment, thus complicating the net effect on unemployment. Second, local minimum wages in some states and cities extend the coverage and in some cases impose a minimum above the federal level. Third, special groups of covered workers can be hired below the minimum wage through exemptions issued by the U.S. Department of Labor.[13] Fourth, compliance with the law is not complete. Fifth, an increase in the minimum wage may take more than a year to have its full impact.

Despite these difficulties, numerous studies in recent years have examined the evidence. Although supporters of the minimum wage used to deny that it increases unemployment, the large rise in the unemployment of young workers is increasingly difficult to disregard as prima facie evidence of such an effect.

In a recent study, Jacob Mincer examined the effect of the minimum wage on employment and labor-force participation separately.[14] He ran time-series regressions from 1954 to 1969 for major subgroups of the labor force. In the regressions various influences on employment and participation are held constant to isolate the effect of minimum wages. We may use Mincer's results to estimate the effects of increases in the ratio of the minimum to average wages from 1956 to 1973. The estimated increase in the unemployment rate was 3.0 percentage points for white teenagers (ages sixteen to nineteen), 5.7

for nonwhite teenagers, 0.8 for young white men (ages twenty to twenty-four), 1.6 for young nonwhites, and 0.2 for white women twenty years of age and over. With the increase in the minimum wage to $2.00 per hour in 1974 the cumulative effects on unemployment were larger.[15] These groups were the only ones for whom Mincer found statistically significant effects. Considering only these groups, the combined effect on the overall unemployment rate was to raise it from 1956 to 1973 by 0.43 percentage points and to 1974 by 0.63 points.[16]

Although Mincer's estimates for employment are similar to those of other studies,[17] his estimates for unemployment are not comparable with those of other studies. Most other studies do not analyze the effect of the minimum wage on labor-force participation separately as Mincer does, an effect which counteracts the employment effect of the minimum wage on unemployment. Other studies examined unemployment directly and did not find an important influence. Mincer's method seems more reliable than those of the other studies,[18] but it could lead to overestimates of the effect of minimum wages. Mincer's estimates may have spuriously incorporated many other influences on young workers which were not allowed for separately. These other influences include increases in job turnover due to less job experience, which results when longer schooling delays permanent work until an older age; increased seasonal employment of the student population induced by the expansion of unemployment insurance; and so forth. Since all of these influences, together with the minimum wage, raise the full-employment rate of unemployment, it is not inappropriate to include them here. Indeed, it is not unreasonable to conclude that all of the rise in unemployment rates of young workers and women relative to the rate for prime-age men occurred for reasons other than a change in aggregate demand. The lower figures given above, however, have the virtue of being estimates of a specified effect.

Other Effects on Unemployment

Other special effects on the unemployment rate may be noted. First, legislation in 1972 required welfare mothers who were able to work to register for work. Some found jobs, but many were added to the unemployment rolls. Subsequent to this legislation their measured unemployment rate increased by 5.8 percentage points.[19] This increase added 0.2 percentage points to the overall unemployment rate. Also, work registration requirements for various other programs, such as food stamps, have become potentially important in raising the measured unemployment rate, but it is not yet possible to determine the magnitude of their effect.

Affecting unemployment in the other direction, federal manpower programs administered by the Department of Labor had an average monthly enrollment of 700,000 in 1973. The effect on unemployment is not clear, since many of the enrollees would otherwise have had jobs or have remained out of the labor force. We might suppose that 25 percent of this number would otherwise have been unemployed. If so, this effect would have reduced the overall unemployment rate in 1973 by 0.2 percentage points. This reasoning underlies Alfred Tella's estimate that such an effect accounted for a reduction in unemployment in 1976 by 0.3 points.[20]

Finally, the measurement of unemployment is subject to response error. Tella has examined response error in the unemployment survey and concludes that the reported unemployment rate understates the rise during periods of high unemployment, recently by as much as 0.75 percentage points, but in times of low unemployment the reported rate shows much less error. His estimate of this understatement is 0.2 percentage points for 1956 and 0.3 points for 1973; consequently, the net effect over two decades has been to reduce the reported rate by 0.1 percentage points.[21]

Summary of Structural Effects on Unemployment

Table 8.1 lists the influences on unemployment for which estimates, however rough, were made above. It indicates that the unemployment rate in 1977 was 1.2 percentage points higher than it was in 1956 for comparable levels of aggregate demand. The 4.1 percent average for 1956 increased to 5.3 percent. It should be emphasized that this is an estimate of the full-employment rate, that is, it does not take into account any additional effects that occur in periods of less than full employment because of extensions of unemployment benefits and special manpower programs. For example, the time limit extension of unemployment benefits in 1975 by twenty-six weeks added, according to one estimate,[22] over one-half of a percentage point to the unemployment rate.

The 1.2 percentage point increase in the full-employment rate

Table 8.1 Estimates of Structural Changes in the Full-Employment Unemployment Rate, 1956–1977 (in percentage points)

Source of Change	*To 1973*		*Change 1974–77*
Change in composition of labor force[a]	+.46		
Extension of unemployment insurance			
Coverage to 1973[b]	+.08		
Seasonal workers in 1975[c]			+.2
Nine million new workers in 1976[d]			+.06
Increase in minimum wage[e]	+.30		+.15
Interaction with composition[f]	+.13		+.05
Work registration of welfare mothers[g]	+.2		
Manpower programs[h]	−.2		−.1
Response error[i]	−.1		
Total	+.87		+.36
Combined total		+1.23	

NOTE: Derivation and sources given at the following text notes: (a) note 3, (b) note 8, (c) note 11, (d) note 9, (e) note 16, (f) note 16, (g) note 19, (h) note 20, (i) note 21.

since 1956 is probably an understatement. The potential magnitude of yet unestimated influences can be gauged by considering the unemployment rate for prime-age men twenty-five to fifty-four as the indicator of aggregate demand. This rate was lower in 1973 than in 1956 by an average of 0.42 percentage points. In 1973 the overall unemployment rate was 0.72 percentage points higher than it was in 1956, which, when adjusted for the lower prime-age rate, results in an increase since 1956 of (0.72 + 0.42) 1.14 percentage points in the overall rate due to influences other than aggregate demand. That figure is 0.37 percentage points higher than the figure for changes up to 1973 noted in table 8.1. If added to the changes up to 1977, the total increase is (1.23 + 0.37) 1.60 percentage points. Even this figure could be an underestimate, because it still omits a possible structural increase in the unemployment rate for prime-age men, and because it does not consider subsequent developments, such as the increased importance of work registration requirements. It is consistent, however, with other recent estimates which treat the increases for the other groups as due to structural developments.[23]

The fact that labor market developments and federal programs have served to raise the unemployment rate does not make them undesirable. Their overall value is usually assessed on other grounds.

The programs are mainly intended to supplement the income of the unemployed. The growing participation of women in the labor force is widely viewed as desirable and, in any case, reflects social developments over which the government of a free society has no control. Even if the resultant increases in unemployment are viewed as undesirable, the management of aggregate demand cannot appropriately provide a remedy. The purpose of demand management is to regulate aggregate demand so that all workers have job opportunities. Long-term influences on the measured unemployment rate unrelated to deficiencies in aggregate demand should be identified and dealt with in other ways.

The Current Noninflationary Rate of Unemployment

The earlier estimate of a 3.5 percent noninflationary rate of unemployment for prime-age men in 1956 was shown to be equivalent to a rate for all workers of 4.6 percent. Table 8.1 indicates that this rate has increased since then by 1.2 percentage points, and, allowing for omitted influences, it may have increased by 1.6 percentage points. Therefore, the 1977 rate of unemployment at which inflation neither increases nor decreases is 5.8 and perhaps 6.2 percent.

In future years the noninflationary rate of unemployment will probably decline because of a declining proportion of youths in the labor force, and because of a more permanent attachment of women to the labor force that will reduce their job turnover. The measured rate of unemployment could also decline through changes in government programs; for example, tighter administration of unemployment benefits, reduced minimum real wages for youths, and increased enrollment in manpower programs. The rate also might increase in the future through, for example, expanded government programs that are designed to alleviate the distress of joblessness but tend to raise the amount of recorded unemployment.

The overall unemployment rate has more often than not been above the noninflationary rate as well as the 4 percent target rate for the past two decades. Since the low target made the unemployment rates of the past appear to be excessively high, some economists attributed the accompanying prevalence of inflation to an "inflationary bias," by which wage increases push up prices at a moderate rate even when excess unemployment exists.[24] But it is now also clear that we have clung to a goal of full employment which, though more relevant in 1956 than it is today, was unrealistic even then, and which can be achieved only with accelerating inflation. The increase in unemployment to 8.9 percent in the first quarter of 1975 was seen as the worst cyclical increase since the catastrophic 1930s. Measured from a noninflationary level of 5.8 percent, the excess was 3.1 percentage points. Yet the increase in unemployment during the 1957–58 recession to 7.5 percent was a comparable 2.9 points in excess of the noninflationary rate then of 4.6 percent. The mid-1977 unemployment rate of 7 percent was in excess of the noninflationary rate by only one percentage point.

If inflation is to decline, unemployment has to average above 6 percent to maintain sufficient slack in the economy. Trends in the labor force and programs designed to alleviate the distress of unemployment have made the former target of 4 percent inappropriate.[25] Future developments in the labor force and government programs may affect the noninflationary full-employment rate, but for the near term they are as likely to raise as to lower it.

Does Inflation Make Unemployment Higher in the Long Run?

One of the regularly extolled triumphs of modern economics is the development of aggregate demand policies to control business activity. Since World War II the government has pursued monetary and fiscal policies to moderate fluctuations in aggregate demand with a view toward keeping the economy at full employment. The avoidance of a severe depression like the one experienced during the 1930s has been an indication of success, while recurring business recessions with associated fluctuations in unemployment are passed off as due to the difficulties of forecasting and of timing policy actions which improvements in technique will gradually overcome.

During the 1950s it became apparent that stimulation of the economy could result in rising prices and to that extent fail to have the desired effect of reducing unemployment. Nevertheless, for some time inflation was viewed as an annoyance to be endured for the sake of keeping unemployment low. That view was formulated in the famous Phillips curve tradeoff, wherein lower unemployment would require higher inflation. While such a tradeoff has been apparent in the short run, *both* inflation and unemployment rates have been rising in the long run. This anomaly forces a change in how the tradeoff is viewed.

Part of the new view is a recognition that continuing inflation comes to be expected and thereby gets built into the price system. The expected rate of inflation determines the trend rate, which then becomes the base rate for further expansions and contractions. For example, if 5 percent is the expected rate of inflation, prices rise 5 percent at normal levels of production; stimulation of aggregate demand raises the rate above, and recessions reduce it below, 5 percent, but 5 percent remains the average rate of inflation. The expected rate changes slowly as experience suggests a different trend rate. Of course, the trend rate cannot persist unless policy accommodates it by producing corresponding growth on the average in nominal aggregate demand. Policy does so or is expected to do so, because any deficiency in demand results in a short-run increase in unemployment with little initial effect on the inflation rate. While continued restraint eventually reduces inflation, this involves the economy in a long and painful adjustment to slower growth in nominal aggregate demand.

The rising trend of inflation since World War II has reflected, in its simplest terms, the adoption of stimulative policies designed to attain low unemployment that ran the economy up to and too often across the threshold of rising inflationary pressures. Periods of overstimulation resulted in bursts of more rapid price increases and successively raised the trend rate of inflation. As the economy adjusted to higher trend rates, the same unemployment rates were associated with higher inflation rates.

This history helps explain the rising rate of inflation but not that of unemployment. According to the revised view of the Phillips curve, overstimulation reduces unemployment in the short run but has no effect in the long run. The Phillips curve is a relation between excess unemployment and, as modified, the difference between the actual and the expected rate of inflation. It is illustrated in figure 8.2.

Excess unemployment is zero when the actual inflation rate equals the expected rate. Deviations of the actual inflation rate from the expected rate trace a downward sloping curve, showing that restraints on aggregate demand initially increase unemployment and reduce inflation below the expected rate. According to the revised view, although the expected rate changes slowly and is not immediately affected by excess unemployment, a reduction in inflation does lead gradually to a lower expected rate, whereupon actual and expected inflation rates can both be lower and equal when unemployment returns to the full-employment level. Therefore, changes in the inflation and unemployment rates are still viewed as inversely related, but only in the short run. The curve is also usually drawn convex to the bottom axis, which means that for further equal increases in excess unemployment the short-run reductions in the inflation rate are successively smaller. That is, the first one percentage point increase in unemployment may reduce the inflation rate by one percentage point (say), but an additional one point of unemployment further reduces the inflation rate by well less than one point, and so on.

Some changes in the inflation rate, of course, reflect changes in materials costs due to international developments (such as the 1973 increase in oil prices) or to domestic deregulation of a controlled price. These effects on prices do not originate from changes in aggregate demand and so affect unemployment, if at all, in a way different from that described by the Phillips curve. Such effects would be reflected in a discrepancy from the relationship in figure 8.2 that would last until they abated or until the expected rate adjusted to the new rate of inflation.

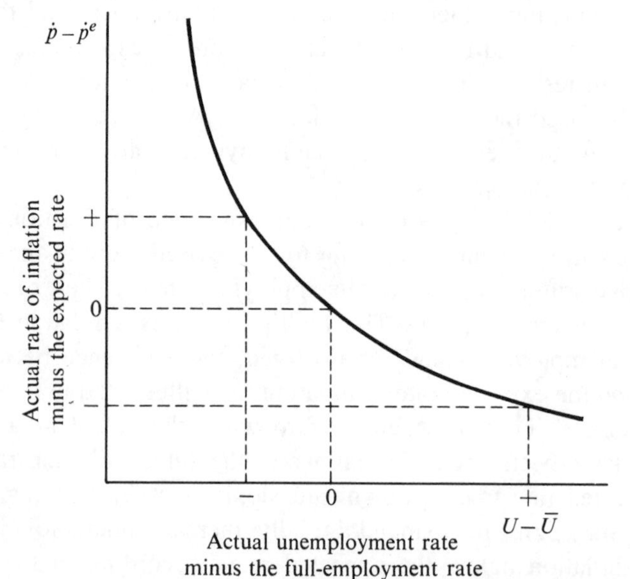

Figure 8.2 The Phillips Curve as the Deviation between Actual and Expected Inflation Rates

Since such disturbances to prices do not directly affect unemployment, and since the inverse relationship depicted in figure 8.2 applies to the short run only, higher rates of inflation which are eventually accompanied by corresponding increases in the expected rate will be associated with the *same* level of unemployment. It is disconcerting, therefore, to note that higher inflation rates since World War II have been accompanied by higher average unemployment rates. Upward trends in unemployment and inflation have also been noted in other Western countries over the past two decades.[26] In the United States changes in the labor force and in government programs are responsible for a rising trend in the full-employment rate. But it is not certain that they account for the entire rise in the average rate of unemployment. Reductions of unemployment after recent recessions have occurred more slowly than after previous recessions. Compare the reductions after 1970 and after 1975 in figure 8.1 with those after 1949, 1954, 1958, and 1960. Unemployment rates during the later business recoveries remained near the high levels of the preceding business recession for longer periods. Such sluggish cyclical recoveries of unemployment tend to make the average unemployment rate over the business cycle higher even if the peak and trough levels reached during the cycle are the same as before.

The reduction of inflation has probably become more difficult than it was two decades ago because expectations of inflation are now firmer and thus force policymakers to impose greater restraint on aggregate demand. In theory, however, firmer expectations do not explain the rising trend of unemployment, because short-run periods of excess unemployment are balanced by periods of low unemployment.

But there is reason to suspect that inflation does result in increased unemployment in the long run, contrary to the short-run relationship. The reason has to do with the observation that higher average rates of inflation have greater variability. This characteristic was typically disregarded in the earlier theoretical literature on inflation in which fluctuations in the rate of inflation were viewed as unimportant. According to that viewpoint, the economy gradually adjusts to the average rate of inflation and is not affected by the magnitude of the rate. Full adjustment of the economy means that the inflation rate is anticipated, that all contracts allow for it, and that inflation itself produces no expected gains or losses, only surprises if the anticipated rate is not realized. Yet experience demonstrates that actual inflation rates are not so easily anticipated. In a cross-section analysis of many countries, a higher average inflation rate is associated with larger short-run fluctuations in the rate.[27] This association has also been apparent in the United States in recent decades.

The increase in the variability of inflation has occurred, despite the intention of governments to avoid or to reduce inflation, because the policies actually pursued have varied considerably with economic circumstances. As a result, the public has come to expect a wide range of possible outcomes, and the behavior of prices is no longer constrained by expectations that actual trends will remain within any particular range. The lack of constraint on expectations affects the complex adjustment system by which prices respond to disturbances and makes the system less stable. Therefore, although monetary and fiscal policies since World War II have been increasingly devoted to stabilizing the economy, they have been less successful in the past decade either because policies were pursued too vigorously and became a source of instability, or because intensifying inflation changed the response of the economy to disturbances. It is not clear whether the disturbances themselves became larger, or whether the response of prices to similar disturbances became larger, or both. Whatever the explanation, the present inflationary environment is volatile with wide swings in the rate of inflation from period to period, where the higher the average rate the wider are the swings.

The higher variability of inflation rates increases uncertainty and lessens the efficiency of the price system in guiding the allocation of resources.[28] Less efficiency means less total output of goods and services. This undesirable effect of inflation is disregarded in much of the literature by the invalid assumption that inflation will gradually be anticipated and adjusted to and then will have no disadvantages. Nevertheless, a reduction in efficiency would not necessarily raise unemployment.

Yet, if the Phillips curve is convex, as is usually assumed, greater variability in inflation rates will produce higher average unemployment. If the inflation rate fluctuates more at higher average rates, and if these fluctuations reflect changes in aggregate demand which also affect unemployment, the increase in unemployment associated with a one-point decline in the inflation rate will be greater than the decrease in unemployment associated with a one-point increase in the inflation rate. This is illustrated by the dotted lines in figure 8.2. Thus, when fluctuations in aggregate demand and the inflation rate are larger, not only are fluctuations in the unemployment rate larger, but the shape of the curve also implies that the *average* unemployment rate will be higher.[29]

Crucial to this argument is the assumed convexity of the Phillips curve. In fact, however, there is little empirical support for any particular shape of the curve. For regression equations of the kind reported in chapter 9, the addition of a quadratic term or reciprocal form of the unemployment rate to show convexity does not add to the explanatory power of the regressions, indicating that the data do not reveal curvature in the relationship.[30] These tests are not conclusive, since the expected inflation rate can be represented in other ways, and since more complicated equations allowing for lagged effects may finally reveal some convexity. Nevertheless, for the range of data observed over the post-World War II period, the shape of the relationship is uncertain.

If convexity could be established, it would suggest that greater inflation has increased the long-run average unemployment rate and that future policy should be conducted more cautiously to avoid producing inflation in the long run. However, the lack of evidence as to the convexity of the Phillips curve leaves uncertain whether the variability of higher average inflation rates has contributed to a long-run rise in unemployment. If the Phillips curve is not convex, the rising trend of unemployment may simply reflect recent policies to reduce inflation and may not be a permanent result of higher inflation rates.

I am inclined to believe that, despite the lack of clear evidence, the Phillips curve is characterized by some convexity. But even without convexity and the implied increase in long-run average unemployment, the costs of inflation are major. The variability of inflation increases uncertainty and interferes with the efficient operation of the economic system. Yet, despite the desirability of reducing inflation, Phillips curve analysis has supported the argument that inflation should be reduced gradually to avoid making the total worker-months of unemployment incurred larger than is necessary. If the curve is not convex, this long-standing policy prescription can be questioned. The convexity of the Phillips curve bears on this issue of policy as well.

Is Gradualism the Best Policy?

Policies to subdue the inflation which began in 1965 have been guided by the principle of gradualism.[31] This principle calls for the imposition of mild restraint on the growth in aggregate demand in order to produce a little slack in the economy, and the endurance of the resulting excess unemployment, until inflation is subdued.[32] In a business recession like that of 1973–75, when the slack in the economy is considered to be far too much, gradualism is consistent with a rapid recovery to reduce economic slack to the desired small amount. Gradualism has been difficult to achieve. Policies designed to produce mild restraint on aggregate demand resulted in a mini-recession in 1967, a mild recession in 1970, and a severe recession in 1973–75. These declines in economic activity were all larger than policymakers considered to be desirable. Gradualism called for smaller declines in economic activity and, consequently, slower reductions of inflation, though the actual reductions of inflation were much slower than was generally expected at the time.

A theoretical justification for the reduction of inflation to be gradual is based on a convex Phillips curve. In figure 8.2, to reduce $\dot{p}$, a policy of restraint holds U above $\bar{U}$, and $\dot{p}$ falls relative to $\dot{p}^e$. A lower actual inflation rate eventually leads to a lower expected rate. If the expected rate adjusts slowly, however, the excess unemployment needed to hold the inflation rate below the expected rate must be endured for a long time. The total unemployment endured can be measured by the time and the amount by which U exceeds $\bar{U}$. Even after $\dot{p}$ is reduced to the desired level, U must still exceed $\bar{U}$ until $\dot{p}^e$ also declines to the desired level. The reduction in $\dot{p}$ is not permanent until $\dot{p}^e$ is also reduced by the same amount. At that point U can return to the level of $\bar{U}$.

If $\dot{p}^e$ adjusts more rapidly, the entire process can be accomplished with less total unemployment. That is why the credibility of a policy to subdue inflation, which can affect $\dot{p}^e$, is important to the success and costs of the policy. The time required to reduce inflation and the optimal policy to adopt depend upon the adjustment speed of expectations and the rate at which excess unemployment dampens inflation. If the inflation rate is held at a given level, changes in the unemployment rate are largely determined by the adjustment speed of expectations and are beyond the control of public policy. But the rate at which policy reduces the inflation rate, given the lags in the system, will influence the amount of unemployment to be incurred in the process.

If the Phillips curve is convex, each successive increase in unemployment is accompanied by a smaller reduction in the inflation rate. A given reduction in the inflation rate can then be achieved with a smaller cost in total unemployment if a mild restraint is applied for a long period than if a strong restraint is applied for a short period. Theoretically, since the least total unemployment is produced by the mildest restraint, the time needed to achieve a desired reduction in inflation approaches infinity. To be realistic, policymakers must select a reasonable time period in which the desired reduction in inflation is to be achieved. A time schedule for reducing inflation is selected which weighs the disadvantages of unemployment against the advantages of reduced inflation.[33] The public concern over unemployment inherited from the 1930s and expressed in the Employment Act of 1946 has until recently outweighed the more remote dangers of uncontrolled inflation. We have therefore tried to subdue inflation gradually by policies of restraint on aggregate demand that were mild in intention if not always in outcome.

If the evidence does not show that the Phillips curve is convex, no basis exists for believing that each successive increase in unemployment is accompanied by a smaller reduction in the inflation rate. If the curve is linear, a given reduction in the inflation rate will result in worker-months of unemployment that sum to the same total whether the reduction is achieved rapidly or slowly, so long as changes in the expected rate of inflation are proportional to the difference between the actual and the expected rate. Then a rapid reduction is preferable, since the disadvantages of inflation are removed sooner.

To be sure, the speed at which we might prefer to reduce inflation has limits even if the Phillips curve is linear over its entire range. A severe depression would be undesirable as a means of subduing inflation, because it could not be properly controlled by policy and the severe unemployment would hit a high proportion of heads of households and become intolerable. However, that is not to say that slow business recoveries may not be a desirable means of reducing inflation as compared with a prolonged period of mild slack in the economy. The latter policy requires an interminable time to reduce inflation and risks setbacks if unforeseen disturbances override the mild restraint and unleash new inflationary pressures. Moreover, the slow rate at which gradualism brings results can cause the public to lose patience and to clamor for other measures which are ultimately ineffective and, in the case of wage and price controls, counterproductive. Based on these arguments, the best anti-inflation policy available lies somewhere between very mild restraint and the opposite extreme.

Assessment of the Policy Alternatives

Post-World War II policies designed to manage aggregate demand have not in general adopted strong anti-inflationary measures in the belief that some inflation had to be allowed in order to keep unemployment low. The first major reassessment of these policies came with the recognition of the role of inflationary expectations. It was realized that a given rate of inflation could not be counted on to stimulate aggregate demand in real terms and increase output and employment. A nominal rise in aggregate demand which is expected has little real effect on the economy. Because output and employment are determined by the expected level of prices and wages in real terms, an effective stimulation of economic activity requires an increase in nominal aggregate demand above the expected increase. An unexpected increase in prices, if continued, will in turn come to be expected, and increasing rates of actual and expected inflation will result from a policy designed to keep unemployment lower than the level at which it settles when actual and expected inflation rates remain equal.

If inflation has no lasting benefit in reducing unemployment, the costs of inflation cannot be so readily brushed aside as they had been when a little inflation was thought to provide considerable benefits. To be sure, if the inflation rate is constant and widely expected, and if the economy adjusts to it completely, the only disadvantage appears to be the inability to compensate holders of currency for the losses in purchasing power due to inflation, which can be dismissed as minor. Inflation might not be a serious concern if it were completely anticipated. But since actual rates of inflation are too volatile to be anticipated with any degree of accuracy, the uncertainty of inflation rates imposes major costs in reduced efficiency of production and resource allocation and in suboptimal saving and investment decisions.

The Phillips curve has served as the theoretical justification for trading off unemployment against inflation in the short run. It is not clear that the objective of keeping unemployment low over the long run is served by focusing on its short-run departures from the full-employment level to the neglect of the long-run consequences, and by primary reliance on the control of aggregate demand to achieve short-run employment targets. Implications of the Phillips curve for long-run employment have been disregarded. The curve is usually thought to be convex, implying that greater variability of inflation rates *increases* average unemployment in the long run—which is a good reason, given the tendency of higher average inflation rates to have greater variability, for avoiding policies that result in long-run inflation.

The evidence on convexity of the Phillips curve is in fact unclear, and the curve may be linear within the range of past experience. A linear curve implies that the long-run average level of unemployment is not affected by the average rate of inflation and its degree of variability. Still, there are other costs of inflation to be avoided, and policymakers remain committed to subduing inflation. Policies have generally been designed to reduce inflation gradually, but they have been pursued erratically and have made disappointing progress. These gradualist policies have been justified by a convex Phillips curve. A linear curve puts a different light on the appropriate degree of restraint. Linearity implies that the cost of reducing inflation in terms of unemployment is the same whether the reduction is rapid or slow. Consequently, a policy that reduced inflation sooner rather than later would be attractive.

The recovery from the 1973–75 recession was widely deplored as being too slow to reduce unemployment. As its first order of business in 1977 the Carter administration proposed additional stimulus to aggregate demand to remove excess unemployment. While the risk of pushing the economy into the zone of increasing inflationary pressures was recognized (and the stimulus was subsequently considered to be unnecessary), strong stimulus was justified at the time by arguing that unemployment was much higher than was needed to reduce inflation. The rationale for this view is based partly on an unrealistically low estimate of the full-employment level of unemployment. But it is also based on the proposition that, while some economic slack serves to reduce inflation slowly, additional slack is comparatively ineffective in reducing it more rapidly.

It is often cynically said that inflation has become inevitable for political reasons because the task of incurring unemployment for the sake of reducing inflation is repeatedly put off for future officeholders to face. What makes that such an unattractive economic policy is that the costs of delaying a reduction of inflation are not compensated by lower overall costs of unemployment. If the Phillips curve is linear, the total unemployment incurred is not reduced by gradualism. If the curve is convex, average unemployment is increased over the long run. Either a convex or a linear Phillips curve justifies, for different reasons, an effective anti-inflationary policy.

9

The Reduction of Inflation by Slack Demand

Current economic policy is directed toward reducing inflation and unemployment. The *Economic Report of the President* in January 1978 states that "We must contain and reduce the rate of inflation as we move toward a more fully employed economy." That has been the unquestioned intention of policy since inflation intensified in 1965, and it was the guiding spirit, even if not always the practical objective, in the previous years since World War II. The method of achieving the objective is to stimulate aggregate demand by monetary and fiscal measures to expand production and jobs up to—but not beyond—the point where new inflationary pressures emerge. The assumption is that it is possible in theory even if difficult in practice to reduce inflation by maintaining some slack in labor and product markets in the aggregate. A period of economic slack is accepted as the cost of subduing inflation.

The maintenance of slack in the economy, with the accompanying excess unemployment, is not, of course, attractive to policymakers. Monetary and fiscal measures designed to reduce inflation result in slack as a by-product, not as an objective, of anti-inflation policy. U.S. policy has faced the dilemma of choosing between inflation and unemployment by targeting a path of aggregate demand which, in deference to political pressures, will produce as little slack as possible and still reduce inflation, even though the reduction of inflation will be slow. The justification for keeping the slack mild and reducing inflation gradually is based on the nature of the assumed

Adapted from an essay originally published in William Fellner, ed. *Contemporary Economic Problems 1978*, pp. 13–43. Washington, D.C.: American Enterprise Institute, 1978.

tradeoff between inflation and unemployed resources. Each addition to the amount of slack is thought to have diminishing effects in reducing the inflation rate. To avoid enduring a large amount of slack for little benefit, therefore, a slow reduction of inflation with mild slack has appeared optimal.[1]

In comparison with the precise objectives of policy, the large discrepancies between the results and the targets, and the wide swings in business activity, have been discouraging. When the Vietnam inflation stepped up in early 1966, it was initially cut down by monetary restraint imposed during the second half of that year. But the monetary authorities, fearful of precipitating a business recession, switched to stimulus in early 1967 and the inflation revived. By 1969 inflation was firmly entrenched and escalating. The monetary restraint applied in 1969 was stronger than in 1966 and this time precipitated a recession in 1970, but the reduction in inflation appeared to be slight up to August 1971 when price and wage controls were imposed. In the meantime, monetary policy stimulated the economy during and following the 1970 recession to remove all but the minimum amount of slack thought sufficient to reduce inflation. The stimulus was carried too far, in part because policy was misled by the umbrella of controls, and by the end of 1972 the overexpansion of domestic aggregate demand was joined by worldwide inflationary pressures to produce an explosion of prices in 1973–74. The ensuing disruption to business activity brought on a severe business contraction from the fourth quarter of 1973 to the first quarter of 1975. The considerable slack remaining in the economy after the contraction was viewed as excessive, and policymakers sought to remove most of it, though the recovery of activity in fact proceeded slowly. Despite policy targets which have consistently called for mild slack in the economy to subdue inflation, the amplitude of fluctuations in activity have been large and increasing. The business contraction of 1973–75 was the most severe since World War II

Although recovery from the 1973–75 contraction was slow and appreciable slack continued at least through the end of 1977, the inflation did not continue to decline (figure 1.1). To be sure, the explosion of prices in 1973–74 reflected in part world influences which proved to be temporary, and the rate of inflation fell sharply during the business contraction. But the average inflation rates for 1976 and 1977, based on the consumer price index, remained in the 5 to 6 percent range, well above the 3.5 percent for 1971–72 and on a par with the previous high rates of 1969–70. At the beginning of 1977 the Council of Economic Advisers predicted that the inflation rate would continue unchanged at 5 to 6 percent for the year, which turned out to be accurate.[2] Inflation rose to higher rates unexpectedly during the severe winter months, but it is not clear whether this made any difference for the year as a whole. The positive deviations of the inflation rate from the basic trend in the winter were subsequently offset by negative deviations later in the year.

The Council's prediction, though correct, departed from the widely accepted view that a slack economy would reduce inflation. The Council chose to ignore previous estimates of the relation between changes in the rate of inflation and excess unemployment based on post-World War II data. These previous estimates had implied that, given the average unemployment rate of 7 percent for 1977, inflation would decline during the year. For 1978 the Council again concluded that, apart from the effect of higher social security taxes and minimum wages, "prices would be expected to rise this year at a rate of 6 percent or somewhat above—the underlying rate for the past 2½ years."[3] Unit labor costs were projected to continue rising at an unchanged rate from 1977, and profit margins did not appear large enough to provide room for a decline which would allow prices to rise less than the rise in unit labor costs. Hence no progress against inflation was seen as likely to occur until these basic trends changed. The Council's projection seemed to imply that inflation would not be reduced by the previously accepted policy of maintaining slack in the economy, nor could inflation even be prevented from increasing in the unlucky event of supply shortages.

The theory that economic slack reduces inflation was unquestioned for over a decade but is no longer widely accepted as viable. In recent years forecasters have predicted little or no decline in inflation despite their predictions of continued slack in the economy. Some prominent economists, doubtful of the desirability of traditional monetary restraints and even of straightforward price and wage controls, proposed a system of taxes and subsidies to induce restraint in wage and price setting.[4] Another prominent economist with experience as a price controls administrator pointed to the regulatory morass and doubtful success of such a system.[5] The fact that these proposals were even seriously considered was a symptom of the low confidence with which the capability of subduing inflation was viewed.

Was the previously widely accepted presumption that the inflation rate is related to the amount of economic slack justified? Casual inspection of the post-World War II data does raise doubts. Apart from the upward trend since 1965, the inflation rate displays a typical pattern within each cycle (figure 1.1). A steep drop in the rate of change during recessions (even below zero in the earlier cycles) is followed by a sharp recovery in the first part of the ensuing business expansion. The recovery in the rate tends to level off in the later stages of expansions and finally to decline, usually before the next downturn in business.[6] This pattern is also characteristic of prices in earlier business cycles.[7]

The two recessions of 1969–70 and 1973–75 display the same pattern but with a delayed peak or trough in the inflation rate. In 1973–75 the rate rose through most of the business contraction; it then declined well into the business recovery, as it did also in 1971–72. The upturn in the rate in 1971–72 was delayed partly or wholly by price and wage controls instituted in August 1971. Price increases may have been hidden because of the controls and not recorded in the data, and many of the increases prevented by the controls were posted later.[8] When most of the controls were removed in January 1973, prices rose sharply. A substantial part of the rise in 1973 and 1974 reflected temporary world influences on basic commodities (feed grains and metals as well as petroleum). When these influences abated in 1975, the inflation rate came down rapidly, which countered the normal tendency of inflation rates to rise in a business recovery. The rise in the inflation rate in the first part of 1978 suggested that the normal tendency was appearing, though this rise also reflected a reduction of economic slack to levels that have traditionally marked the beginning of renewed inflationary pressures. The altered timing in these two cycles may therefore reflect special developments and not indicate a change in cyclical pattern that will be repeated.

Whether the cyclical pattern has changed or not, it is evident from the historical record that the rate of inflation is not to be explained simply by the amount of slack in the economy. Full employment of resources is not normally reached until late in business expansions. If a simple relation existed between the inflation rate and economic slack, the rate would continue to decline until the later stages of business expansions when slack finally begins to disappear. Actually, as figure 1.1 showed, the inflation rate fluctuates over business cycles in a procyclical pattern and begins to rise early in business recoveries at or shortly after the trough in activity. The only continuing declines in the rate, apart from business contractions, were in 1951–52 following the sharp run-up of prices at the outbreak of the Korean War and in the early recovery stage of the last two cycles. The first of the latter two exceptions appears to be attributable to price controls and the second to foreign influences.

The theory that the reduction of inflation depends upon the amount of economic slack evolved in the 1960s from earlier theories of price behavior. The 1960s theory was a departure from traditional views and appeared for a time to rectify certain of their deficiencies. Its own deficiencies have in turn led to new theories of price behavior.

Old and New Theories of Price Behavior

Standard economic theory teaches that markets adjust to demand and supply with a rise in prices when demand exceeds potential supply and a decline in prices when demand falls short of potential supply. This was the virtually universal view of price behavior up to the 1930s and is still, with qualifications, commonly held. Strictly interpreted, it implies that the level of prices should generally rise in business expansions and decline in business contractions, propelled by associated fluctuations in aggregate demand. Such behavior is most clearly exemplified by prices sold on organized exchanges, such as agricultural products and basic commodities, and those sold in highly competitive markets. These prices are highly flexible, even volatile, and respond quickly to the shifting forces of demand and supply.

It has long been recognized, however, that prices of many other products, particularly manufactures and services, display considerably less flexibility and often decline quite slowly in the face of slack market conditions. Price inflexibility has often been viewed as somehow unnatural. In the 1930s Gardiner Means gained attention with his theory that inflexible prices were "administered" by producers in disregard of market conditions and thus did not respond to cyclical changes in demand.[9] Such behavior was attributed to the ''market power'' of producers, which they wielded to enhance their profits (exactly how was never clear). The prime example of inflexibility, of course, is wages, which have always displayed an extreme stickiness in the face of declining employment and even mass unemployment. It was no doubt the inflexibility of wages in Britain during the mass unemployment of the 1920s that led Keynes largely to ignore cyclical changes in prices and wages in his influential *General Theory of Employment, Interest, and Money,* published in 1936. He assumed that wages and prices were constant when aggregate demand declined; and, though he acknowledged that they often increased when aggregate demand rose, the increase played no role in his theory. As so often happens with an influential work, the assumption made for simplification became widely accepted as fact and extended. For years thereafter theoretical economics usually treated price and wage levels in macro models of the economy as generally fixed until aggregate demand becomes excessive and then pulls them up. This view gained further currency in the 1950s with the notion that downward rigidity characterized wages and many prices—which meant that they never declined, even when markets were slack. Such price behavior was condemned in the 1950s as the major reason for the creeping inflation of that decade. If prices rose in the later stages of business expansions when demand was strong and failed to decline during business contractions, the price level would rise from cycle to cycle, and its long-run trend would be persistently and inexorably upward.[10] Shifts in demand among sectors of the economy, increasing prices in some and failing—because of downward rigidity—to reduce them in others, would have the same effect of raising the overall level of prices.[11] Downward rigidity was thought to be at variance with the normal behavior of prices in competitive markets; it reflected the inertia of custom in economic behavior and, since the 1930s, allegedly the growth of labor unions, product oligopolies, and the institutional rigidities of regulation.

By the end of the 1960s it began to appear that downward rigidity was only half the problem. Prices and wages could continue rising, and not merely fail to decline, when demand was slack. The theory that developed to account for such behavior combined a Phillips curve with price expectations. As described by the Phillips curve, prices respond to excess or deficient demand too slowly to keep markets cleared. A shortfall in aggregate demand, for example, produces a gap at prevailing prices between demand and the potential supply of output. The slack generates pressures for prices to fall below their trend path. Since prices respond slowly, markets in the meantime remain slack. What prevents prices and wages from adjusting rapidly to clear markets and reduce the gap to zero? The main reasons usually given are that changes in market conditions may at first be viewed as temporary, and firms find it costly and awkward to adjust prices to temporary fluctuations in demand and supply; that explicit and more often implicit contracts bind firms to offer their products and purchase resources at a predetermined price or to make changes only under specified conditions, particularly with respect to wages; and that firms in all but highly competitive industries seek to coordinate prices (without overt collusion) so as to avoid the confusion to buyers and the disarray in the market of selling the same product at different prices. For all these reasons prices are constrained from deviating from the expected equilibrium path. Unanticipated disturbances and short-run fluctuations in demand are largely ignored, and firms base selling prices on their unit costs of production at a standard level of output. They rely on these unit costs as an indicator of the long-run equilibirum path of prices likely to prevail in the industry.

The gradual response of prices to a gap between demand and supply is expressed in the Phillips relationship by the dependence of the rate of change of prices upon the size of the gap. But this dependence does not explain why prices rise when demand falls short of potential supply and is deficient by any reasonable measure. Such behavior is explained by expectations. When the growth trend of nominal aggregate demand exceeds that of output, the expected equilibrium path of wages and prices has an upward trend. Economic decisions are geared to this expected upward trend of prices. Deviations of aggregate demand from the expected trend are generally not anticipated. A fall in aggregate demand in a business recession, for example, reduces the actual rate of price increases below the trend rate. Unless the recession is unusually severe, however, most prices continue rising, though at a slower rate. During business expansions prices rise faster than the trend rate. As long as the growth trend in aggregate demand does not change from cycle to cycle, long-run expectations are confirmed and the trend rate is maintained. A persistent deviation above or below the trend would indicate a change in the trend, however, and lead gradually to the revision of expectations.

Expectations are also influenced by the monetary regime and political environment in which monetary and fiscal policies operate. The gold standard was less inflationary than managed currencies, and expectations under the present managed currency system undoubtedly take that difference into account. There is evidence that prices have gradually become less responsive to changes in aggregate demand in the business cycles since World War II (chapter 3). This diminishing responsiveness is caused in part, no doubt, by a decline in the expected capability of monetary and fiscal policies to contain inflation, as demonstrated by the accommodation of higher and higher rates of inflation. Although the statistical analysis reported below ignores changes over time in the way expectations are formed, there is no intention to deny the importance of such changes.

The rate of change of prices at any time, $\dot{p}_t$ (where the overhead dot denotes the rate of change), may therefore be represented by two influences: (1) the pressure of the concurrent gap between demand and potential supply—deficient or excess demand as measured by the difference between the actual rate of unemployment of resources, U_t, and the full-employment rate of unemployment, $\bar{U}$; and (2) the anticipated trend path of prices, $\dot{p}^e_t$, which has been incorporated into wage contracts and past pricing decisions and so raises input costs as it is passed along the production pipeline:

$$\dot{p}_t = F(U_t - \bar{U}) + \dot{p}^e_t. \quad [1]$$

This is the standard Phillips curve combined with expectations. F is a function which declines as $U_t - \bar{U}$ increases. The coefficient of $\dot{p}^e$ is unity on the assumption that there is no long-run tradeoff between inflation and unemployment. The equation summarizes the view that policy can reduce the inflation rate by restraining aggregate demand, in which the amount of restraint is measured by the amount of slack that results. If $\dot{p}$ is thereby kept below $\dot{p}^e$, $\dot{p}^e$ will eventually be revised downward, after which the slack can be removed and $\dot{p}$ and $\dot{p}^e$ will be equal at a reduced rate of inflation.

When applied to experience in 1977, such an equation, as noted earlier, seems to suggest that inflation should have declined. In that year $\bar{U}$ was about 6 percent of the total labor force. This may seem high by past standards, but the rate of unemployment at which inflation neither increases nor decreases has been rising because structural changes in the labor force have added to recorded unemployment. The actual unemployment rate averaged 7 percent in 1977, giving unemployment in excess of $\bar{U}$ of one percentage point. (Most estimates of excess unemployment for 1977 were even higher.) With this excess unemployment the actual rate of inflation should have been below the expected rate, which would then gradually decline, thus reducing the actual rate for any given amount of excess unemployment. But the inflation rate did not decline in 1977. The consumer price index increased at the same 4.3 percent annual rate from the third to the fourth quarters of both 1976 and 1977. Year over year the rate actually rose, from 4.9 percent in 1976 (December to December) to 6.7 percent in 1977. (Most forecasts for 1978, including the Council's, predicted no decline in the inflation rate, but, as noted, this is not inconsistent with the above equation. Unemployment fell to the 6 percent level in the first part of 1978, which by the preceding estimate of $\bar{U}$ is the full-employment level and put the economy at the threshold of increasing inflationary pressures.)

What explanation can be given for a rise in the *rate* of inflation or even constancy early in business recoveries, when aggregate demand still falls short of the potential supply? Prices of crude materials, which are highly sensitive to market conditions, contribute to this rise (see figure 1.1). They typically decline sharply in business recessions (that is, have negative rates of change) and then begin to rise as the forces of recovery spread through the economy. They exemplify the behavior that economic theory attributes to competitive prices. Their fluctuations contribute to procyclical movements in the rate of change of a general price index. But they do not dominate the behavior of the general price level and by themselves cannot account for its procyclical fluctuations. The inflation rate for most intermediate and finished goods also displays a procyclical pattern. Crude materials make up too small a part of the total cost of production of most intermediate and finished goods to dominate the movements in their input costs.

One explanation for a rising inflation rate when slack demand exists pertains to the price expectations term in equation [1]. A reduction in $\dot{p}^e$ is presumed to occur whenever $\dot{p}$ falls below $\dot{p}^e$. If $\dot{p}^e$ changes too slowly, however, the cyclical fluctuations in the first term of equation [1] will dominate to produce a procyclical pattern in $\dot{p}$. A slack-induced reduction of inflation that outlasts the business cycle therefore requires that $\dot{p}^e$ respond to $\dot{p}$ and that the net effect be downward. If over the business cycle $\dot{p}$ rises above $\dot{p}^e$ as much as it falls below, there will be no net reduction in $\dot{p}^e$. Inflation has escalated since 1965 because U on the average has been below $\bar{U}$. The reduction of inflation requires that for a while U be above $\bar{U}$ on the average.

This relationship can be expressed in simple mathematical terms which provide a form for regression analysis. If price expectations are revised gradually, an adaptive revision may be described by

[2] $$\frac{d\dot{p}^e_t}{dt}=b(\dot{p}_t-\dot{p}^e_t),$$

which by [1] equals bF. The coefficient b may change over time, but for simplicity it is assumed to be constant. In theory it can be any positive number. To incorporate such adaptive expectations into the modified Phillips relationship, equation [1] is differentiated with respect to time,

[3] $$\frac{d\dot{p}_t}{dt}=F'\frac{dU_t}{dt}+\frac{d\dot{p}^e_t}{dt}$$

and [2] substituted into [3],

[4] $$\frac{d\dot{p}_t}{dt}=F'\frac{dU_t}{dt}+bF$$

If the F function is a simple proportional relationship $F=a(U_t-\bar{U})$, and differentials are treated as discrete first differences, and $\bar{U}$ is constant, then

[5] $$\dot{p}_t-\dot{p}_{t-1}=a(U_t-U_{t-1})+ba(U_t-\bar{U}).$$

An indication of the effect of slack demand on the inflation rate that outlasts the business cycle is given by estimates of ba, which is the product of the speed of revision of price expectations, b, and the cyclical effect of slack on the inflation rate, a. Estimates of this effect of slack demand are presented below.[12]

A different way of formulating the effect of slack demand on inflation is suggested by the new theory of rational expectations. This theory starts from the presumption that expectations formed about economic developments make full use of all available information. Given the incentives for market participants to use information to full advantage, expectations of price changes and other variables will not be subject to repeated errors of forecast in the same direction insofar as available information could avert such biased forecasts, though errors can of course be large because of developments that no one is able to foresee. The theory evolved in reaction to the assumption, commonly made in economic analysis, that expectations adjust slowly to new developments as new information is absorbed gradually through an adaptive error-learning process. Slow revisions of expectations produce a series of similar and avoidable errors during the time in which new information is being acquired by economic agents and behavior has not yet fully adjusted to it. Such lags in response may pertain to habitual behavior, though under conditions of imperfect knowledge they may be quite "rational" and may describe actual behavior quite well. However, under conditions when profits are to be made by fully utilizing new information, economic agents will try to avoid lags in revising expectations and may succeed in doing so. New information will thus be reflected rapidly in prices for which expectations of future developments play a role. Rapid—virtually instantaneous—use of new information is certainly characteristic of commodity and financial exchanges, where expectations of future movements are critical and new information is extremely important. Analysis of price movements on exchanges indicates that errors of expectations, insofar as they can be measured, are unsystematic, essentially unpredictable, and reflect only new developments which were not foreseen. Such prices are characterized by jumps from one position to another, because everyone is aware of a new development that justifies a change in price, and all transactions occur immediately at the changed price.

In its extreme form the theory of rational expectations requires that prices clear markets at every moment. Since a price that does not equate demand and supply is subject to pressures to change until it does so, market participants acquire and make rational use of information about such pressures and do not transact at a price that they know is subject to further change in a particular direction. Prices so determined always equate all demand and supply offers at the moment. The theory offers no explanation for most prices and wages in the economy, which change smoothly and usually follow the same trend for months at a time in markets often characterized by persistent slack or excess demand. Most prices and wages either are subject to institutional constraints or, if influenced by "rational" expectations, are not as yet fully understandable by economic theory.

But a modified form of the theory can be espoused which seems more realistic and accommodates prices which do not clear markets. Faced with a fall in demand, an individual firm or industry, given its costs of production and the desire to maximize profits or minimize losses, will not cut prices far enough to prevent a decline in its sales in real terms and the necessity of reducing its output. Explicit or implicit contracts to supply labor and materials at predetermined wages and prices are one reason for lack of market clearing and a decline in sales, but it seems doubtful that such contracts are the only reason. Another likely reason is the sheer complexity of a full adjustment of the entire price system to changes in demand. The restoration of demand to its original level in real terms only through changes in prices, after a general fall in aggregate demand in a recession, would require a quite large decline in the *general level* of prices and wages, in which each individual firm and industry plays a small part.[13] Individual firms and industries do not know to what extent deflation in the whole economy will reverse a decline in aggregate real demand, and we may suppose that they act on the basis of the demand they face at the moment. There is no reason to suppose that rational expectations of developments elsewhere in the economy, of which individual firms and industries can have only limited knowledge, would significantly affect prices in individual markets, nor that such knowledge would therefore imply an immediate fall in all prices to a level that would restore a shortfall in demand to its original real level. When demand falls, individual firms and industries will cut prices and output, and their action may still be based on rational expectations in that their estimate of sales and the prices that will prevail is neither high nor low on the average. Their reduction of output will, of course, contribute to a continuation of the decline in aggregate demand. With each fall in demand, prices and output will be cut further. If expectations are rational, however, there is no systematic delay in the response of prices to changes in demand. Hence the level of demand will determine the level, not the rate of change, of prices.[14] Such a relationship is formulated as follows.

Rational expectations may thus be made consistent with the existence of slack markets, but an explanation of rising prices in a recession is still missing. To explain that anomaly, we may also suppose that the anticipated long-run trend of prices is upward, and price changes over the business cycle occur as cyclical deviations from the trend. Then it is possible that cyclical declines in prices combined with the rising trend can produce prices that rise in a recession—a rise that is less than the trend, to be sure, but a rise nonetheless. The long-run trend would presumably also be subject to rational expectations. The long-run expectations would be based on the anticipated trend of prices from cycle to cycle, after the cyclical ups and downs are netted out. An upward trend would affect prices in recessions as well as expansions for at least two reasons. First, an anticipated rising trend would be incorporated into price and wage contracts for resource inputs and would continue to inflate costs in recessions. Second, the price trend would influence the cyclical price at which storable materials and goods as well as some labor services would be supplied; sellers would withhold supplies as prices in a recession fell further and further below the anticipated trend price. The withholding of supplies would limit the decline in prices during a recession and would even cause prices to continue rising if the anticipated trend were rising fast enough.

Under rational expectations, the anticipated trend of prices would presumably not be influenced by anticipated developments within the business cycle that were reflected in cyclical price changes; rational expectations allow for cyclical fluctuations. But trends can and do change without being clearly foreseen. Rational economic agents will revise their expectations of the price trend when they become aware of a change occurring or about to occur; for example, a business recession more severe or a period of slack demand more prolonged than expected. Hence slack demand may also affect anticipated price trends under rational expectations, but the effect would depend upon the amount of slack in the economy both currently and in the past. Certainly it would not depend upon the current amount only, since the current amount would be largely indistinguishable from expected cyclical fluctuations. This means that the expected trend of prices would be related to the cumulative amount of slack over an extended period. Such a relation contrasts with the modified Phillips equation, in which expected price changes can be related to the discrepancy between actual and expected changes (and this discrepancy can in turn be related to the current amount of slack). The two theories differ because, in accordance with the slow adjustment of prices underlying the Phillips curve, economic decisions are based, not on rational expectations of current price movements, but on an adaptive error-learning process in which current price movements contain relevant unused information for the revision of expectations.

We can express the theory of price behavior under rational expectations in a mathematical form for regression analysis. The theory implies that the *level* of prices depends upon both the expected price level and the *level* of demand or, equivalently, the gap between demand and potential supply as indicated by unemployed resources; namely,

$$[6] \qquad p_t = G(U_t - \bar{U}) + p_t^e,$$

where the symbols are the same as those introduced above and G is a function which declines when $U_t - \bar{U}$ increases. When differentiated with respect to time, the relationship becomes

$$[7] \qquad \dot{p}_t = G' \frac{dU_t}{dt} + \dot{p}_t^e,$$

where as above the overhead dots denote the rate of change on the assumption that the price variables are measured in logarithms.

On the proposition that the expected price trend is influenced by the cumulative amount of slack over an extended period,

$$[8] \qquad \dot{p}_t^e = [\text{noncyclical trend of prices}] + c_0(U_t - \bar{U}) + c_1(U_{t-1} - \bar{U}) + \ldots + c_n(U_{t-n} - \bar{U}).$$

The noncyclical trend of prices may be represented by the average inflation rate over the length of a typical business cycle, which is roughly four years. Whether the average is a little more or less than four years will not materially affect the results. Substituting [8] into [7] and assuming a proportional G function and discrete first differences, we have

$$[9] \quad \dot{p}_t - \sum_{i=1}^{16} \frac{\dot{p}_{t-i}}{16} = a(U_t - U_{t-1}) + c_0(U_t - \bar{U}) + c_1(U_{t-1} - \bar{U}) + \ldots + c_n(U_{t-n} - \bar{U})$$

where the average rate of inflation, which has a coefficient of unity, has been transferred to the left side of the equation. The coefficient a

of the first term reflects the temporary effect of changes in slack demand on the inflation rate. The lasting effect over a business cycle is given by the sum of the c coefficients.[15]

Collecting terms into a form suitable for regression analysis, we have

$$[10] \quad \dot{p}_t - \sum_{i=1}^{16} \frac{\dot{p}_{t-i}}{16} = (a + c_0)\,(U_t - \bar{U}) + (c_1 - a)\,(U_{t-1} - \bar{U}) + c_2(U_{t-2} - \bar{U}) + \ldots + c_n(U_{t-n} - \bar{U}).$$

In theory n should be the length of a business cycle, but for statistical convenience most of the estimates of this equation, presented below, are based on only six U terms. Results for fifteen and seventeen terms, however, are not dissimilar.

The difference between rational and adaptive price behavior is illustrated in figure 9.1. The price at any particular time is influenced by the expected shift in demand and supply schedules owing to inflation and by deviations of the actual schedules from the expected ones. Only one set of expected schedules is shown in the figure, al-

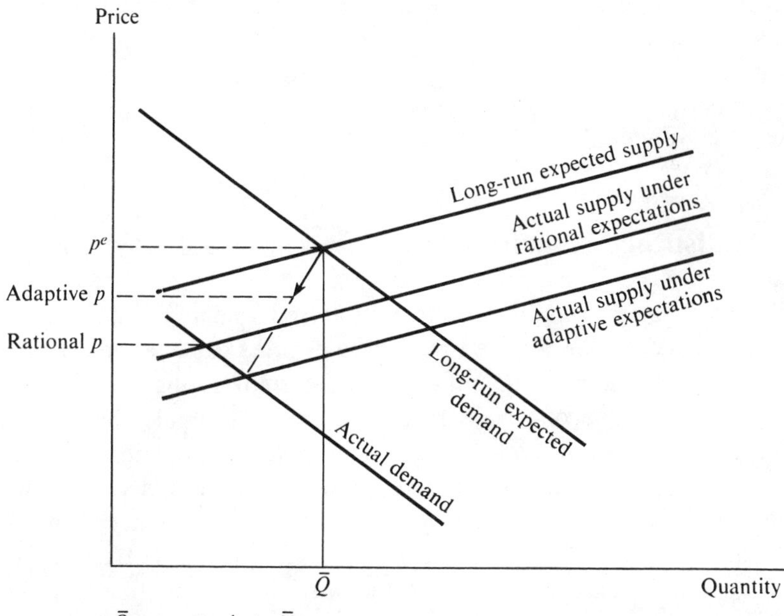

$\bar{Q}$ corresponds to $\bar{U}$.

Figure 9.1 Response of Price to Downward Shifts of Demand and Supply: Adaptive and Rational Expectations

though rational and adaptive expectations would not ordinarily have the same set. Given the expected price under either theory of behavior, the actual demand and supply will cause the price to deviate from the expected price. The adaptive response will result in a price that partially reflects the actual change in demand and supply in relation to the expected change. The rational response will result in a price which equates actual demand and supply. As argued above, this rational price will not ordinarily prevent a fall in output because real demand has shifted leftward and also because contracts predetermine some prices and supplies may be held off the market in anticipation of more favorable prices in the future.

Therefore, when the earliest and the most recent theories of price behavior are modified to account for procyclical fluctuations in the inflation rate, they are not necessarily inconsistent with a Phillips type of relation between the inflation rate and the amount of excess capacity. As suggested above, however, the correlation between procyclical fluctuations in the inflation rate and in the amount of excess demand is evidence of only a temporary effect of slack in reducing inflation. For a lasting effect economic slack must reduce the expected trend rate of inflation. Let us examine the record for evidence of an effect of economic slack on price expectations. In estimating this effect, we shall analyze the data in terms of the two theories discussed above.[16]

Statistical Estimates of the Effect of Slack Demand

The two theories formulated above allow for a noncyclical effect of slack demand on the inflation rate through price expectations. In the first theory the *current* amount of slack determines long-run expectations, but in the second it does not because it is largely reflected in short-run expectations and the current price level. Equations [5] and [10], each based on one of the two theories, were designed to distinguish the cyclical and noncyclical effects of slack demand on the inflation rate. Statistical regressions of these equations were fitted to U.S. quarterly data beginning in the first quarter of 1953, which avoids the large price swings associated with the Korean War, and ending in the fourth quarter of 1977, the latest date available, and alternatively in 1969 to exclude the last two business cycles. Various series were used to provide a broad indication of how the parameter estimates are affected by different measures of prices and slack demand. The results are presented in appendix tables B and C.

The regression equations do not in general fit the data closely, as is evidenced by the low levels of significance of many of the regression coefficients. (The total correlation coefficients are high simply because they include an adjustment for serial correlation in the error terms; they have not been reported.) Our principal interest here is the values of the coefficients as estimates of the effect of slack demand on the inflation rate. The lack of a close fit does not appear to mean that the estimates of the coefficients are biased and so does not invalidate the statistical results, though it does of course widen the range of error of the estimates.

Table 9.1 Estimates of Changes in Various Measures of the Inflation Rate from Excess Unemployment, Equation [5] (change per quarter in annual percentage rate from excess unemployment of one percentage point)

Measures of the Inflation Rate	*Period of Estimate*	*Total Change (ba)*	*Total Due to*		*Estimated Change in Inflation Rate for 1977 over 1976*
			a	*b*	
Consumer price index	1953–69	−0.17	−0.70	0.24	−0.02
	1953–77	−0.23	−0.95	0.24	−0.21
GNP deflator	1953–69	0.01	−0.26	−0.04	–
	1953–77	−0.12	−0.57	0.21	+0.03
Wholesale crude materials	1953–69	−0.43	−0.23	1.87	−0.88
	1953–77	−0.02	−0.06	0.67	+0.33
Wholesale intermediate goods	1953–69	0.02	−0.58	−0.03	–
	1953–77	−0.13	−2.38	0.05	+1.44
Wholesale finished goods	1953–69	−0.20	−0.66	0.30	−0.13
	1953–77	−0.28	−1.22	0.23	−0.10
Average hourly earnings	1953–69	−0.05	−0.56	0.09	+0.10
	1953–77	−0.11	−0.52	0.21	−0.06

SOURCE: Based on regressions in appendix table B, for unemployment rate of prime-age men.
NOTE: The value of b is derived by dividing ba by a. Estimated change for 1977 over 1976 is $a(-0.65) + 4ba(4.6 - \overline{U})$, where $\overline{U}$ for each row is given in appendix table B. (The unemployment rate for prime-age men in 1977 was 4.6 percent, and the decline in the average level from 1976 to 1977 was 0.65.) Dash (–) indicates not calculated because estimates of ba and b are of wrong sign.

For equation [5] the estimates of *ba* represent the noncyclical effect of slack demand on the inflation rate. These are reproduced in table 9.1 for the regressions using the unemployment rate to measure slack demand.[17] The estimated effect of slack demand is similar for the consumer price index and wholesale finished goods prices (and is statistically significant, as shown in appendix table B, except for the wholesale price series over the shorter period). The estimated effect differs for the other price measures. The estimates for wholesale crude and intermediate materials prices are erratic and reflect their lack of regular cyclical pattern. The estimates for average hourly earnings are quite small, reflecting the lower response of wages to the business cycle. The estimated effect for the GNP deflator is also small (and actually nonexistent in the 1953–1969 regression), apparently because of its broader coverage of industries.[18] Many of the results are not strongly significant for the basic reason that moderate slack works slowly and its effect is hard to identify. But it seems to exist overall in these data, and the estimates appear credible in magnitude.

If we tentatively accept the results for the consumer price index and wholesale finished goods, which are statistically the strongest, as the clearest indication of the size of such an effect, the estimates are around 0.2 and imply that excess unemployment maintained at one percentage point would reduce the annual inflation rate by 0.2 percentage points per quarter and by 0.8 percentage points per year. By this evidence the noncyclical trend of inflation is reduced by economic slack, but quite slowly when the amount of slack is moderate. The slowness of the effect reflects the small revision of the expected price change per period of time, shown by the value of *b*. The immediate effect, shown by *a*, is larger, but the part of the effect that has not been translated into a reduction of the expected price change disappears when the slack is removed.[19]

The failure of the inflation rate to decline continually when slack exists is reflected in the large negative value of *a*, which represents the cyclical effect of changes in slack and which dominates the noncyclical effect. In a business expansion the continued existence of slack works to reduce the expected rate of inflation, but, until the decline in slack slows down, the net effect can be no change or even an increase in the current inflation rate. The last column of table 9.1 gives the change in the inflation rate as estimated by each regression for 1977. Despite the existence of substantial slack in the economy in 1977, but because of the decline in amount of slack, most of the estimates show only a slight decline—practically no change—in the inflation rate for the year. Actually, the inflation rate increased in 1977; this upward deviation from the equation suggests that the severe winter generated direct upward pressures on prices which were accommodated by aggregate-demand policy but did not affect the measures of excess unemployment.

The results for equation [10], based on rational expectations, are presented in appendix table C, and summarized in table 9.2. The sum of the *c* coefficients gives the lasting effect of slack demand in reducing the expected trend of prices. The additional *c* coefficients beyond the first two are not collectively significant statistically, and this remains true when the number of them in the regression is increased. Consequently, the estimate of their sum is subject to a wide range of error. The lack of significance may also mean that rational expectations are an inappropriate basis for describing these data, or it may possibly mean that expectations of the inflation trend cannot be adequately represented by past unemployment. We may nevertheless

Table 9.2 Estimates of Changes in Various Measures of the Inflation Rate From Average Excess Unemployment, Equation [10] (change per indicated period in annual percentage rate from excess unemployment of one percentage point)

Measures of the Inflation Rate	*Period of Estimate*	*Sum of c Coefficients* (*1*)	*Effect per year* (*0.37 × col.* [*1*])[a] (2)	*Effect over Business Cycle, Continuous Adjustments* (*1.72 × col.* [*1*])[a] (*3*)
Consumer price index	1953–69	−0.80	−0.30	−1.38
	1953–77	−1.46	−0.54	−2.51
	1953–77	−0.99[b]	−0.37	−1.70
Wholesale finished goods	1953–69	−0.88	−0.33	−1.51
	1953–77	−1.87	−0.69	−3.22
Average hourly earnings	1953–69	−0.84	−0.31	−1.44
	1953–77	−0.78	−0.29	−1.34

SOURCE: Appendix table C.

[a] See note 20, this chapter.

[b] Estimated from regression with fifteen terms of U.

examine these estimates as an alternative indication of the effect of slack demand on inflation, since they suggest a slower response than does the adaptive expectations model.

The estimates of the sum of the c coefficients in table 9.2 vary from 0.8 for the shorter period 1953–69 to over 1.5 for the full period 1953–77. The larger sum for the full period probably reflects the unusual fluctuations of 1973–75, however. As the number of U terms in the regression is increased to provide a longer perspective on the cumulative effect of slack demand, the sum declines toward unity (third row of table). We may therefore take a value of unity or a little lower as the central estimate of the effect. The implications for the average inflation rate are shown in columns (2) and (3) of the table. Column (2) shows the effect per year for an assumed four-year business cycle. Column (3) shows the cumulative effect over a full business cycle of any length, under the likely assumption that adjustments in the expected trend are made continuously.[20] For the central estimate of the sum of c coefficients of unity in the third row, the annual inflation rate would be reduced by 0.37 percentage points per year for each one percentage point of average slack maintained over a business cycle, and reduced as much as 1.70 percentage points over the entire business cycle with continuous adjustments. This effect is about a half or less of the effect estimated above for adaptive expectations over the same length of time. Rational expectations have a smaller effect because it is assumed that most of the cyclical fluctuation in slack demand is expected and already incorporated in the expected trend, and that only the cumulative amount of slack, if more or less than expected, affects the expected trend of prices.

Although these estimates show a small effect of slack demand, they pertain to the initial effect within the span of a business cycle; the longer-run effect could well be larger. Presumably the slack produced by a business recession will not reduce the expected trend of prices very much if it is expected that the pressure on prices of slack markets in the recession will be offset in the subsequent expansion. The recent cyclical fluctuations, in which the final stages of the expansion have encountered increasing inflationary pressures, give a historical basis for such an expectation. For policymakers to restrain inflation effectively given the recent history of failures, they must demonstrate over the course of a business cycle that the restraint will persist. Once this is demonstrated for one business cycle, however, the effect is likely to be considerably stronger in the next.[21] In the late 1950s the inflation rate was widely viewed as intractable because it was not eliminated by the recession of 1957–58 (see figure 1.1). Yet the subsequent business expansion did not overshoot, and the inflation rate remained lower than it had been in the previous expansion. Although the inflation stubbornly resisted further decline in the subsequent business contraction of 1960–61, it rapidly disappeared during the second half of 1961 when the business recovery proved to be mild. With the benefit of hindsight, it appears that the inflation of the 1950s was finally conquered not so much by the business recessions as by the avoidance of renewed inflationary pressures during the business expansions.

The adaptive and rational models imply different time patterns for the effects of slack demand on the expected rate of inflation. The effects under adaptive expectations occur faster and, for a given initial period of excess unemployment, appear to be about twice as large. Given the cyclical fluctuations in slack demand over the business cycle, however, the initial change in the expected inflation rate will be partially or fully offset over a full cycle. Under rational expectations, although slack demand has an immediate effect on price levels, its effect on the expected trend of prices is slight initially, may even be negligible during a recession, and occurs mainly with a lag the length of the business cycle. But the response of the expected rate of inflation to slack demand is likely to be stronger—and this applies to adaptive expectations as well—when a change in aggregate-demand policy demonstrates that the change will be maintained by outlasting the course of a business cycle.

Although our statistical results slightly favor adaptive over rational expectations, it is not clear which model describes economic behavior more accurately. Actual behavior may well be a mix of both.

The Political Problem of Reducing Inflation

The statistical results add an important qualification to the proclaimed policy goal of reducing both inflation and unemployment. The goal can be accomplished only if the reduction of unemployment is not carried all the way to full employment but stops short of that goal and maintains some excess unemployment for a long period. No such limitation has been evident in the pursuit of the goal over the past decade. Business expansions, whether intended by policy or not, have carried aggregate demand up to and beyond the zone of increasing inflationary pressures. Policymakers have also set up an unattainable goal by claiming that cyclical rates of both inflation and unemployment can be reduced at the same time.

Although there are no economic barriers to reducing inflation, a political problem of indecisiveness has erected a barrier. The problem centers on two implications of the economic relation between inflation and slack demand. First, changes in the amount of slack reflect cyclical fluctuations in aggregate demand which produce cyclical fluctuations in the rate of inflation. Restraint imposed on the growth in aggregate demand increases the amount of economic slack and reduces the inflation rate. But while the restraint is being applied the rate declines far more than can be maintained after the economy begins to recover. As the amount of slack declines, the inflation rate increases, which makes it appear as though the hard-earned gains against inflation are slipping away. In fact, however, most of those gains are temporary cyclical fluctuations and cannot be counted as reductions in the long-run inflation rate. The real progress against inflation is to be measured by the rate that prevails after slack has declined to an acceptable level. At that point the inflation rate can be somewhat lower, compared with the average for the previous cycle, because of the cumulative effect of economic slack during the business contraction and recovery. It is conceivable that fluctuations could be avoided by imposing an amount of slack which, once reached, is kept constant thereafter until the long-run rate of inflation has declined to an acceptable level. But fluctuations in business activity owing to policy measures as well as to other sources of cyclical fluctuations in the economy have not been avoided in the past and are well beyond our capability of avoiding in the foreseeable future. Since cyclical fluctuations in the inflation rate will surely continue, a "true" reduction in the rate would mean that the *expected* rate has declined, as implied by a decline in the actual rate between corresponding business cycle stages in which the amount of slack is the same.

A second implication of the relation between inflation and slack demand is an obvious one with touchy political consequences.

It is that the reduction of inflation "almost" certainly requires slack demand. The qualification is added to cover the possibility implied by the theory of rational expectations that an announced and widely believed change in policy which reduced the growth path of nominal aggregate demand would immediately reduce the expected growth path and thereby its contribution to the trend of prices. An argument sometimes made for controls is that, if accompanied by announced restraints in aggregate-demand policy, they could help to reduce expected price changes along with the targeted decline in the inflation rate, thus avoiding the period of slack demand produced by a discrepancy between actual and expected price changes. The purpose of the controls would be to make the announced change in aggregate-demand policy believable, though in the light of past experience it is questionable whether they ever have or now would have such an effect. There is no doubt, however, that the stance and credibility of policy affects expectations. Market decisions about wages and prices are guided at least in part by rational expectations of the direction of policy. To the extent that prices behave according to the theory of rational expectations, the trend rate of inflation can persist in the face of slack demand and the proclaimed desire of policymakers to subdue inflation only if they are generally not believed to be capable of translating the desire into effective action. Since the evidence suggests that the economic capability exists, the lack of credibility concerns the political capability. In such circumstances and in view of our past experience, the desire to subdue inflation is obviously not enough and must be confirmed by performance. The conclusion appears inescapable, therefore, that the reduction of inflation requires the maintenance of slack demand, and the less that policy hides an intention to maintain slack, the faster the reduction will be.

The lack of a clear intention to subdue inflation becomes even more important if the public suspects that the government accepts inflation as a means of resolving political pressures to expand expenditures without legislating higher tax rates. Large continuing budget deficits could be financed without inflationary policies, but in practice they are partially monetized, thus producing inflation, in part because of pressures to hold down interest rates. In addition, for indecisive governments, inflation has the appealing property of not only financing expenditures without taxing or borrowing but also of providing an automatic reallocation of government expenditures in real terms without explicit legislative action, since rising prices reduce the real value of dollar allocations for which no increase is mandated. Thus the government may increase the expenditures favored by pressure groups and through inaction allow all others to decline in real terms without the necessity of explicitly legislating nominal cutbacks in any expenditures. Of course, some groups have the political influence to gain automatic increases in nominal benefits to maintain their real value. For example, social security benefits have been indexed to the cost of living, while most other expenditures and the income brackets for step increases in income tax rates have not.

The disadvantage of the lack of a clearly stated policy of subduing inflation is that it misleads economic agents into expecting higher inflation than policy measures are designed to allow, thus slowing down the reduction in the expected rate of inflation and holding back the reduction in the actual rate. In addition, policymakers are trapped into publicly adopting targets of economic slack which are unrealistic and, if pursued, unable to reduce inflation. The 4 percent level of unemployment held as a goal in the Humphrey-Hawkins bill can no longer be considered a reasonable estimate of the noninflationary rate of full employment—if it ever was. Budget projections in 1978 were still based on a full-employment rate of less than 5 percent. More realistic estimates, as noted, indicate that this rate is now close to 6 percent. If these higher estimates are correct and if policymakers mistakenly try to achieve a lower unemployment rate, it will not be possible to reduce the actual unemployment rate much below 6 percent. Nor will the widely deplored high rates for youths and minority groups be reduced much by any degree of economic stimulation that would conceivably be undertaken. But the attempt to achieve these unattainable goals would, of course, push the economy into the zone of increasing inflationary pressures. Even if realism prevails in the adoption of goals and the maintenance of a credible amount of slack demand is acknowledged as necessary, the chances of success are greatly diminished by targeting too little slack, because the slightest disturbance raising aggregate demand or restricting supplies can rapidly eliminate a small amount of slack and set off new inflationary pressures. In times past, when the general price level was relatively stable, such disturbances were not important because the response of prices to them was weak; but in recent years, when experience with inflation alerts everyone to the likelihood of new outbursts, the response is rapid.

Although the maintenance of slack demand is necessary to subdue inflation, the imposition of slack can give the appearance of not working, because it takes time and is dominated by cyclical fluctuations that inevitably accompany the attempt to restrain the growth in aggregate demand. This behavior of the inflation rate is hardly ideal for maximizing political statesmanship or for resisting the political temptation to make promises whose impracticality is revealed much later. But despite all the hand wringing over the political obstacles to subduing inflation, it is still true that avoidance of new outbursts of inflation is viewed as politically acceptable and that the rising trend of inflation has largely reflected the failure of policy to contain new outbursts. The evidence gives more support than denial to the traditional view that, without outbursts and with the maintenance of some slack in the economy, inflation will gradually decline. There is a basis for hope that each of the various kinds of mistakes which allow the economy to overheat will be made only once, and that eventually policymakers will proceed without further serious mistakes to bring inflation effectively under control.

Appendix Tables

Table A. Measures of the Frequency Distribution of Wholesale Prices by Industry in Post-World War II Recessions (recession rates minus preceding expansion rates in percent per year)

		No. of Series		*Mean*					*Percent Declining*					*Standard Deviation*				
BLS Code	*Industry*	*1948–1961*	*1969–1970*	*1948–1949*	*1953–1954*	*1957–1958*	*1960–1961*	*1969–1970*	*1948–1949*	*1953–1954*	*1957–1958*	*1960–1961*	*1969–1970*	*1948–1949*	*1953–1954*	*1957–1958*	*1960–1961*	*1969–1970*
1	Farm prod.	70	62	−16.3	−5.3	3.6	3.1	−8.3	78.6	58.6	41.4	51.4	62.9	24.7	18.7	28.6	19.6	22.3
2	Proc. foods	110	100	−12.7	−2.2	6.6	7.7	1.9	70.0	60.0	40.0	30.0	36.0	20.0	15.3	15.2	18.5	12.8
3	Textiles	114	114	−9.2	−3.7	−2.6	−3.1	−0.7	79.8	74.6	71.1	59.6	50.9	14.3	5.0	6.0	8.7	4.6
4	Leather	36	35	−2.2	−12.1	−6.9	−12.8	−6.3	63.9	88.9	72.2	91.7	85.7	13.8	18.7	13.5	14.1	14.4
5	Fuels	33	33	−41.1	−11.7	−18.3	6.8	13.1	100.0	93.9	93.9	33.3	18.2	25.3	15.1	20.0	9.1	22.7
6	Chemicals	150	149	−9.3	−0.3	−1.6	2.0	1.8	74.0	65.3	61.3	30.0	36.2	23.6	17.6	17.9	12.9	14.8
7	Rubber	30	30	−6.4	−5.0	−7.2	−11.4	0.8	83.3	80.0	70.0	60.0	33.3	8.3	5.2	14.5	27.1	14.9
8	Lumber	57	55	−20.4	−7.2	−3.5	−11.4	−11.0	93.0	91.2	82.5	91.2	94.5	15.0	6.7	7.4	12.8	10.4
9	Paper	43	43	−13.6	−5.6	−1.1	−3.8	1.2	90.7	93.0	74.4	58.1	39.5	17.8	5.1	7.9	6.7	6.1
10	Metals	131	124	−15.6	−5.4	−6.8	−3.2	1.2	90.0	86.3	89.3	77.1	37.1	15.1	9.1	11.2	7.8	7.8
11	Machinery	242	239	−8.9	−3.2	−2.1	−1.8	1.3	90.5	83.9	64.9	66.9	32.6	8.5	4.0	5.6	6.0	4.8
12	Furniture	46	46	−8.0	−3.3	−1.4	−1.0	−0.7	84.8	84.8	73.9	65.2	60.9	5.3	2.9	4.5	2.3	3.8
13	Minerals	30	30	−7.8	−2.5	−3.2	−0.4	0.8	96.7	86.7	63.3	60.0	30.0	5.5	2.4	9.5	4.7	3.9
15	Misc.	46	46	−3.9	−2.4	−1.4	0.8	1.2	63.0	82.6	67.4	32.6	43.5	7.0	4.3	6.4	4.4	3.9
	All items	1138	1106	−11.7	−4.0	−2.2	−1.1	0.1	82.7	78.0	66.9	56.9	43.7	17.5	11.4	13.9	12.9	11.9

Table B. Estimated Effect of Economic Slack on Inflation, Assuming Adaptive Expectations

Regression for Eq. [5]: $\dot{p}_t - \dot{p}_{t-1} = a\left(\frac{U_t - U_{t-2}}{2}\right) + ba\left(\frac{U_t + U_{t-1} + U_{t-2}}{3} - \bar{U}\right)$

Price Series	*Period*	*Regression Coefficients (and t values)*		
		a	*ba*	$\bar{U}$
	U: Unemployment rate			
Consumer price index	1953–69	−0.70 (2.7)	−0.17 (2.1)	3.9
	1953–77	−0.95 (3.4)	−0.23 (2.6)	3.7
GNP deflator	1953–69	−0.26 (0.7)	+0.01 (0.1)	–
	1953–77	−0.57 (1.8)	−0.12 (1.2)	3.9
Wholesale crude materials	1953–69	−0.23 (0.1)	−0.43 (0.9)	4.0
	1953–77	−0.06 (0.0)	−0.02 (0.0)	8.2
Wholesale intermediate goods	1953–69	−0.58 (1.2)	+0.02 (0.1)	–
	1953–77	−2.38 (2.0)	−0.13 (0.3)	4.4
Wholesale finished goods	1953–69	−0.66 (1.6)	−0.20 (1.6)	3.9
	1953–77	−1.22 (2.0)	−0.28 (1.5)	3.8
Average hourly earnings	1953–69	−0.56 (1.5)	−0.05 (0.4)	3.3
	1953–3/77	−0.52 (1.4)	−0.11 (0.9)	3.7
	U: Excess capacity			
Consumer price index	1953–69	−0.07 (1.2)	−0.05 (2.3)	17.7
	1953–77	−0.15 (2.6)	−0.08 (3.4)	17.6
GNP deflator	1953–69	−0.05 (0.7)	+0.01 (0.2)	–
	1953–77	−0.11 (1.7)	−0.04 (1.7)	17.8
Wholesale crude materials	1953–69	+0.01 (0.3)	−0.08 (0.6)	19.0
	1953–77	−0.22 (0.4)	+0.06 (0.3)	–
Wholesale intermediate goods	1953–69	−0.25 (2.4)	+0.01 (0.2)	–
	1953–77	−0.77 (3.3)	−0.06 (0.6)	18.9
Wholesale finished goods	1953–69	−0.16 (1.7)	−0.06 (1.7)	18.0
	1953–77	−0.34 (2.8)	−0.09 (2.0)	17.8
Average hourly earnings	1953–69	−0.11 (1.3)	−0.02 (0.7)	16.2
	1953–3/77	−0.11 (1.5)	−0.04 (1.3)	17.4
	U: Potential in excess of actual GNP (CEA)			
Consumer price index	1953–69	−0.17 (1.4)	−0.08 (2.1)	2.7
	1953–77	−0.27 (2.2)	−0.12 (3.4)	2.9
GNP deflator	1953–69	−0.21 (1.3)	−0.01 (0.2)	9.2
	1953–77	−0.19 (1.4)	−0.07 (1.8)	3.1
Wholesale crude materials	1953–69	+0.16 (0.2)	−0.14 (0.7)	3.3
	1953–77	−1.12 (1.1)	−0.05 (0.2)	5.9

Table B (Concluded)

Price Series	*Period*	*Regression Coefficients (and t values)* *a*	*ba*	$\bar{U}$
		U: Potential in excess of actual GNP (CEA) (cont.)		
Wholesale intermediate goods	1953–69	−0.48 (2.2)	−0.03 (0.4)	5.3
	1953–77	−1.36 (2.7)	−0.20 (1.3)	3.2
Wholesale finished goods	1953–69	−0.28 (1.4)	−0.10 (1.7)	2.8
	1953–77	−0.60 (2.4)	−0.16 (2.3)	3.0
Average hourly earnings	1953–69	−0.19 (1.1)	−0.03 (0.6)	1.7
	1953–3/77	−0.07 (0.4)	−0.04 (1.0)	2.8
		U: Potential in excess of actual GNP (St. Louis)		
Consumer price index	1953–69	−0.21 (1.7)	−0.08 (2.2)	2.4
	1953–2/77	−0.37 (3.0)	−0.11 (2.9)	3.1
GNP deflator	1953–69	−0.19 (1.2)	−0.01 (0.2)	7.1
	1953–2/77	−0.23 (1.6)	−0.06 (1.5)	3.0
Wholesale crude materials	1953–69	−0.07 (1.0)	−0.12 (0.6)	3.4
	1953–2/77	−1.46 (1.4)	+0.03 (0.1)	–
Wholesale intermediate goods	1953–69	−0.41 (1.9)	−0.01 (0.1)	14.7
	1953–2/77	−1.72 (3.3)	−0.13 (0.8)	3.2
Wholesale finished goods	1953–69	−0.31 (1.6)	−0.08 (1.4)	2.7
	1953–2/77	−0.81 (3.1)	−0.13 (1.7)	3.3
Average hourly earnings	1953–69	−0.17 (0.9)	−0.04 (0.8)	1.2
	1953–2/77	−0.09 (0.5)	−0.06 (1.2)	2.2

SOURCE: Consumer price index (all items), wholesale prices, average hourly earnings of production workers (adjusted to exclude overtime and interindustry shifts), and unemployment rate of prime-age men aged twenty-five to fifty-four are from the Department of Labor, Bureau of Labor Statistics. GNP deflator is from the Department of Commerce, Bureau of Economic Analysis. Excess capacity in manufacturing (the complement of capacity utilization) is from the Federal Reserve Board. Potential in excess of actual GNP as estimated annually by the Council of Economic Advisers (logarithmic interpolations used to derive quarterly data) is given in the *Annual Report, 1978,* p. 84, and as estimated quarterly by the Federal Reserve Bank of St. Louis is given in Rasche and Tatom (1977), p. 80.

All series are seasonally adjusted.

NOTE: The values of the *t* statistic omit negative signs and were not calculated for $\bar{U}$. For explanation of regression equation, see note to table C.

Dash (–) indicates not calculated because of wrong signs.

Table C. Estimated Effect of Economic Slack on Inflation, Assuming Rational Expectations

Regression for Eq. (10): $\dot{p}_i - \sum_{i=1}^{16} \frac{\dot{p}_{t-i}}{16} = (a + c_0)\,(U_t - \bar{U}) + (c_1 - a)\,(U_{t-1} - \bar{U}) + \sum_{i=2}^{5} c_i (U_{t-i} - \bar{U})$

U: Unemployment rate

	Regression Coefficients (and t Values)							
Period	$a+c_0$ (1)	c_1-a (2)	c_2 (3)	c_3 (4)	c_4 (5)	c_5 (6)	$\bar{U}$ (7)	Sum of cols. (1)–(6) (8)
			p: Consumer price index					
1953–69	0.08	−1.03	0.14	−0.20	0.10	0.12	4.1	−0.80
	(0.2)	(1.8)	(0.3)	(0.4)	(0.2)	(0.3)		
1953–77	−0.26	−1.00	0.26	0.22	−1.01	0.33	3.9	−1.46
	(0.7)	(2.0)	(0.5)	(0.5)	(2.1)	(0.9)		
			p: Wholesale finished goods					
1953–69	−0.80	0.27	−0.22	−1.00	1.51	−0.67	3.6	−0.88
	(1.1)	(0.3)	(0.2)	(1.0)	(1.5)	(1.0)		
1953–77	−0.84	−1.09	1.65	−1.50	−0.17	0.08	3.7	−1.87
	(0.9)	(0.8)	(1.2)	(1.1)	(0.1)	(0.1)		
			p: Average hourly earnings					
1953–69	−1.24	1.04	−0.67	−0.43	0.48	−0.01	3.3	−0.84
	(2.4)	(1.3)	(0.8)	(0.6)	(0.6)	(0.0)		
1953–77	−1.10	1.39	−1.01	−0.17	0.09	0.03	3.7	−0.78
	(2.2)	(1.7)	(1.3)	(0.2)	(0.1)	(0.1)		

SOURCE AND NOTE: Same as for table B.

Tables B and C

Regressions were fitted to quarterly data by the Cochrane-Orcutt method, which adjusts for first-order serial correlation in the residuals. (The total correlation coefficient is made misleadingly high by this adjustment and is not shown.) The period of fit began with the first quarter and ended with the fourth quarter of the years indicated, with certain exceptions because of unavailability of data. Units of inflation rates are percent per year, and of unemployed resources are percent. Hence units of coefficients are the change per quarter in annual percentage rate for each unit of quarterly change in U for a and for each unit of excess U for ba and the c's. The noninflationary rate of unemployed resources, $\bar{U}$ in percent, is estimated by the constant term of the regressions divided by ba in table B and by the sum of c's in table C. The method of calculating the variables was as follows.

$\dot{p}_t$ is the rate of change between quarterly levels of the price series in t and $t-1$.

U_t is an average for the quarter. For equation [5] in Table B, where the dependent variable is the change in the inflation rate, the two independent variables representing the change and level of unemployed resources have three-quarter spans. Thus all the variables in equation (5) have the same span of coverage. For equation [10] in table C, even though $\dot{p}_t$

covers two quarters of data and U_t only one quarter, a comparable span was not necessary because the set of six lagged U variables covers six quarters.

The unemployment rate of prime-age men aged twenty-five to fifty-four years was used in preference to the rate for all workers, because structural changes in the labor force have affected the total rate but are far less important for prime-age men (chapter 8). This rate was about half the rate for all workers in 1977.

Notes

Chapter 1. Emergence of the "Problem" of Inflation

1. Statement of Arthur F. Burns before the Joint Economic Committee, July 23, 1971, reprinted in *Federal Reserve Bulletin* (August 1971), 57:656.

2. See Moore (1961), p. 104, table 3.6; and (1973), p. 18. See also Fabricant (1972).

3. See, for example, Poole and Lieberman (1972).

4. On the profit rate, see Eckstein and Fromm (1959).

5. Stigler and Kindahl (1970), pp. 71–74.

6. Eckstein and Fromm (1959), p. 12, table 3.

7. See Barro and Grossman (1971).

8. See Humphrey (1937) and Tucker (1938).

9. In economic theory a condition of profit maximization is that price equal marginal cost times $\xi/(\xi - 1)$, where ξ is the price elasticity of demand to the firm in absolute terms. Except under perfect competition, ξ would be greater than unity and less than infinity. Under this condition prices rise if ξ declines or if marginal cost rises. There is no reason for ξ to decline in recessions; if anything, it might rise. It is not clear what role the term $\xi/(\xi - 1)$ plays in short-run price behavior, and it has been disregarded here.

Marginal cost changes when movements occur along the cost schedule due to shifts in demand or when the cost schedule shifts due to changes in unit factor prices. If demand shifts are unimportant, very likely so are movements along the cost schedule, and only shifts in the schedule are important for short-run price behavior.

10. For a survey of empirical studies, see Nordhaus (1972).

11. See Eckstein (1964) and Nordhaus (1972).

12. See Moore (1971).

13. See Moore (1975) and Hultgren (1965).

14. ". . . the world we now live in is one in which the monetary system has become relatively elastic, so that it can accommodate itself to changes in wages, rather than the other way about. Instead of actual wages having to adjust themselves to an equilibrium level, monetary policy adjusts the equilibrium level of money wages so as to make it conform to the actual level. It is hardly an exaggeration to say that instead of being on a Gold Standard, we are on a Labour Standard." Hicks (1955), p. 391.

15. Wilson (1959). See also Selden (1959).

16. Means (1935), (1939).

17. Mills (1927), pp. 485–93, appendix tables 2 and 4; and Mitchell (1938), p. 42, table 7.

18. Weiss (1966), (1971).

19. Perry (1966), (1967), and Perry et al. (1969).

20. Cagan (1975).

21. "With inflation, the demand curves of the firm and industry are moving persistently to the right. Under these circumstances there will normally be an incomplete adaptation of oligopoly prices. Prices will not be at profit-maximizing levels in any given situation, for the situation is continually changing while the adaptation is by deliberate and discrete steps. . . . I should like to argue that under quite commonplace conditions the lag in adaptation will be considerable and the unliquidated short-run monopoly gains substantial." Galbraith (1957), p. 127.

"So, only one course of action remains. This is some form of public intervention in the part of the economy where full employment or an approach to full employment means inflationary price and wage increases. . . .

"We are coming to accept the need for such intervention. The recent survey of professional economists by the Joint Economic Committee shows that between 40 and 50 percent of those interviewed or surveyed accepted the need for wage and price regulation as at least a reserve weapon against inflation." Galbraith (1959), p. 4390.

22. Burns (1957) and Schultze (1959).

23. Since real wages rise with the growth of labor productivity over the long run, unit wage costs can decline so long as money wages rise less than the growth in productivity. In a period of slack demand, however, productivity usually does not rise, in which case a reduction of labor costs requires a fall in money wages.

24. This behavior was attributed to oligopolistic industries by Sweezy (1939). Sweezy's interpretation of price rigidity was criticized by Stigler (1947).

25. Stigler and Kindahl (1970).

26. Solow and Samuelson (1960).

27. Tobin (1972), p. 10.

28. Friedman (1968).

29. Rees (1970).

30. Perry (1970), Gordon (1970) and (1971), Fellner (1971).

31. Sargent (1971), Lucas (1972), and Cargill and Meyer (1974).

32. See, for example, Phelps (1972).

33. Alchian and Klein (1973).

34. Klein (1975).

35. Public dissatisfaction with inflation appears to have affected voting in congressional elections from 1896 to 1970 (Stigler, 1973).

36. "The fact of the controls, plus their initial success [in 1971], had reduced inflationay expectations, held down total spending, restrained the tendency to boost wages and prices, and permitted output to rise more rapidly than it would otherwise have done." CEA (1974), p. 99.

37. Gordon (1972), (1973). See also Wachter (1974).

Chapter 2. Monetary versus Cost-Push Theories of Inflation

1. Discussed in Cagan (1965), ch. 6.

2. Letter to the *Economist,* May 8, 1869, reprinted in Jevons (1894).

3. See also Horwich (1966).

4. Cagan (1956).

5. For a discussion of the evidence, see Cagan (1969).

6. The rate of change of the money stock can be expressed in terms of three proximate determinants, high-powered money, the reserve ratio, and the currency ratio (see Cagan, 1965, ch. 1). The last one—the ratio of currency held by the public to the total money stock—does not change rapidly, except perhaps in banking panics, and has rarely been responsible for continuing rapid growth in the money stock.

7. Phillips (1958).

8. Friedman (1966) and Phelps (1967).

Chapter 3. Changes in the Cyclical Behavior of Prices

1. The Bureau of Labor Statistics index begins in 1890. The Warren-Pearson index of wholesale prices covering 1854 to 1890 (not shown) rose in the final two (1887 and 1890) of the seven recessions in that period.

2. The 1973–75 recession, not covered in these tables, was atypical, in that rates of price change increased dramatically during most of the recession period and fell sharply in the first part of the recovery. See chapter 6.

3. There are some differences between tables 1.1 and 3.1 and figures 3.1 and 3.2. In the figures, the first expansion after World War II was shortened to February 1947 through November 1948, because of the unavailability of earlier data for many of the product prices, and the last expansion was dated from December 1965 rather than from the 1961 trough, because the inflationary second half of this unusually long phase seemed more appropriate than the full period.

The rates for each expansion and recession phase were calculated for each series from the three-month average surrounding each peak and trough month, except that calendar-year averages were used for the beginning of the two expansions in 1921 and 1924, because not all the needed monthly data have been published. The series in the figures were not seasonally adjusted, which produces distortion mainly for the highly seasonal farm prices in recessions of length other than twelve months (all but 1970).

4. The dispersion of changes in rates of price change across the economy is shown by the slope of the distributions. A perfectly flat distribution would occur if all price responses were located in the two outside intervals of less than −20 and of +10 percent or more per year; a steep distribution reflects a clustering of changes in a narrow range. The distributions for the 1920s and for 1949 are much flatter than those for later cycles, indicating a one-time decline in dispersion after 1949. (Evidence presented below indicates that a general decline in dispersion occurred for all product groups except raw materials.) Data for earlier recessions, back to the 1890s, suggest that dispersion had long been about the same as in the 1920s (see Mills, 1927, p. 421, table 139). Since the distributions cover the same set of price series, this decline in dispersion since the 1920s cannot be due to the inclusion of less volatile prices or other changes in composition that can affect the behavior of the aggregate index.

Reported wholesale prices do not catch secret rebates and price shading in weak markets. If these practices have spread in recent decades, they could produce a misleading appearance of a decline in flexibility. This possible bias in the data, which is examined further below, does not appear to explain the overall changes in price behavior.

5. Stigler and Kindahl (1970), p. 23.

6. These data cover total shipments of establishments in the industry and therefore cover all products, not just the main one on which classification of the establishment is based. This produces some error in the classification of prices.

7. The fraction of total industry shipments by the four largest firms was used. In a few cases where the four-firm ratio for 1963 was not available, the concentration ratio for 1958 was used if the eight-firm ratio suggested that the concentration of the industry had not changed much between 1958 and 1963.

8. Demsetz (1973).

9. Means (1935), (1939), and (1959), p. 143.

10. Friedman (1966) and Phelps (1967).

Chapter 4. The Beginning of Inflation in 1965 to the Imposition of Price Controls in 1971

1. This description of the actual policy is based on figures for the money supply which have been revised several times since then and which do not necessarily agree closely with the data available to the committee at the time. But in general, and for this period in particular, the revisions have not altered the overall picture of monetary developments.

2. Salant et al. (1963).

3. The actual increase was 11.5 percent, and all of this came in the first three quarters.

4. *Business Review,* September 1969.

5. Hamburger (1973).

6. Most of this discrepancy was due to differing treatment of the housing sector (Triplett and Merchant, 1973).

7. American Statistical Association, "Third Quarter Survey of the Economic Outlook," mimeographed, 1971.

8. See U.S. Congress, Joint Economic Committee, *Report on the January 1970 Economic Report of the President,* pp. 19–20. 91st Congress, 2d session, March 25, 1970.

9. According to a Federal Reserve survey, state and local governments were forced to cut back desired long-term borrowing by $5.2 billion from mid-1969 to mid-1970, a reduction of 28 percent (Petersen, 1971).

10. Their figures pertain to money including time deposits, whereas the lags reported above are for the narrow definition of money excluding time deposits. The choice of definition influences the results somewhat, but the mixing of two different definitions here seems appropriate. Time deposits were not clearly distinguished from demand deposits in banking data before the 1930s and are best not excluded for that earlier period. In recent years, however, time deposits have undergone large fluctuations as a result of the ceilings on interest payable on deposits; time certificates of deposit, which have expanded rapidly since 1960, are particularly close substitutes for Treasury Bills and commercial paper and therefore are highly affected by changes in interest-rate differentials. For the recent period the inclusion of time deposits seems to introduce a misleading source of fluctuation.

11. American Statistical Association, "Third Quarter Survey of the Economic Outlook," mimeographed, 1969.

12. Teigen (1970), p. 102. See also CEA, 1963, p. 48.

The Federal Reserve–MIT econometric model indicated that a 10 percent tax increase would raise revenues $4 billion initially and decrease GNP by $10 billion in three quarters and $15 billion in six quarters. For a $10 billion increase in revenue, the corresponding effect on GNP would be $25 and $37.5 billion, respectively. These calculations do not hold the money stock completely constant, however, and so are somewhat overstated for present purposes. See de Leeuw and Gramlich (1968).

This model has an unusually large multiplier. For a personal tax cut, its multiplier after three years is 4.2. For the Brookings model the corresponding multiplier is 1.2, for the Wharton model 2.4, and for the Michigan model 1.7 (*ibid.*, p. 28, table 6).

13. This explanation is given by Wallich (1970).

14. Okun (1971a), table 1. Okun argues that the effect of the surcharge was delayed because of the lagged effect of income on consumption.

Chapter 5. The Economy under Controls 1971–1973

1. A favorable assessment of the guideposts by Perry (1967) was that they reduced manufacturing wage increases by about 2 percentage points per year for the period 1962–66. Difficulties with this estimate suggest that it is too high (Perry et al. 1969).

2. Schiff (1971).

3. Bosworth (1972), table 4.

4. CEA, 1972, p. 81. The freeze specified that prices could not rise above the highest level of substantial transactions (10 percent or more) in the previous thirty days or above the level of May 1970 if higher, with special provisions for seasonal or seldom-traded goods.

5. Bosworth (1972), table 5; and CEA, 1973, p. 62.

6. An econometric study by Gordon (1972), table 5, found the reduction in the rate of inflation due to controls to be 1.75 percentage points per year. The estimated effect on wage increases was .75 percentage points per year. While these results seem to underplay the effect of slack demand in curtailing inflation, they are consistent with the view that controls mainly affected profit margins.

7. There were special problems in lumber due to the profit ceilings (''Lumber: Fumblings of the Visible Hand,'' First National City Bank, 1972). For other difficulties see Fiedler (1973) and Poole (1973).

8. CEA, 1972, p. 69.

9. In a Lou Harris poll of 1,537 households reported on May 14, 1973 in the *New York Post* (p. 6), 65 percent said that middlemen and processors were a ''major cause'' of the rise in food prices and an additional 21 percent said they were a ''minor cause.''

Chapter 6. Foreign Influences in the Inflationary Outburst of 1973–1974

1. Fand (1975).

2. Same source as for table 6.1. The estimates are biased upward by the assumption that the input weights for each industry are constant and that the rise in prices of domestic substitutes is the same as that of the corresponding imports. The estimates may be biased downward, on the other hand, by a failure to allow for increases in all substitutes.

3. In the study cited for table 6.1, the Federal Reserve's econometric model was simulated to measure demand as well as cost effects. In the simulation the estimated effect of the depreciation of the exchange rate on the consumption deflator was 2.8 percentage points, compared with less than one point by the input-output analysis noted in the text. The estimated effect of the extraordinary increases in import *and* export prices was 4.5 percentage points, the same as the estimate by input-output analysis noted in the text for import prices alone, apparently because deflationary demand effects exactly offset the added inflationary effects.

4. A time-series regression estimate (Modigliani and Papademos, 1976) found the underlying inflation rate in 1974 to be from 4 to 5 percent and thus attributed slightly more than half the total rate to foreign influences.

The domestic inflation rate of 5.1 percent may have partly reflected a measurement catch-up from the removal of Phase II price controls (Darby 1976) and so may have overstated the "true" rate. In that event the remainder attributable to the foreign influences would have been more than half of the total "true" inflation rate.

In the light of these studies, the mid-1973 inflation rate, and the fact that the Joint Economic Committee estimate is probably low, the half-and-half assumption in the text for the division between foreign and domestic influences seems to represent a reasonable order of magnitude.

5. The Federal Reserve capacity utilization index was 83 percent in 1973, a bit below its level of 87 percent in the first three quarters of 1969. The Wharton index was 96 percent in the three final quarters of 1973, about equal to the percentage in the first three quarters of 1969.

6. American Statistical Association, "Fourth Quarter Survey of the Economic Outlook," mimeographed, 1972.

7. A price rise of 10.5 percent reduces real money balances to 1/1.105 = .905 or by 9.5 percent.

8. Modigliani and Papademos (1975), especially p. 159; Phelps (1975); and Tobin (1975).

9. The tax rebates of 1975 offered an opportunity to increase the money stock quickly through Treasury operations (see Phelps 1975). The rebates did shift Treasury holdings into public hands, a fact that accounts for the rise in monetary growth in early 1975. But the Federal Reserve did not favor this result, and subsequent growth was low in order to offset the rebate increase.

Chapter 7. Recovery from the Recession of 1973–1975

1. *The Budget of the U.S. Government* (Washington, D.C.: Government Printing Office, 1976), p. 41.

2. Modigliani and Papademos (1976) and Benjamin M. Friedman (1976).

3. Modigliani and Papademos (1976).

4. The corresponding target for M_2 was 8.5 to 10.5 percent and for M_3 was 10 to 12 percent. *Federal Reserve Bulletin,* May 1975, p. 286; August 1975, p. 495; and November 1975, p. 747. The successive extensions of the target did not, however, allow for corrections of previous divergences.

5. *Federal Reserve Bulletin,* February 1976, pp. 119–25. This target for M_1 was changed again in May to 4.5 to 7 percent, and to 7.5 and 10 percent for M_2 and left unchanged (since November 1975) at 10 to 12 percent for M_3. (The Federal Reserve's definitions of M_1 and M_3 were given in the note to figure 6.4. M_2 is M_1 plus time deposits at commercial banks other than large negotiable CDs).

Chapter 8. The Reduction of Inflation and the Magnitude of Unemployment

1. CEA, 1962, p. 46.

2. Modigliani and Papademos (1976), p. 10. Most other estimates of the full-employment rate of unemployment simply *assume* that it was equal to the actual unemployment rate in 1956, though allowance is now usually made for increases since then.

3. A change in the overall unemployment rate U can be decomposed as follows: For 1956, $U^{56} = \sum_i w_i^{56} U_i^{56}$ where i denotes the various sex and age subgroups and w_i is their relative weight in the labor force. (The age subgroups are 16–19, 20–24, 25–54, 55–64, and 65 and over.) For a later year t, where the change in the subgroup rates and weights from 1956 to year t is denoted by $\underset{t}{\Delta}$,

$$U^t = \sum_i (w_i^{56} + \underset{t}{\Delta} w_i)(U_i^{56} + \underset{t}{\Delta} U_i) = U^{56} + \sum_i (w_i^{56} \underset{t}{\Delta} U_i + U_i^{56} \underset{t}{\Delta} w_i + \underset{t}{\Delta} w_i \underset{t}{\Delta} U_i).$$

For $t = 1973$, these quantities are, in percent,

$$4.85 = 4.13 + .04 + .46 + .22.$$

The compositional change given in the text for $t = 1973$ is

$$\sum_i U_i^{56} (w_i^{56} + \underset{73}{\Delta} w_i) - U^{56} = \sum_i U_i^{56} \underset{73}{\Delta} w_i = .46.$$

The constant-weight unemployment rate calculated by the CEA (1975), p. 95, for 1973 is

$$\sum_i w_i^{56} (U_i^{56} + \underset{73}{\Delta} U_i) = 4.17.$$

When this amount is subtracted from U^{73}, the remainder shows the implied effect of changes in composition:

$$\sum_i U_i^{56} \underset{73}{\Delta} w_i + \sum_i \underset{73}{\Delta} w_i \underset{73}{\Delta} U_i = .46 + .22.$$

This is greater than the first figure for compositional change above by the amount of the interaction term,

$$\sum_i \underset{73}{\Delta} w_i \underset{73}{\Delta} U_i = .22.$$

The interaction term is important here because of the rise in unemployment rates of youths and women combined with their growing importance in the labor force. The rising proportion of these groups in the labor force can itself cause their unemployment rates to increase because of the time necessary for the demand for labor to adjust to the expansion of labor supply groups which are not perfect substitutes for other groups. Because of the difficulty of measuring this effect, the interaction term may be kept separate from the direct effect of changes in composition.

4. Mincer (1966) and Simler and Tella (1968).

5. Feldstein (1973) found that unemployment insurance accounts for half or more of the volume of job layoffs. Such temporary or seasonal layoffs add to the average amount of unemployment.

Chiswick (1976) estimated that unemployment insurance increased the average unemployment rate in agriculture in 1975 by one percentage point.

6. Coverage and benefits are for all federal and state programs (CEA, 1975, pp. 281 and 122).

7. Classen (1975). This study was based on an analysis of survey data collected by the Pennsylvania Department of Labor and Industry. The period 1967–68 was chosen because the maximum weekly benefits in Pennsylvania increased on January 1, 1968 from $45 to $60. It was possible to measure the effect of benefits on the duration of unemployment because of substantial differences in dollar benefits among similar claimants over a short period. This study might even understate the effect, because higher benefits also foster more temporary layoffs which tend to be of short duration.

Two other studies which gave different results may be cited. A study of four subgroups of the labor force using the National Longitudinal Survey for the second half of the 1960s (Ehrenberg and Oaxaca 1976) found the increase in the duration of unemployment due to unemployment insurance to be from two and one-half to six weeks, and for one subgroup nineteen weeks. From a comparison of insured and uninsured workers in 1969, Marston (1975) concluded that the duration of unemployment increased by from one-half to one-and-one-half weeks.

8. The number of workers receiving benefits is reported in U.S. Department of Labor, *Unemployment Insurance Statistics,* various monthly issues. Nonstate unemployment programs, which comprise 8 percent of the total, are excluded here.

9. CEA, 1977, p. 50.

10. Holen and Horowitz (1974).

11. Tella (1976a).

12. When the weighting takes into account the proportion of covered teenage employment in each sector, the increase is from 21.0 percent to 40.1 percent (Gavett 1970, p. 12, table 1.6).

13. In 1976 certificates were issued for about 600,000 students working in educational institutions and for 200,000 other youths (CEA, 1977, p. 142).

14. Mincer (1976).

15. These estimates are based on the change from 1956 to 1973 and to 1974 in the ratio of the minimum wage to average hourly earnings in private nonfarm sectors, weighted by the proportion of all workers or of teenagers covered by the minimum wage in each sector. This variable, used by Mincer in the regressions, was published for the years up to 1968 in Gavett (1970), p. 12.

For 1973 and 1974 the ratio was approximated using the industrial distribution of covered workers in 1974 (Elden 1974, p. 35, table 2) and of teenagers in 1968 (Gavett 1970). For 1973, when the minimum wage was $1.60 per hour, the ratio was 34.6 percent for covered workers and 34.9 percent for teenagers. For 1974, when the minimum wage was $2.00 per hour, it was 40.0 and 42.1 percent, respectively.

16. These figures weight the increases in unemployment for each subgroup according to the composition of the labor force in 1973 and 1974. As weighted by the 1956 composition, the increases are 0.30 and 0.45 percentage points, respectively. The difference between the use of weights for 1956 and 1973 or 1974 can be attributed to the interaction between the effects of compositional changes and the minimum wage (see note 3).

17. Goldfarb (1974).

18. Similar results were found for the 1963–72 period by Ragan (1977). Gramlich (1976) reported that the extension of minimum wage coverage has had no effect on unemployment, but this finding is open to question (see Gordon, 1977, esp. pp. 207–8).

19. CEA, 1976, pp. 97–98.

20. Tella (1976a).

21. Tella (1976b), table 5.

22. O'Neill et al. (1974).

23. Hall (1974), p. 345; Wachter (1976a) and (1976b); Gordon (1977); and CEA, 1977, p. 51. Tella (1976a) gives a total increase of 2 percentage points or more, but he includes additional influences which occur mainly in the high-unemployment stages of the business cycle.

All such studies which estimated the rise in the full-employment unemployment rate since the 1950s accepted the actual 1956 rate as representing the full-employment level.

24. Tobin (1972) and Rees (1970).

25. The price stability and declining unemployment of the early 1960s suggest that the inflationary pressure set off by rising aggregate demand may be less when expected price changes are very low. Hence it may be possible to achieve lower unemployment after a period of price stability than after a period of prolonged inflation.

26. In his Nobel lecture Milton Friedman (1977) presented evidence of such a relationship for several countries.

27. Okun (1971b) and Logue and Willett (1976).

28. Higher inflation rates are also associated with greater fluctuations in relative prices. See Vining and Elwertowski (1976).

29. Lipsey (1960) pointed out that convexity in the Phillips curve and fluctuations in demand among sectors of the economy affect aggregate unemployment.

Greater variability of inflation rates could cause firms to attribute most shifts in demand to nominal rather than real effects, and thus to respond largely by changing prices rather than by changing output and employment. The effect is to reduce the slope of the Phillips curve (see Lucas 1973). It is not clear, however, how this would affect the convexity of the curve. If a steeper curve also had less convexity (as seems plausible), the greater variability of higher average inflation rates might, after the period of transition to a steeper curve, produce little increase in average unemployment. At the same time, there would be less fluctuation in unemployment despite the greater fluctuation in inflation rates. We do not observe smaller fluctuations in unemployment in the United States, but such effects might yet occur if inflation continues to be highly variable.

30. A linear function fits the data examined in chapter 9 slightly better than a convex function does, though not significantly according to the usual statistical criteria. Papademos (1977) also tested the shapes of various versions of the Phillips curve and found that none is statistically superior to the linear form.

In an earlier study, Perry (1966), p. 55, found the reciprocal form of the unemployment rate to fit slightly better than the linear form. His data ended with 1960. Conceivably, convexity exists but the data after 1960 do not reveal it because of greater statistical "noise."

Since the definition of unemployment does not admit negative values, the Phillips curve must show convexity as unemployment approaches zero. But that arithmetical constraint does not mean that the curve cannot be linear within the usual range of values experienced.

31. Although the term gradualism was coined by the Council of Economic Advisers in 1969 to describe administration policy (which as a staff member at the time I fully agreed with) and then dropped when the 1970 recession ensued, the criterion of policy described by it has persisted.

32. "Subdued" inflation has never been precisely defined. In practice it does not mean a zero rate of inflation but a rate that, by the standards of the day, is not "excessive." It is easy to forget that, in the late 1950s, 3 percent appeared excessive.

33. The optimal path calls for a constant rate of unemployment until the inflation rate reaches the desired level. The reason for a constant unemployment rate is that a higher rate of unemployment in one quarter does not produce a sufficiently greater reduction in inflation to justify the lower rate of unemployment then possible in a later quarter. However, in a more sophisticated analysis, with discounting of the disadvantages of future inflation and unemployment, a constant unemployment rate may no longer be the optimal path. Papademos (1977) analyzes the optimal path of inflation reduction under a variety of assumptions.

Chapter 9. The Reduction of Inflation by Slack Demand

1. See discussion in ch. 8, "Is Gradualism the Best Policy?"

2. CEA, 1977, p. 41.

3. CEA, 1978, p. 80.

4. Heller et al. (1978). See also Jianakoplos (1978).

5. Ackley (1978).

6. This pattern of price behavior has long been noted by business cycle analysts. For example, see Moore (1971) and (1977), esp. pp. 141–58.

7. Mills (1927).

8. Darby (1976).

9. Means (1935), (1939), and (1959).

10. Burns (1957).

11. Schultze (1959).

12. A similar equation was derived by Papademos (1977), p. 23 (his equation 23). The equation given in the early Phillips curve literature was quite different in theory and implications. It had the same right side as equation [5] above but with the inflation rate rather than its change on the left. (For a review of empirical work in the literature, see R. A. Gordon, 1975.) The equation in the literature was unable to explain rising prices in a recession since both variables are then positive, and, given the appropriate negative coefficients, the two terms will be negative. What the standard Phillips curve lacked was a term representing *long-run* price expectations, which equation [5] includes.

Much of the literature reports that the rate of change of wages is more closely related to changes in the unemployment rate than to the rate itself (see Kuh, 1967). An effect of the change in the unemployment rate on the rate of change of wages has been interpreted as reflecting *short-run* expectations of changes in demand (see Bowen and Berry, 1963). This implies a relation between changes in the rate of change of wages and the second derivative of the unemployment variable. Such a relation has no importance for the effect of slack demand on inflation as formulated here.

13. This is the implication of the theory of aggregate disequilibrium. The spillover effects of reduced output and employment in one industry make demand lower in other industries. The restoration requires an increase in the purchasing power of money balances through a decline in the price level—an increase sufficient to raise the demand for goods and services to the original level of expenditures in real terms.

14. A rational expectations model with this relationship is presented by Meltzer (1977).

15. An alternative formulation suggested by other rational expectations models would be to use past monetary growth and other basic determinants of the price level, known to rational economic agents, as indicators of the expected trend of prices. Then, in theory, slack demand would be superfluous in the equation and would not itself affect the inflation rate. (For example, see Meltzer, 1977). In such models, however, a decline of monetary growth and consequent reduction in inflation still produces a period of slack demand. Equation [9] can be interpreted as reflecting the amount of slack which is associated in such models with reductions in the expected trend of prices.

16. Although equations [5] and [10] have many apparent similarities, they differ crucially in the form of the left-hand variable. This difference does not, however, provide an acceptable statistical test for choosing between the two theories. The fit of these equations to the data is not sufficiently close to produce a clear preference for one or the other, nor to indicate whether or not certain forms of the variables or their lags should be included in the regression equation. A satisfactory test of the two theories of price behavior requires different techniques and evidence from that provided here. Nevertheless, we may examine the reasonableness of the estimates from the two theories for the effect of slack demand on the inflation rate.

17. The other measures of slack give similar results if we note that they register the same slack with two-and-a-half to three times the magnitude shown by the unemployment rate.

18. Results for the GNP deflator of the private nonfarm sector (not shown) are similar. In a

recent study of 1954–71, R. J. Gordon (1975) also found, for the GNP chain deflator of the private sector excluding food and energy, that current and lagged changes in the GNP gap affect the inflation rate but the current and past levels do not.

19. The results in table 9.1 seem to suggest that the effect of slack on inflation has increased in recent years; the estimates of *ba* generally have larger negative values for the full than for the shorter period. The larger values, however, may simply reflect the large rise and subsequent decline in the inflation rate in 1973–75 stemming from the extraneous foreign influences. The estimates for average hourly earnings also suggest that *b* is higher for the full period, but the overall effect shown by *ba,* though larger, remains low, indicative of the smaller and slower response of wages to economic slack compared with the response of prices. It is doubtful that the effect of slack in reducing inflation has increased, although there is no indication here of a decrease either. (The evidence presented in chapter 3, which did not cover the 1973–75 recession, suggested a decrease.)

20. The sum of the *c* coefficients gives the estimated effect of excess unemployment on the difference between the current inflation rate and the noncyclical trend. For a business cycle of *n* periods in which this difference is maintained at *C*,

$$\dot{p}_t - \sum_1^n \frac{\dot{p}_{t-i}}{n} = \sum_0^n c_i(U_{t-i} - \bar{U}) = C,$$

the cumulative effect can be expressed by

$$\dot{p}_{t+n} = C\left(1 + \frac{1}{n}\right)^{n-1} \text{ and } \sum_1^n \frac{\dot{p}_{t-i}}{n} = C\left(1 + \frac{1}{n}\right)^{n-1} - C.$$

For $n = 16$ quarters, the average rate is 1.48*C* or .37*C* per year.

The estimate of *C* is not affected greatly by changes in *n* beyond a small number, and we may assume *C* remains the same as *n* increases. In particular, we may derive the effect for continuous adjustments where the periods approach zero in length and *n* approaches infinity, for which the limit of $\left(1 + \frac{1}{n}\right)^{n-1}$ is *e* or 2.72. Hence the total effect for a full cycle of continuous adjustments, which is independent of the length of the cycle, is 1.72*C*.

21. This is emphasized by Fellner (1976).

References Cited

Ackley, Gardner. 1978. "Okun's New Tax-Based Incomes-Policy Proposal," in *Economic Outlook USA* (Winter), pp. 8–9. University of Michigan, Survey Research Center.

Alchian, Armen A. and Benjamin Klein. 1973. "On a Correct Measure of Inflation," *Journal of Money, Credit and Banking* (February), 5(1):173–91.

Barro, Robert J. and Herschel I. Grossman. 1971. "A General Disequilibrium Model of Income and Employment," *American Economic Review* (March), 61:82–93.

Berner, R., P. Clark, J. Enzler, and B. Lowrey. 1975. "International Sources of Domestic Inflation," U.S. Congress, Joint Economic Committee, *Studies in Price Stability and Economic Growth,* Paper no. 3. 94th Congress, 1st session, August 5.

Bosworth, Barry. 1972. "Phase II: The U.S. Experiment with an Incomes Policy," *Brookings Papers on Economic Activity,* no. 2, pp. 343–83.

Bowen, William G. and R. Albert Berry. 1963. "Unemployment Conditions and Movements of the Money Wage Level," *Review of Economics and Statistics* (May), 45:163–72.

Burns, Arthur F. 1957. *Prosperity Without Inflation.* New York: Fordham University Press.

Cagan, Phillip. 1956. "The Monetary Dynamics of Hyperinflations," in Milton Friedman, ed., *Studies in the Quantity Theory of Money.* Chicago: University of Chicago Press.

—— 1965. *Determinants and Effects of Changes in the Money Stock 1875–1960.* New York: National Bureau of Economic Research.

—— 1969. "Interest Rates and the Reserve Ratio—A Reinterpretation of the Statistical Association," in Jack M. Guttentag and Phillip Cagan, eds., *Essays on Interest Rates,* 1:223–71. New York: National Bureau of Economic Research.

—— 1975. "Inflation and Market Structure 1967–73," *Explorations in Economic Research* (Spring), 2:203–16.

Cargill, Thomas F. and Robert A. Meyer. 1974. "Wages, Prices, and Unemployment: Distributed Lag Estimates," *Journal of the American Statistical Association* (March), 69:98–107.

(CEA) *The Annual Report of the Council of Economic Advisers.* Washington, D.C.: U.S. Government Printing Office.

Chiswick, Barry. 1976. "The Effect of Unemployment Compensation on a Seasonal Industry: Agriculture," *Journal of Political Economy* (June), 84:591–602.

Classen, Kathleen. 1975. "The Effects of Unemployment Insurance: Evidence from Pennsylvania." Arlington, Va.: The Public Research Institute of the Center of Naval Analyses (April), processed.

Darby, Michael. 1976. "The U.S. Economic Stabilization Program of 1971–74," in *The Illusion of Wage and Price Controls.* Vancouver, B.C.: Fraser Institute.

de Leeuw, Frank and Edward Gramlich. 1968. "The Federal Reserve–MIT Econometric Model," *Federal Reserve Bulletin* (January), pp. 11–40.

Demsetz, Harold. 1973. *The Market Concentration Doctrine.* AEI-Hoover Policy Study 7. American Enterprise Institute.

Eckstein, Otto. 1964. "A Theory of the Wage-Price Process in Modern Industry," *Review of Economic Studies* (October), 31:267–83.

Eckstein, Otto and Gary Fromm. 1959. "Steel and the Postwar Inflation." U.S. Congress, Joint Economic Committee, *Study of Employment, Growth, and Price Levels,* Study Paper no. 2. 86th Congress, 1st session, November 6.

Ehrenberg, Ronald G. and Ronald L. Oaxaca. 1976. "Unemployment Insurance, Duration of Unemployment, and Subsequent Wage Gain," *American Economic Review* (December), 66:754–66.

Elden, Peyton. 1974. "The 1974 Amendments to the Federal Minimum Wage Law," *Monthly Labor Review* (July). Washington, D.C.: Bureau of Labor Statistics.

Fabricant, Solomon. 1972. "The 'Recession' of 1969–70," in *The Business Cycle Today,* pp. 89–136. New York: National Bureau of Economic Research.

Fand, David I. 1975. "World Reserves and World Inflation," *Banca Nazionale del Lavoro Quarterly Review* (December), no. 115.

Feldstein, Martin S. 1973. "The Importance of Temporary Layoffs: An Empirical Analysis," *Brookings Papers on Economic Activity,* no. 3, pp. 725–44.

Fellner, William. 1971. "Phillips-type Approach or Acceleration?" *Brookings Papers on Economic Activity,* no. 2, pp. 469–83.

—— 1976. *Towards a Reconstruction of Macroeconomics.* Washington, D.C.: American Enterprise Institute.

Fiedler, Edgar R. 1973. "The Case Against Rigid Controls," *The Wall Street Journal,* April 19, p. 20.

First National City Bank. 1972. *Monthly Economic Letter* (December). New York.

Friedman, Benjamin M. 1976. "Monetary Policy for the 1976 Recovery," *New England Economic Review* (January–February), pp. 3–16. Federal Reserve Bank of Boston.

Friedman, Milton. 1966. "What Price Guideposts?" in G. P. Schultz and R. Z. Aliber, eds., *Guidelines, Informal Controls, and the Market Place.* Chicago: University of Chicago Press.

——. 1968. "The Role of Monetary Policy," Presidential Address, *American Economic Review* (March), 58:1–17.

—— 1977. "Inflation and Unemployment," Nobel lecture, *Journal of Political Economy* (June), 85:457–72.

Galbraith, John Kenneth. 1957. "Market Structure and Stabilization Policy," *Review of Economics and Statistics* (May), 39:124–33.

—— 1959. Statement, U.S. Congress, Senate Subcommittee on Antitrust and Monopoly, *Administered Prices,* part 10, p. 4390. 86th Congress, 1st session, March 11.

Gavett, Thomas W. 1970. "Introduction," in *Youth Unemployment and Minimum Wages.* Washington, D.C.: Bureau of Labor Statistics Bulletin no. 1657.

Goldfarb, R. S. 1974. "The Policy Content of Quantitative Minimum Wage Research," *Proceedings of the Twenty-Seventh Annual Meeting,* pp. 261–68. Madison, Wisc.: Industrial Relations Research Association.

Gordon, R. A. 1975. "Wages, Prices, and Unemployment, 1900–1970," *Industrial Relations* (October), 14:273–301.

Gordon, Robert J. 1970. "The Recent Acceleration of Inflation and Its Lessons for the Future," *Brookings Papers on Economic Activity,* no. 1, pp. 8–41.

—— 1971. "Inflation in Recession and Recovery," *Brookings Papers on Economic Activity,* no. 1, pp. 105–58.

—— 1972. "Wage-Price Controls and the Shifting Phillips Curve," *Brookings Papers on Economic Activity,* no. 2, pp. 385–421.

—— 1973. "The Response of Wages and Prices to the First Two Years of Controls," *Brookings Papers on Economic Activity,* no. 3, pp. 765–78.

—— 1975. "The Impact of Aggregate Demand on Prices," *Brookings Papers on Economic Activity,* no. 3, pp. 613–62.

—— 1977. "Structural Unemployment and the Productivity of Women," *Journal of Monetary Economics* (supplement), 5:181–229.

Gramlich, Edward. 1976. "Impact of Minimum Wages on Other Wages, Employment, and Family Incomes," *Brookings Papers on Economic Activity,* no. 2, pp. 409–51.

Hall, Robert E. 1974. "The Process of Inflation in the Labor Market," *Brookings Papers on Economic Activity,* no. 2, pp. 343–93.

Hamburger, Michael J. 1973. "The Demand for Money in 1971: Was There a Shift?" *Journal of Money, Credit, and Banking* (May), 5:720–25.

Heller, Walter, Arthur Okun, Robert Solow, James Tobin, Henry Wallich, and Sidney Weintraub. 1978. "Economy: Toward a 'Carrots' and/or 'Sticks' Cure," *New York Times,* March 12, op–ed page.

Hicks, John R. 1955. "Economic Foundations of Wage Policy," *Economic Journal* (September), vol. 65.

Holen, Arlene and Stanley A. Horowitz. 1974. "The Effect of Unemployment Insurance and Eligibility Enforcement on Unemployment," *Journal of Law and Economics* (October), 17:403–31.

Horwich, George. "Tight Money, Monetary Restraint, and the Price Level," *Journal of Finance* (March), pp. 15–33.

Hultgren, Thor. 1965. *Costs, Prices, and Profits: Their Cyclical Relations.* New York: National Bureau of Economic Research.

Humphrey, Don D. 1937. "The Nature and Meaning of Rigid Prices, 1890–1933," *Journal of Political Economy* (October), 45:651–61.

Jevons, Stanley. 1894. *Investigations in Currency and Finance.* London: Macmillan, pp. 155–158.

Jianakoplos, Nancy A. 1978. "A Tax-Based Incomes Policy (TIP): What's It All About?" *Federal Reserve Bank of St. Louis Review* (February), 60:8–12.

Klein, Benjamin. 1975. "The Measurement and Social Costs of Inflation: The Recent Inflation and Our New Monetary Standard," *Economic Inquiry* (December), 13:461–84.

Kuh, E. 1967. "A Productivity Theory of Wage Levels—An Alternative to the Phillips Curve," *Review of Economic Studies* (October), 34:333–60.

Lipsey, Richard G. 1960. "The Relation Between Unemployment and the Rate of Change of Money Wage Rates in the United Kingdom, 1862–1957: A Further Analysis," *Economica* (February), 27:1–31.

Logue, Dennis E. and Thomas D. Willett 1976. "A Note on the Relation Between the Rate and Variability of Inflation," *Economica* (May), 43:151–58.

Lucas, Robert E. 1972. "Econometric Testing of the Natural Rate Hypothesis," in Otto Eckstein, ed., *The Econometrics of Price Determination.* Washington, D.C.: Social Science Research Council and Board of Governors of the Federal Reserve System.

—— 1973. "Some International Evidence on Output-Inflation Tradeoffs," *American Economic Review* (June), 68:326–34.

Marston, Stephen R. 1975. "The Impact of Unemployment Insurance on Job Search," *Brookings Papers on Economic Activity,* no. 1, pp. 3–48.

Means, Gardiner C. 1935. *Industrial Prices and Their Relative Inflexibility,* Senate Document 13. 74th Congress, 1st session.

—— 1939. In *The Structure of the American Economy.* Washington, D.C.: National Resources Committee (June), part 2, p. 143.

—— 1959. Statement, U.S. Congress, Senate Subcommittee on Antitrust and Monopoly, *Administered Prices,* part 9, pp. 4745–60. 86th Congress, 1st session, January 24.

Meltzer, Allan H. 1977. "Anticipated Inflation and Unanticipated Price Change," *Journal of Money, Credit, and Banking* (February), 9:182–205.

Mills, Frederick C. 1927. *The Behavior of Prices.* New York: National Bureau of Economic Research.

Mincer, Jacob. 1966. "Labor-Force Participation and Unemployment: A Review of Recent Evidence," Robert A. Gordon and Margaret S. Gordon, eds., *Prosperity and Unemployment,* pp. 73–112. New York: Wiley.

—— 1976. "Unemployment Effects of Minimum Wages," part 2, *Journal of Political Economy* (August), 84:87–104.

Mitchell, Wesley C. 1938. *The Making and Using of Index Numbers.* Washington, D.C.: Bureau of Labor Statistics Bulletin 656 (March).

Modigliani, Franco and Lucas Papademos. 1975. "Target for Monetary Policy in the Coming Year," *Brookings Papers on Economic Activity,* no. 1, pp. 141–63.

—— 1976. "Monetary Policy for the Coming Quarters: The Conflicting Views," *New England Economic Review* (March–April), pp. 2–35. Federal Reserve Bank of Boston.

Moore, Geoffrey H. 1971. *The Cyclical Behavior of Prices.* Washington, D.C.: Bureau of Labor Statistics Report 384.

—— 1973. "New Work on Business Cycles," in *53d Annual Report* (September). New York: National Bureau of Economic Research.

—— 1974. "Price Behavior During Growth Recessions," in *Perspectives on Inflation,* pp. 25–37. Ottawa: The Conference Board of Canada.

—— 1975. "Productivity, Costs, and Prices: New Light from an Old Hypothesis," *Explorations in Economic Research* (Winter), 2:1–17.

—— 1977. "Lessons of the 1973–1976 Recession and Recovery," in William Fellner, ed., *Contemporary Economic Problems 1977.* Washington, D.C.: American Enterprise Institute.

Moore, Geoffrey H., ed. 1961. *Business Cycle Indicators,* vol. 1. Princeton, N.J.: Princeton University Press for National Bureau of Economic Research.

Nordhaus, William D. 1972. "Recent Developments in Price Dynamics," in Otto Eckstein, ed., *The Econometrics of Price Determination.* Washington, D.C.: Social Science Research Council and Board of Governors of the Federal Reserve System.

Okun, Arthur M. 1971a. "The Income Tax Surcharge and Consumer Demand, 1968–70," *Brookings Papers on Economic Activity,* no. 1, pp. 167–204.

—— 1971b. "The Mirage of Steady Inflation," *Brookings Papers on Economic Activity,* no. 2, pp. 485–98.

O'Neill, David, Kathleen Classen, and Arlene Holen. 1974. "Effects of the 1974 UI Extensions on Unemployment." Arlington, Va.: The Public Research Institute of the Center for Naval Analyses. December, processed.

Papademos, Lucas. 1977. "Optimal Aggregate Employment Policy and Other Essays." Ph.D. dissertation, Massachusetts Institute of Technology.

Perry, George L. 1966. *Unemployment, Money Wage Rates, and Inflation.* Cambridge, Mass.: MIT Press.

—— 1967. "Wages and Guideposts," *American Economic Review* (September), 57:897–904.

—— 1970. "Changing Labor Markets and Inflation," *Brookings Papers on Economic Activity,* no. 3, pp. 411–41.

Perry, George, Paul S. Anderson, Michael L. Wachter, and Adrian W. Throop. 1969. Comments on Perry and Reply, *American Economic Review* (June), 59:351–70.

Petersen, John E. 1971. "Response of State and Local Governments to Varying Credit Conditions," *Federal Reserve Bulletin* (March), pp. 209–32.

Phelps, Edmund S. 1967. "Phillips Curves, Expectations of Inflation, and Optimal Employment over Time," *Economica* (August), 34:254–81.

—— 1972. *Inflation Policy and Unemployment Theory: The Cost-Benefit Approach to Monetary Planning,* New York: Norton.

—— 1975. "Creating Money for Tax Rebates." *New York Times,* January 25, op–ed page.

Phillips, A. W. 1958. "The Relation between Unemployment and the Rate of Change of Money Wage Rates in the United Kingdom, 1861–1957," *Economica* (November), 25:283–99.

Poole, William. 1973. "Wage-Price Controls: Where Do We Go From Here?" *Brookings Papers on Economic Activity,* no. 1, pp. 285–99.

Poole, William and Charles Lieberman. 1972. "Improving Monetary Control," *Brookings Papers on Economic Activity,* no. 2, pp. 293–335.

Ragan, James F., Jr. 1977. "Minimum Wage Legislation and the Youth Labor Market," *Review of Economics and Statistics* (May), 59:129–36.

Rasche, Robert H. and John A. Tatom. 1977. "Potential Output and Its Growth Rate—The Dominance of Higher Energy Costs in the 1970s," in *U.S. Productive Capacity: Estimating the Utilization Gap,* p. 80. Working Paper 23, Center for the Study of American Business, Washington University, St. Louis, December.

Rees, Albert. 1970. "The Phillips Curve as a Menu for Policy Choices," *Economica* (August), 37:227–38.

Salant, Walter S. et al. 1963. *The United States Balance of Payments of 1968.* Washington, D.C.: The Brookings Institution.

Sargent, Thomas. 1971. "A Note on the Accelerationist Controversy," *Journal of Money, Credit, and Banking* (August), 3:721–25.

Schiff, Eric. 1971. *Incomes Policies Abroad.* Washington, D.C.: American Enterprise Institute.

Schultze, Charles L. 1959. "Recent Inflation in the United States." U.S. Congress, Joint Economic Committee, *Study of Employment, Growth and Price Levels,* Study Paper no. 1. 86th Congress, 1st session, September.

Selden, Richard T. 1959. "Cost-Push versus Demand-Pull Inflation, 1955–57," *Journal of Political Economy* (February), 67:1–20.

Simler, N. J. and Alfred Tella. 1968. "Labor Reserves and the Phillips Curve," *Review of Economics and Statistics* (February), 50:32–49.

Solow, Robert M. and Paul A. Samuelson. 1960. "Analytical Aspects of Anti-Inflation Policy," *American Economic Review* (May), 50:177–94.

Stigler, George. 1947. "The Kinky Oligopoly Demand Curve and Rigid Prices," *Journal of Political Economy* (October), 55:432–49.

—— 1973. "General Economic Conditions and National Elections," *American Economic Review* (May), 63:160–67.

Stigler, George and James Kindahl. 1970. *The Behavior of Industrial Prices.* New York: National Bureau of Economic Research.

Sweezy, Paul M. 1939. "Demand under Conditions of Oligopoly," *Journal of Political Economy* (August), 47:569–73.

Teigen, Ronald L. 1970. "The Determination of National Income." In Teigen and Warren L. Smith, eds. *Readings in Money, National Income, and Stabilization Policy.* Homewood, Ill.: Irwin.

Tella, Alfred. 1976a. "Analyzing Joblessness." *New York Times,* October 27, op–ed page.

—— 1976b. *Cyclical Behavior of Bias-Adjusted Unemployment.* Methods for Manpower Analysis No. 11, W. E. Upjohn Institute for Employment Research. Kalamazoo, Michigan, April.

Tobin, James. 1972. "Inflation and Unemployment," Presidential Address, *American Economic Review* (March), 62:1–18.

—— 1975. "Monetary Policy and the Control of Credit," in A. T. Sommers, ed.,

Answers to Inflation and Recession: Economic Policies for a Modern Society. New York: The Conference Board.

Triplett, Jack E. and Stephen M. Merchant. 1973. "The CPI and the PCE Deflator: An Econometric Analysis of Two Price Measures," *Annals of Economic and Social Measurement* (July), vol. 2.

Tucker, Rufus. 1938. "Reasons for Price Rigidity," *American Economic Review* (March), 28:41–54.

Vining, Daniel R. and Thomas C. Elwertowski. 1976. "The Relationship Between Relative Prices and the General Price Level," *American Economic Review* (September), 66:699–708.

Wachter, Michael L. 1974. "Phase II, Cost-Push Inflation, and Relative Wages," *American Economic Review* (June), 64:482–91.

—— 1976a. "The Changing Cyclical Responsiveness of Wage Inflation," *Brookings Papers on Economic Activity,* no. 1, pp. 115–59.

—— 1976b. "The Demographic Impact of Unemployment: Past Experience and the Outlook for the Future," in National Commission for Manpower Policy, *Demographic Trends and Full Employment,* Special Report No. 12 (December), pp. 27–99.

Wallich, Henry C. 1970. "Fiscalists vs. Monetarists," *Financial Analysts Journal,* September–October.

Weiss, Leonard W. 1966. "Business Pricing Policies and Inflation Reconsidered," *Journal of Political Economy* (April), 74:177–87.

—— 1971. "The Role of Concentration in Recent Inflationary Movements: A Statistical Analysis," *Antitrust Law and Economics Review* (Spring), pp. 109–21.

Wilson, Thomas A. 1959. "An Analysis of the Inflation in Machinery Prices," U.S. Congress, Joint Economic Committee, *Study of Employment, Growth and Price Levels.* Study Paper no. 3. 86th Congress, 1st session, November 6.

Index